A

i

THE VIOLENT EARTH

To
Valerie Jiles
A Token of Friendship

THE VIOLENT EARTH

FRANK W. LANE

Salem House
Topsfield, Massachusetts

Printed and bound in
Italy

Page 2 *The red glow of
approaching destruction as
fountains of lava shoot
skywards from Heimaey,
Iceland during the 1973
eruption.* (Sigurgeir
Jónasson)

Opposite *The billowing
ash cloud, dwarfing
9,000-feet high St Helens
volcano, towers twelve miles
high. The eruption blasted
away 1,300 feet of the
mountain's summit.* (John
Lynch)

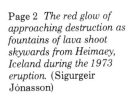

072934

Contents

Preface

During the Second World War I wrote a book about the extremes of natural violence – *The Elements Rage* (1945). It went through four editions in Great Britain and was published in five other countries. It is now out of print everywhere.

Since the last edition, in 1968, much has happened in the relevant sciences. These changes are reflected in this book, which is so different, both in text and illustrations, from the earlier versions that a new title is justified.

The importance of the book's subject matter can hardly be exaggerated. A report of the United Nations dealing with disaster relief says: 'Increasingly heavy losses are inflicted on the world economy by the effects of natural disasters, despite all existing efforts to remedy the situation. Indeed, it is likely that this worsening trend will continue.' (UNDRO News, May/June 1983)

I could not have written this book if I had described only my own experiences; death would have come long before I had witnessed a minute fraction of the incidents recorded here. I have therefore used the writings of a multitude of people, both scientists and laymen, and have corresponded with scores of experts in a dozen countries. Most of these were professional scientists; to very few did I appeal in vain.

Alice's query 'What is the use of a book without pictures?' is particularly relevant to a volume which deals with Nature in her most spectacular moods. Much time, thought and effort have been devoted to acquiring the work of numerous photographers who, sometimes at the risk of their lives, have obtained permanent records of Nature's violence and the effects left on the earth.

To the scientists, authors and photographers who made this book possible I am deeply indebted.

The book ranges over the sciences of meteorology, astronomy and geology, and has references to history, physics and mathematics. Much of the subject matter is highly technical. I have had to take the scientist's technicalities and translate them into the language of Everyman. Consider the following sentences from one specialist treatise:

> Although the tornado may have nonuniform reflectivity we assume (for simplicity) the reflectivity to be either uniformly distributed throughout the pulse volume or to have a Gaussian-shaped profile with control over the peak position and width. . . . A von Hann weighting function (raised cosine) was applied to data prior to a discrete Fourier transform. The von Hann weight offers a good compromise between the width of the spectral main peak and the size of sidelobes. Specifically, the rapid sidelobe decay reduces contamination of high velocity peaks by strong signal, low velocity components.'

Fortunately all the specialist works I consulted were not so recondite, but coping with technicalities has been the hardest part of my task, especially as there is considerable disagreement among experts. One scientist said of another I had quoted: 'Don't trust anything [he] publishes!'

The specialist may feel that I have sometimes oversimplified. I have, however, tried to give a *general* picture as I believe that too many qualifications take all the life out of writing. That great populariser in another field, Sir Winston Churchill, recognised this danger. In his *A History of the English-speaking Peoples* he says: 'The reserve of modern assertions is sometimes pushed to extremes, in which the fear of being contradicted leads the writer to strip himself of almost all sense and meaning.'

Scientists will criticise, as they have the right and duty to, whatever they consider the technical faults of the book. But I ask them to remember that any scientist who wrote a book on such wide-ranging subjects would be a layman himself outside his own discipline.

This book is not a detailed treatise and much of it concerns facts and observations which, although often dismissed by specialists as irrelevancies, are of considerable general interest. I hope this material will help to sugar the pill of the inevitable technicalities.

I have tried to keep theorising to an acceptable minimum. Sometimes there is no generally accepted theory to account for phenomena; ball lightning is an example, and some scientists even claim there is no such thing. Readers wanting more information should consult the technical volumes and papers listed in the bibliography of this book and, for earlier references, *The Elements Rage*.

I have not considered it necessary to give authorities and references for widely accepted facts and statements. Generally the source of anecdotes, quotations and other statements requiring authentication can be identified in the bibliography by the author's name. Dates are given after names only when it is necessary to distinguish between different publications of the same author. All dates are given in the bibliography.

Some details about the writing of this book may be of interest. Research, writing and checking have been spread over six years. Over 2,000 letters have been exchanged. Altogether about 80 people have read the manuscript in whole or in part.

In fairness to the host of helpers who have given so generously of their time and knowledge, I must stress that ultimate responsibility for everything in this book is mine. I have not accepted every suggestion and criticism, and some material has been added after the critical readings.

The book is being published internationally. It is, however, probable that the majority of English-speaking readers are more at home with imperial than metric units; I have therefore used the former. Conversion tables appear on page 210.

F.W.L.
Pinner, Middlesex, England

Acknowledgements

The bibliographies of this book and its predecessor, *The Elements Rage*, contain some 1,500 entries and indicate the extent of my indebtedness to published sources. These bibliographies are, as far as I know, the most extensive on natural violence in any general book so far published. The onerous task of setting out titles and other publishing details in correct form has been done by Mr Michael Sargent ALA, who also compiled the index.

Each chapter has been read by at least four professional scientists, some by eight or more. To list everybody who has helped would be tedious, but it would be churlish not to thank publicly any of those who have given so generously of their time and knowledge. I particularly wish to thank the following: Dr R. D. Adams (Earthquakes); Mr Oliver M. Ashford (all meteorological chapters); Professor Howard B. Bluestein (all meteorological chapters); Dr K. A. Browning (Tornadoes and Hail), Mr Eric Crew (all chapters); Professor Larry Gedney (Earthquakes); Dr Joseph Golden (Waterspouts); Dr Robert Holcomb (Volcanoes); Dr G. T. Meaden (all meteorological chapters); Dr Peter M. Millman (Meteoroids); Dr Joseph E. Minor (Hurricanes, Tornadoes and Waterspouts); Professor Herbert Riehl (Hurricanes); Miss Susanna van Rose (Earthquakes and Volcanoes); Dr Peter Ryder (Hail and Lightning); Dr John A. Shanahan (Tornadoes).

I thank the editors of the *National Geographic* for permission to quote from articles they have published. I also thank the *Reader's Digest* for permission to quote from an article by Colin Fletcher which appeared in the British edition for July 1963.

I also wish to thank the following for permission to quote from the books mentioned: George Allen & Unwin Ltd, London, *Great Earthquakes* by Charles Davison; Ernest Benn Ltd, London, *Excavations at Ur* by Sir Leonard Woolley; Harvard University Press, Cambridge, Mass., *Between the Planets* by Fletcher G. Watson; Her Majesty's Stationery Office, London, *Observer's Handbook*; William Kimber & Co. Ltd, London, *The Destruction of Dresden* by David Irving; Oklahoma Press, Norman, Oklahoma, *Tornadoes of the United States* and *Hailstorms of the United States* by Snowden D. Flora; Oxford University Press, London. From *History of U.S. Naval Operations in World War II*, Volume XIII, *The Liberation of the Philippines*, by Samuel Eliot Morison. Copyright © 1959 by Samuel Eliot Morison; Princeton University Press, Princeton, New Jersey, *Earthquakes* by Nicholas H. Heck; Raleigh Press, Newton Abbot, *Lynmouth Flood Disaster* by E. R. Delderfield; Mrs J. Rasmussen (Mrs J. Kingdon-Ward) and A. D. Peters & Co., *My Hill So Strong* by Mrs J. Kingdon-Ward; Alvin Redman Ltd, London, *Johnstown, The Day The Dam Broke* by Richard O'Connor; The Williams and Wilkins Co., Baltimore, *Meteors* by Charles P. Olivier.

Like many British authors, I owe much to the magnificent service of the public library system. The Northwood Hills Library – with its pleasant and helpful staff – proved the 'Open Sesame' to more than 100 million volumes which line the shelves of our public libraries, and to the runs of technical journals held in the National Lending Library for Science and Technology.

I owe much to the staff, past and present, of my Photographic Agency: my secretary, Mrs Kathleen Dennis; my daughter, Jean; Mrs Joan Jones and Mrs Averil Lewis. Their help, cheerfulness and enthusiasm have helped to lighten a long and arduous task.

I wish also to thank my publishers for all they have done, not only in producing such a handsome volume, but in friendly co-operation as well.

Finally I desire to thank my wife, Barbara. Authors, especially when in the throes of composition, are not the easiest people to live with. In addition to coping with my vagaries, she has borne more than her fair share of family responsibilities, thus freeing me to spend more time on this book.

HURRICANES

Wind is air in motion. In any study of wind, therefore, it is desirable to have a clear idea of what air is – a mixture of gases. At sea level dry air consists, by volume, of about 78% nitrogen, 21% oxygen, 0.9% argon and minute quantities of several other gases. It is slightly sticky, having a tendency to adhere to solid bodies.

Air is surprisingly heavy: at ground level a cubic yard of it – a large bathtubful – weighs 2 pounds. The air in a tank $30 \times 25 \times 20$ feet (15,000 cubic feet – about the size of a six-roomed house) weighs about half a ton. We live on the floor of an immense ocean of air, vastly greater in volume than all the seas of the world.

The first tenuous beginnings of the atmosphere are at least 500 miles above the earth, but 75% of the air is within about 7 miles of the earth (the troposphere). The total weight of the earth's atmosphere is estimated to be some 5,000 million million tons, equal to a mass of granite roughly 1,250 miles long, 1,000 miles wide and 1 mile thick. So there is about a *ton* of air on every square foot of earth's 197 million square miles. This means that the average man has above his head about half a ton of air every moment of his life, and when he lies down there are about 5 tons of it above his body. *That* is atmospheric pressure. It is not felt because the air and fluids inside the body press outward with the same force. In view of such facts, it is somewhat misleading to say 'as light as air'. It is the very heaviness of air that accounts for the tremendous force it exerts when moving at high speed.

The primary force in the circulation of the air, and therefore in the production of wind, is the sun. In general, the air is heated in the tropics, rises, and flows towards the polar regions, eventually falling towards the earth. It then flows back to the tropics. The rotation of the earth and other influences, however, are constantly at work, and it is these which occasionally cause millions of tons of air to sweep wildly across the face of the earth.

Wind speed varies with height above ground: in Gt. Britain, the standard exposure for an anemometer is at a height of 33 feet in an open situation. It is estimated that a wind which has a speed of 40 mph at 33 feet will blow at about 50 mph at 100 feet, but at only 30 mph at 6 feet above the ground.

Meteorologists have evolved several scales for indicating wind speed. The best-known is the Beaufort Scale, invented by Captain (later Admiral) Sir Francis Beaufort in 1805. It was originally a force scale for recording operating conditions in ships' logs. In the original table no reference was made to actual speeds; the British Meteorological Office added these in 1906. Modifications and additions – from force 11 onwards – were made in 1944. There are several versions of the scale; that given in the British *Observer's Handbook* (1975) is reproduced at the end of this chapter.

In older versions of the scale, any wind which exceeded 72 mph was defined as a hurricane-force wind: 'that which no canvas could withstand' according to Beaufort. In fact, winds which have nothing to do with hurricanes often exceed 72 mph. Some of the best-known of these occur in Europe when the wind sweeps down through breaks in mountain ranges – the Föhn, the Mistral and the Bora; these winds rarely exceed 100 mph, although gusts sometimes reach 125 mph.

A hurricane is a special type of windstorm, the most destructive of all. Although not so violent as tornadoes, hurricanes cover a much wider area and last much longer: some cover half a million square miles and last three weeks. The total destruction is therefore greater. Sometimes a hurricane generates tornadoes on the fringes of its path. Lightning occasionally occurs also.

The word *hurricane*[1] is apparently derived from the Spanish *huracan* which, in turn, is thought to have originated from the Caribbean Indian word for 'big wind'. The same wind is also called typhoon and cyclone (mostly in Asia), tropical cyclone and baguio. There are no records of fully developed hurricanes in the South Atlantic or Southeast Pacific.

Since the end of the Second World War, and particularly after the devastating storms of 1954 and 1955, much more study has been devoted to hurricanes. The National Hurricane Research Project, set up in 1956 in the United States, has been responsible for an immense

Wind-sculptured Manuka ('tea tree') shows effect of prevailing winds at Muriwai, New Zealand. The tree is exposed to the south-west winds blowing off the Tasman Sea. (G.J.H. Moon)

amount of detailed investigation into these awesome storms. Such great interest is understandable: in the first 60 years of this century hurricanes took 17,000 American lives and caused property damage of 5,000 million dollars.

In later years the number of deaths has been drastically reduced, due largely to better warning services, but the economic loss is still great. Today, a single severe hurricane can cause damage costing 3,000 million dollars (inflation, of course, must be taken into account when comparing with earlier figures). In other lands, the loss of life from hurricanes is often worse than in North America: for example, 300,000 died in the catastrophic typhoon of November 1970 in Bangladesh (see pages 27–8).

Hurricanes form over warm oceans, generally when the sea temperature is 80°F or above, within about 5 to 30 degrees north and south of the equator. Somehow thousands of millions of tons of warm, moist air rise and the Coriolis force (deflecting effect of the earth's rotation) makes the whole mass whirl. At the equator the Coriolis force is zero, so hurricanes do not form there. In the Northern Hemisphere the winds in a hurricane always revolve in a counterclockwise direction; in the Southern Hemisphere they rotate clockwise.[2] This is because the Coriolis force acts to the right of the direction of motion of winds in the north; to the left in the south.

What starts the hurricane-forming process? Even today, with all the intensive research, there is no generally accepted answer. If there were it would be a great aid to forecasting, and possibly to hurricane control. Virtually every day the general weather situation is favourable for a hurricane somewhere in the tropics yet – fortunately – only a few form each year. In 1914 not one Atlantic hurricane was recorded. It is obvious, therefore, that there is a rare and elusive factor (or factors) which fires the meteorological engine to produce one of these storms.

True hurricanes never form in European waters. The reasons appear to be the lower moisture content of the atmosphere, the lower temperature of the sea surface and the stronger force of the earth's rotation in the middle latitudes. Despite these considerations, however, Tor Bergeron says: 'Disturbances sometimes occur showing such a rare intensity and small horizontal extent that they may be regarded as a kind of extra-tropical hurricane.'

What fuels the vast energies of a hurricane? Essentially a hurricane is a heat engine. The energy comes mainly from the heat which is released when water vapour from the warm, moist air in the centre of the hurricane condenses on meeting the cooler, drier air of the surrounding atmosphere.

The heat released in a large hurricane of some 30,000 cubic miles is equivalent to that from a conflagration continuously burning some 3 million tons of coal. It is an energy equivalent of a megaton hydrogen bomb exploded every minute. A large hurricane releases slightly more energy every 24 hours than all the electricity used in the United States *in a year*.

Some hurricanes take a week to reach maximum intensity, while others mature in a day or so. During this time another may be at full blast 1,000 miles away.

The rate at which a hurricane moves varies considerably, depending on conditions and area; sometimes one remains almost stationary. The

average speed of movement for an Atlantic hurricane is about 12 mph, although speeds of 5 mph and 25 mph have been recorded. The rate usually increases when the hurricane moves northward out of tropical waters. The famous hurricane of September 1938 travelled through New England at about 1 mile a minute.

The average life of an Atlantic hurricane is about nine days, during which it travels some 3,000 miles. Some, however, last three weeks and travel 10,000 miles. The great San Ciriaco hurricane of 1899 is believed to have lasted from about 3 August to 7 September. Beginning in the Cape Verde region, it passed over Puerto Rico and the Bahamas, was observed off Cape Hatteras, and finally died near the Azores.

When viewed from the land, one of the first signs of an approaching hurricane is the storm swell. Far out at sea, the winds furrow the ocean into giant windrows. Travelling at 30 mph or more, these waves spread out and traverse great distances, carrying their warning of impending disaster to mariner and shoreman alike. Sometimes the storm swell breaks upon the shore 400 or 500 miles ahead of the hurricane.

These swells have a slower beat than ordinary waves: roughly four to the minute instead of seven or more. They pound against the shore with a roar that is sometimes heard for several miles inland. In the New England hurricane of September 1938, the trembling of the earth as the seas fell on the shore was recorded on seismographs in Alaska, 3,000

An infrared image, taken from a satellite, of hurricane Camille as it crossed the Mississippi coast on 18 August 1969. Colours enable meteorologists to gauge temperature and rainfall in different parts of the hurricane and to estimate its strength, maturity and course. Camille was one of the most destructive hurricanes ever to ravage the United States: nearly 1½ thousand million dollars' worth of damage, 258 deaths. (NASA)

13

miles away. So, when slow heavy waves start crashing on the beach, ''ware hurricane!'

The shape of a hurricane is like a gigantic gramophone record, or a monstrous mobile doughnut with a small centre. The winds spiral several miles high, and often cover a circle 500 miles or more in diameter, although hurricane-force winds do not occur over the whole of the area. The great Atlantic hurricane of September 1944 was about 800 miles wide, but the fiercest winds occurred within an area only some 200 miles in diameter. The famous Labor Day storm on 2 September 1935 had fierce winds in an area only about 40 miles in diameter, but it was one of the most violent hurricanes on record, killing 408 people in Florida.

Once a hurricane moves inland, and is thus deprived of the fuelling effect of the warm ocean surface, it begins to break up. Some hurricanes, however, have caused considerable damage for hundreds of miles before they finally blew themselves out.

Confusion over hurricanes sometimes arises in people's minds because the rotary and progressive movements of the winds are not differentiated. If the hurricane is compared to a spinning top, this difficulty is resolved. The swift spinning of the top is the equivalent of the hurricane's spiralling winds; the changing position of the top relative to the ground is comparable to the progression of the hurricane across the sea.

The winds composing a hurricane whirl at very high speeds. At the extreme edge they are light to moderate, but as they move inward the speed increases, and those blowing around the centre whirl violently. The winds are faster over the sea, where there is a minimum of surface friction, than over the land.

During the Galveston hurricane of September 1900, an anemometer disintegrated after recording about 100-mph winds. Speeds of over 150mph have been measured for continuous periods of five minutes. During the great New England hurricane of September 1938, an anemometer at Blue Hill Observatory near Boston recorded 121 mph for five minutes, and 186 mph for a shorter period. It must be remembered, however, that the accuracy of anemometers decreases with increasing wind speed. From structural damage to buildings, engineers estimate that hurricane winds sometimes exceed 225 mph.

The highest instrumental wind speed was recorded on 12 April 1934, on 6,288-foot-high Mount Washington, New Hampshire. According to the US Weather Bureau, the wind blew at 231 mph for 1.17 seconds. No hurricane was involved. The highest official wind speed for Great Britain is 144 mph, recorded on 6 March 1967 at Cairn Gorm, Scotland, but in British tornadoes this speed has been greatly exceeded (see page 41).

(see page 41).

When a hurricane is fully formed, its maelstrom of winds moves in a vast spiral around the centre of the storm – hence 'cyclone' (one of the popular names for a hurricane) meaning 'coil of the snake'. The 'eye', as it is called, is one of the characteristics of a hurricane – the hole in the gramophone record – but it is not always in the centre. It is an oasis of comparatively calm air and sometimes sunshine, although the sea remains confused as waves converge from all directions, making it very dangerous for ships.

The eye of a hurricane averages some 14 miles in diameter, although there are wide variations: 4 to 25 miles. Even greater diameters have been reported, while in some hurricanes an eye does not appear to form at all. The eye is but a short interlude between the two halves of the storm, just a breathing space to the battered victims of the hurricane. After it has passed, the winds blow again, but from the opposite direction.

When the eye passes over a ship, birds, and occasionally insects, sometimes land on the deck and rigging. Some ships have been covered with such aerial visitors. The pilots of weather planes observing hurricane Carla in September 1961 reported that the eye was so filled with birds that they dared not fly through it (*Ibis*, October 1962). The winds are so violent that any living thing caught in them is powerless, and is carried willy-nilly wherever they blow. As the winds spiral towards the centre, anything caught in them will eventually reach the calm eye and, once there, will be unable to break out and must remain until the hurricane subsides. When, therefore, the eye passes over a ship, it is natural that any living creatures should land on the vessel to rest from their life-and-death struggle with the elements. Birds sometimes travel great distances in the eye: tropical birds have been found in New England after a hurricane – a distance of 2,000 miles.

One of the best descriptions of what it is like in the eye of a hurricane is that given by R. H. Simpson, who flew into the eye of hurricane Marge on 15 August 1951, on a reconnaissance flight:

'The plane flew through bursts of torrential rain and several turbulent bumps. Then, suddenly, we were in dazzling sunlight and bright blue sky. Around us was an awesome display. Marge's eye was a clear space 40 miles in diameter surrounded by a coliseum of clouds whose walls on one side rose vertically and on the other were banked like galleries in a great opera house. The upper rim, about 35,000 feet high, was rounded off smoothly against a background of blue sky. Below us was a floor of low clouds rising to a dome 8,000 feet above sea level in the center. There were breaks in it which gave us glimpses of the surface of the ocean. In the vortex around the eye the sea was a scene of unimaginably violent, churning water.'

Variations of atmospheric pressure are noticed as a hurricane approaches and recedes. Sometimes there is a rise before the storm, indicating a pressure greater than normal (which is about 30 inches). As the hurricane comes closer, the atmospheric pressure begins to fall, and is lowest in the eye. The lowest reading recorded on the American continent was at Long Key, Florida, on 2 September 1935: 26.35 inches. On rare occasions, even lower figures are recorded at sea. The *Guinness Book of Records* says that on 16 September 1945, off Okinawa in the Pacific Ocean, a ship recorded 25.55 inches in the eye of a typhoon (hurricane).

Such differences may seem small, but for every inch drop in pressure about 70 pounds is lifted off every square foot of surface. Thus, a drop in atmospheric pressure from 29.92 to 27.92 inches removes a load of some 2 million tons from each square mile.

Although tropical hurricanes do not scourge the British Isles, violent storms with continuous high-speed winds have left their scars on British history. In the first 60 years of this century, 20 gusts exceeding 100 mph were registered by anemometers. On 16 February 1962, a freak windstorm, with gusts of up to 96 mph, pounded Sheffield for about eight hours; the wind then dropped to 40–50 mph, but continued for many more hours. Enormous damage was done to property: over 90,000 houses were damaged, 48 wrecked beyond repair; 170 schools were damaged, 89 seriously, and 5,500 trees were destroyed (Henry Smith).

The greatest recorded British windstorm raged across England and Wales from the Wash to the English Channel in November[3] 1703. To quote Macaulay: 'The only tempest which in our latitude has equalled the rage of a tropical hurricane.' Some meteorologists believe that this storm was a West Indian hurricane that had crossed the Atlantic and somehow became rejuvenated in its old age.[4] There were strong southwest winds from about 10 November, then during the night of 26 November the storm reached its utmost fury, with winds reaching an estimated 120 mph. There was little rain, but a roaring that would sound in men's ears as long as they lived. Details of the storm can be found in the writings of Daniel Defoe, George M. Trevelyan, and Carr Laughton and V. Heddon. Below I have outlined the worst of the damage.

On the Welsh coast the storm drove a great tide up the River Severn which, with the accompanying winds, left the port of Bristol in ruins. For days afterwards boats were rowing through the surrounding countryside, rescuing people from roofs and treetops.

Hitting the mainland, the storm left a trail of fallen chimneys and church spires, and ruined houses. Boats were blown out of rivers, carriages flung off the highways and into fields. Trees fell by the tens of thousands – 4,000 in the New Forest alone. Lead was stripped off hundreds of church and cathedral roofs, wrapped 'like a parchment roll', and carried away. The damage in London alone was put at £1 million; 100 citizens were reported killed in the ruins of their houses, and the next morning London looked like a city that had been bombarded. The total loss of life was over 8,000.

Wind and wave took a heavy toll at sea. The newly built Eddystone Lighthouse off Plymouth was flung down and all inside, including its builder, were killed. Vessels of all sizes were wrecked, sunk or damaged – how many no-one knows. A report from Deal said: 'We find missing of our Merchant Men upwards of 70 sail.' Some ships on the east coast which ran before the storm were carried across the North Sea, ending their enforced voyage on the Norwegian coast.

The storm was particularly hard for the Royal Navy. Fifteen warships were lost, and one admiral and 1,500 seamen drowned. England was at war with France and could ill afford such losses, which would have been even greater save for 'the skill and courage of the crews of innumerable vessels, fighting the greatest naval battle of the war against no mortal foe' (Trevelyan).

To encounter a hurricane at sea is a terrifying experience. Weston Martyr, an ocean-going yachtsman, describes what it feels like to be caught in an Atlantic hurricane:

'Do you know that you cannot breathe with a hurricane blowing full in your face? You cannot see, either; the impact on your eyeballs of spray and rain flying at over 100 miles an hour makes seeing quite impossible. You hear nothing except the scream and booming of the wind, which drowns even the thunder of the breaking seas. And you cannot move except by dint of terrific exertions. To stand up on deck is to get blown away like a dead leaf. You cannot even crawl; you have to climb about, twisting your arms and legs around anything solid within reach.'

Others who have survived a hurricane at sea say that it is impossible to speak, because the wind blows your mouth out of shape. Sometimes the clothes are ripped off men's backs as they struggle across exposed parts of the deck. And many a man has been washed overboard when caught by wind-whipped giant waves which rise 20, 30 and occasionally 40 feet above the normal sea. When the *Aquitania* was caught in a hurricane in September 1922, ten ports on the B deck – 50 feet above the water line – were smashed. Even 50 feet is exceeded by some monstrous waves: the British meteorological ship, *Weather Reporter*, recorded a wave in the Atlantic 86 feet high.

An official on the *Mauretania* told me that heavy seas easily break the inch-thick glass of the portholes. The plate glass used to screen the bridges of ships has sometimes been shattered during a hurricane, the splinters penetrating wooden bulkheads like glass daggers.

The most strongly built ship can be seriously damaged by a hurricane. When the *Phemius* encountered a hurricane in November 1932, her funnel was carried away, she became unmanageable, and was swept along like driftwood. Hatches were blown overboard, derricks and boats wrecked, upper and lower bridges stove in. The maximum

Twin hurricanes Ione and Kirsten photographed from a satellite over the Pacific on 24 August 1974. (NOAA)

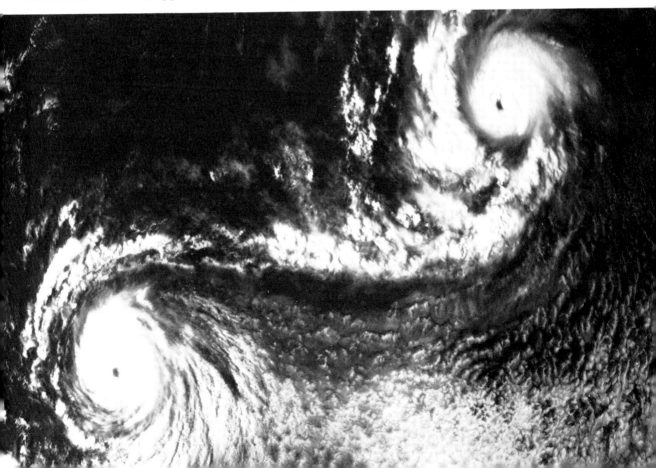

wind speed was estimated at 200 mph. Eventually the *Phemius* was taken in tow by another vessel (Ivan Ray Tannehill).

Even a modern battle fleet is in hazard when a hurricane strikes. This was tragically demonstrated when Task Force 38 of the United States Third Fleet encountered a typhoon off the Philippines on 17–18 December 1944. The typhoon, to quote Samuel Eliot Morison, was 'young, small and tight'. The highest wind speed recorded was 124 knots (142 mph) and the barometer fell to 27.30 inches.

Owing to various factors, the typhoon caught Task Force 38 unawares and in the middle of refuelling, which meant that many ships were low in ballast and in no condition to fight the storm. A few captains prudently filled their empty oil tanks with sea water, a standing order for destroyers when encountering rough weather, but the operation is extremely hazardous under typhoon conditions.

When the typhoon struck, the 90 or so ships were spread over 3,000 square miles of the Pacific Ocean. At the height of the storm some were unmanageable; they were unable to head downwind or into the wind and took it abeam. The wisest captains followed an ancient dictum of the seas: 'You can't fight a typhoon', and hove to. A vivid description of the fleet during the height of the storm on the afternoon of 18 December is given by Morison:

'Except in the case of the battleships, all semblance of formation had been lost. Every ship was laboring heavily; hardly any two were in visual contact; many lay dead, rolling in the trough of the sea; planes were crashing and burning on the light carriers. From the islands of the carriers and the pilot houses of destroyers sailors peered out on such a scene as they had never witnessed before, and hoped never to see again. The weather was so thick and dirty that sea and sky seemed fused in one aqueous element. At times the rain was so heavy that visibility was limited to three feet, and the wind so powerful that to venture out on the flight deck a sailor had to wriggle on his belly. Occasionally the storm-wrack parted for a moment, revealing escort carriers crazily rising up on their fantails or plunging bow under, destroyers rolling drunkenly in hundred-degree arcs or beaten down on one side. The big carriers lost no planes, but the extent of their rolls may be gauged by the fact that *Hancock*'s flight deck, 57 feet above her waterline, scooped up green water.'

The destroyers suffered most. The *Hull* was pounded until her deck was swept clean of nearly everything movable. Then a gust estimated at nearly 130 mph pinned her down on her beam ends; the raging sea poured into her funnels, and she sank. The few survivors had their life-jackets torn from their backs by wind and sea.

The heavy destroyer *Spence*, very low in fuel – only 15% of capacity – was in no condition to fight a typhoon. On the morning of 18 December she began to roll heavily to port; water poured in through ventilators and the rudder jammed; then at 11.10 a.m. she rolled deeply, recovered, rolled again – and sank. The fuel tanks of *Monaghan* were three-quarters full but, like *Spence*, she also rolled over and sank.

In this typhoon the fleet lost three destroyers, 146 aircraft and 790 men; 18 ships suffered major damage and many others needed repairs.

War plans had to be altered while the fleet recovered. After such happenings as this, it is hardly surprising to learn that since the war the United States Navy has studied the possibility of 'steering' typhoons towards an enemy fleet!

When a hurricane's colossal energy turns inland, it causes enormous destruction: sometimes thousands are killed, and material damage may run into many millions of dollars. In some of the most severe hurricanes, 50,000 people have perished. Not surprisingly, the Roman Catholic Church once decreed that *Ad repellendam tempestatis* should be intoned during the hurricane season.

There are three main causes of destruction by a hurricane: wind, rain, and waves, especially storm surges. In islands and coastal areas, of course, all three combine to destroy.

WIND

The fierce gusts deliver blows of 25 to over 100 pounds per square foot. Such winds develop both positive and negative forces: pushing from the front, and pulling (suction) from the rear and on top (especially on flat roofs).[5] Conditions, of course, vary greatly with the speed and direction of the wind, and with the shape, location and structure of the building, but sometimes the local pressures tending to lift a roof are several times greater than the direct pressure of the wind. Another factor is that, to quote Herbert Riehl (1962): 'The resistance capacity of many structures appears to become exhausted rapidly when the winds exceed 75 to 85 m.p.h.'

During the Galveston, Texas, hurricane of September 1900 roofs were ripped off, and as they whirled through the streets along with other objects carried by the wind they acted as battering rams to knock down other structures to leeward. A hurricane's winds have been known to pick up pieces of shingle, hurl them through the air like bullets, and embed them in the trunks of hardwood trees. During a violent hurricane which passed over Florida on 2 September 1935, a beam of wood 18 feet long and 6 × 8 inches in cross-section was blown 300 yards, then smashed through a house, wrecking it like an artillery shell (J. E. Duane). In the same hurricane, two heavy land turtles, one weighing 165 pounds, were swept 20 miles across the Gulf of Florida: C. H. Townsend, of the New York Zoological Society, considers that they must have drawn their heads and legs tightly under their hard protective shells and have been rolled across the tempestuous seas; they must have travelled at about 20 mph, because at a lesser speed they would have sunk.

It sounds fantastic, yet it is true, that some towns have been blown away by hurricanes. The old city of Santo Domingo, which admittedly was composed of flimsily constructed dwellings, was destroyed in the hurricane of 3 September 1930. During the night of 27 September 1955, hurricane Janet blew down Chetumal, Mexico, a township of 2,500 inhabitants; when morning came, only four battered buildings were left upright.

It was primarily wind which gave New Englanders their first experience in 70 years of a major hurricane: the famed 'Long Island Express'[6] of 21 September 1938, named from the speed – about 60 mph – with which it swept up the eastern seaboard. At Blue Hill Observatory, Massachusetts, 600 feet up, wind for a five-minute period was timed at

121 mph and one gust at 183 mph. The anemometer on the 1,200-foot Empire State Building registered gusts of 120 mph. All over eastern New York State the wind caused havoc. Steel towers and radio masts were toppled to the ground, and thousands of wooden houses blew over or were crushed like matchboxes under the pressures of 30 and more pounds to the square foot.

In Vermont and New Hampshire the wind played tenpins with forest timber. Wherever the shape of the terrain served to intensify wind speeds, there were tremendous blow-downs, trees lying in swaths. This great hurricane also moved oyster beds at the bottom of the ocean; 'picked' 4 million bushels of apples; tossed ocean-going vessels into the streets of Bridgeport and New London; sent cartloads of onions floating down the Connecticut River; and smashed enough plate-glass windows 'to cover 17 football fields' (George Ainley, F. Barrows Colton). The wind carried sea salt 120 miles inland to whiten windows in Vermont.

An aerial reconnaissance of part of the devastated area was made by Rudy Arnold, who says:

'Acres of trees were scattered about like matchsticks. Automobiles were lying on their sides, half buried in sand. Houses [mostly wooden] were flattened out as though they had been crushed under steam rollers. . . . At one spot, nearly 15 houses were whirled together as though they had been in the grip of a giant eggbeater. At another place, a yacht was resting on a front lawn with a five-foot hedge between it and the sea. Near Madison, Connecticut, there was the strangest sight of all – a two-storey house which had been blown half a mile and had come to rest upside down without a single window-pane broken!'

Twenty-six thousand cars, 20,000 miles of electric lines, and 275 million trees were destroyed or damaged. Hurricane-felled trees knocked down lines to some 600,000 New England telephones. At one time so many wires were down that telegrams from Boston to New York City were being sent via London! About 600 lives were lost; the figure would have been higher but for the heroic and alert rescue services.

When I visited New England in 1951, the scars of the hurricane were still visible. I saw the ruins of houses, and skeleton trees which had been stripped of their bark by the rasping effect of wind-whipped sand. The same hurricane had sandblasted all the paint from cars and scrubbed painted houses down to the plain wood.

RAIN

As a hurricane's spiralling winds pass over the ocean they suck up enormous quantities of water vapour, which is later released in the form of torrential rain, sometimes in so-called cloudbursts. Large hurricanes lift thousands of millions of tons of water vapour every 24 hours. Some estimates range as high as 200,000 million tons. It was the rain floods of hurricane Agnes of June 1972 that made it the most costly natural disaster in America's history. As much as 17 inches fell in some locations, causing disastrous floods from Virginia to New York. Estimates of damage range from 3,000 million to 4,000 million dollars.

The water comes down in rain bands that spiral towards the eye. Between these bands rainfall is comparatively light, and at the circumference there is frequently no rain at all. Where a mountain mass stands in the way of a hurricane, especially heavy rains occur on the windward side. In temperate latitudes, a rainfall of 1 inch in 24 hours is considered heavy; a hurricane sometimes pours down 20 inches in 24 hours! Exceptionally, however, there are hurricanes which produce only a little rainfall.

In the most violent hurricanes the intense rain is driven by 150-mph winds in a blinding horizontal sheet that sweeps roads and thoroughfares clear of every living thing. One eye-witness of a great hurricane said: 'The air had turned into a milky green swirl of mud, water, coconuts and sheets of galvanized roof, like flying razor blades.'

The weight of rain poured down is measured in millions of tons. It was estimated that in the 1900 Galveston hurricane 2,000 million tons of rain a day came down. During the hurricane in August 1899, the total weight of rainfall on Puerto Rico alone was estimated to be 2,300 million tons. In the great Florida hurricane of 1947, it was computed that on 17 September over 10,000 million tons of rain fell. Great floods are often an aftermath of severe hurricanes. Hurricane Flora of 1963 pummelled Haiti with such cataracts of rain that 5,000 people died – swept away by the rain-induced floods.

WAVES

The suction effect of the hurricane's winds sometimes causes the sea to rise far above normal levels. The French call the phenomenon *raz de marée*, 'rise of the sea'. It is often referred to as 'tidal waves', but in fact has nothing to do with tides in the ordinary sense of the word.

As this dome of water moves into shallow coastal areas it becomes a storm surge, rising high above normal sea level. If the surge, whipped by 150-mph winds, coincides with a high tide, the water rises catastrophically – 25 feet above normal level in hurricane Camille. Isaac M. Cline, chief of the United States Weather Bureau in Galveston at the time of the great hurricane, said that the sea rose 4 feet in four seconds. It is no wonder that water and waves cause the large majority of hurricane deaths.

Waves are the sea's battering rams and, with all the weight of the sea behind them, their destructive power is enormous. Sometimes they break against sea works – harbours, piers, breakwaters – at 30 mph, and, rarely, at double this speed. Even in a moderate storm there are sometimes 600 waves an hour crashing against sea works, each striking with a 1-ton blow for every foot of the obstruction.

Waves do not only have a battering effect; in addition, the rapid subsidence of the mass of water sometimes produces a partial vacuum which, in turn, causes sudden differential pressure. That is why a lighthouse door is sometimes broken *outward* after the fall of a monstrous wave.

Marine engineers measure the force of a wave by spring dynamo-meters fixed into sea walls which, when struck by a wave, record the pressure in pounds per square foot. The same instruments are also used to measure the suction force of a wave, and the force exerted when wave water falls from a height.

French engineers have made careful studies, using refined techniques, of waves striking on sea walls at Dieppe and Le Havre. Reporting on these experiments, R. R. Minikin says: 'The highest intensity of pressure so far [1963] recorded is no less than 6.6 tons per square foot at a point just above the base of the wall.'

When heavy waves crash against vertical obstacles, water sometimes shoots upward at 200 mph, reaching 200 feet with spray flying 20–30 feet higher. Tons of water fall with such force that 12-inch timbers are broken like the proverbial matchsticks.

Sometimes waves entrap air against sea walls. The surrounding water compresses it until there is a minor explosion as the air bursts free. The force of such an explosion may be gauged from the fact that the granite facing on part of the Admiralty Pier at Dover is frequently blown out by the compressed air of breaking waves.

These facts about wave-action should be borne in mind when considering the following story about the breakwater at Wick, on the northeast tip of Scotland, otherwise there will not be a 'willing suspension of disbelief', and I shall be classed with the fiction writers to whose work that mental attitude rightly applies. The seaward end of this breakwater was protected by a cap of rubble, stone and cement welded together with 3½-inch-diameter iron rods; the total weight was about 1,400 tons. Then came the great storm of 1872: as the then resident engineer, D. M. Donald, watched from a nearby cliff, this great mass, under the impact of successive mountainous seas, slewed round until it broke away as a unit and rested at right angles to its original position. This is remarkable enough, but during the violent storm of 1877 a replacement cap with a total weight of about 2,600 tons was also carried away.

So much for waves in general. Hurricane waves are the fiercest of all – apart from some of those caused by seismic disturbances, which have nothing to do with meteorology.

In hurricanes, waves up to 20 feet high dash against the shore at anything up to 40 mph, surge over all but the highest and most strongly built sea walls, and sweep miles inland to swell the rain floods. Thus, to the havoc caused by the hurricane's wind and rainfall is added that of inundation. On the rare occasions when a storm wave coincides with a seasonal high tide, the destruction is sometimes catastrophic. The weight and force of the water wash out the foundations of buildings so that they collapse, turn turtle or float away – and sometimes all three. Inundation is responsible for more than three-quarters of the deaths from hurricanes.

The most deadly hurricane in North America this century sent immense waves surging into Galveston, Texas, in the Gulf of Mexico in September 1900. They destroyed 3,600 houses and killed 6,000 people, about one-sixth of the population. This disaster, the worst recorded to strike the North American continent, had one good result: Galveston was made the best hurricane-protected city in the world. Today, between Galveston and the sea, there is an immense barrier nearly 11 miles long. There is a riprap (loosely piled barrier of granite) 20–40 feet wide and 3 feet high at the foot of the sea wall, which is founded on 30-foot timber piles and covered with concrete. It is 16 feet wide at the base and rises 17–20 feet in a backward-sloping concave curve.

On 11 September 1961, Carla, the worst Texas hurricane for 60 years, raged against Galveston. Fortunately the hurricane centre was 100 miles away, so the town was spared Carla's wildest fury, in which winds reached 175 mph. Despite this, Galveston was flooded from water which swept around the wall and entered the city from inside the defences. Such, however, was the strength of the wall and the efficient warning system that only two people died, although seven others were killed by a tornado associated with Carla.

It is obvious that the Galveston engineers have not been over-cautious. Consider what happened to the sea forts at Guadeloupe in the tremendous hurricane which struck the island on 4 August 1666. Mountainous seas pounded at the fortifications until all the batteries, with their 6-foot-thick walls, were destroyed and the 14-pounder guns were washed away.

Admiral Sir George Rodney says of the hurricane that swept over Barbados in early October 1780:

'The strongest buildings and the whole of the houses, most of which were of stone, and remarkable for their solidity, gave way to the fury of the wind, and were torn up to their foundations; all the forts destroyed, and many of the heavy cannon carried upwards of 100 feet from the forts. Had I not been an eye-witness, nothing could have induced me to have believed it.'

Although Sir George blames the damage on the 'fury of the wind', it was undoubtedly the storm surge which was responsible. Why are such strongly built structures unable to withstand the waves? Some reasons have already been given, but, apart from thousands of tons of fast-moving water, the debris which the waters carry along with them acts like a concentration of battering rams. Telegraph and telephone poles, heavy beams, tree trunks, pieces of masonry, and large rocks smash continuously against any structure barring their path. It has been

Overleaf Lashed by hurricane David's 150 m.p.h. winds, huge waves batter shorelines in the Caribbean. Spawned in the warm waters off West Africa in August 1979, David spiralled 3,000 miles across the Atlantic to slam into the islands of the Caribbean. Before it blew itself out near the Canadian border David's winds, rain and waves left tens of thousands homeless, over 1,000 dead. (John Hillelson)

estimated that, in a violent hurricane, the total forces – wind, rain, storm surge and debris – constantly pummelling a building 100 feet tall and 100 feet wide amount to 8,000 tons.

When hurricane Hazel of October 1954 smashed into Garden City, South Carolina, a two-storey concrete-block store, 80 × 40 feet, near the beach was pounded until its lower floor disintegrated; Hazel's waters then hurled the upper storey, almost intact, 300 feet. It was here that Hazel levelled 20-foot, grass-covered sand dunes, then went on to smash homes and houses – complete with concrete-slab floors – until they just disappeared.

Nowhere, however, was destruction so complete as at Long Beach, North Carolina. Dunn and Miller say:

'Everything on the island was destroyed. Where 300 homes existed at daybreak, all had disappeared by noon – far worse than the destruction of a tornado. Well-built concrete-block buildings with concrete floors and paved driveways were carried away. No litter or debris remained – it had been swept clean. The homes had been built in a space of some 75 to 100 yards between the beach and the highway, but after the hurricane the beach reached the highway and beyond.'

Three years after Hazel, hurricane Audrey struck. On 27 June 1957, it swept up the Gulf of Mexico and battered Louisiana with wind, rain and – above all – storm surges. The little town of Creole was washed out of existence: one concrete building remained; four others floated away, but came to rest within the city limits; of the remainder there was nothing but debris.

East of Creole a house was wrenched off its foundations, floated intact for several miles and then, ballasted with tons of mud, sank into marshland. It is still there, an incongruous country mansion in the middle of nowhere, whose only residents are marshland wildlife, especially rats and cottonmouth moccasins. One of the zoological hazards of sitting out a hurricane is that poisonous snakes compete with people for the available accommodation: during Carla's rampage in September 1961, there was a plague of rattlesnakes in Texas City.

Audrey's waters carried some houses 30 miles. In addition, and typical of the macabre happenings when the earth is violent, coffins, encased in concrete tombs, were washed out of burial grounds and carried 15–20 miles (Dunn and Miller).

Over 20 years later, in September 1979, hurricane David came near to razing the Dominican Republic in the Caribbean. Spanning some 300 miles, David's 150-mph winds slammed into Rosea, the capital, and flattened it in a five-hour assault which left 60,000 homeless. Other towns were similarly battered. The banana crop, mainstay of the island's economy, was totally destroyed. In all, at least 1,000 people were killed and 150,000 rendered homeless. The damage was estimated at 1,000 million dollars.

It may be thought that the Dominican towns suffered so severely because the buildings were of comparatively flimsy construction. This is probably true, but consider what happened to the modern city of Darwin, chief seaport of the Northern Territory, Australia. On Christmas Day 1974, hurricane Tracy slammed into Darwin and left it a rubble-strewn ruin, with 48 known dead and about 20 missing. 'Some of the suburbs were virtually annihilated; the comparisons that come to mind are inevitably Dresden and Hiroshima.' (Peter Durisch and Robert Howarth)

The United States National Weather Service has compiled *The Hurricane Disaster – Potential Scale*. The most potently disastrous category is No. 5, which reads:

'Winds greater than 155 miles per hour. Shrubs and trees blown down, considerable damage to roofs of buildings; all signs down. Very severe and extensive damage to windows and doors. Complete failure of roofs on many residences and industrial buildings. Extensive shattering of glass in windows and doors. Some complete building failures. Small buildings overturned or blown away. Complete destruction of mobile homes. Or: storm surge greater than 18 feet above normal. Major damage to lower floors of all structures less than 15 feet above sea level within 500 yards of shore. Low-lying escape routes inland cut by rising water 3 to 5 hours before hurricane center arrives. Massive evacuation of residential areas on low ground within 5 to 10 miles of shore possibly required.' (*Weatherwise*, August 1974)

Only twice this century have No. 5 hurricanes made landfall in the United States: the Labor Day hurricane of 2 September 1935 which killed 408 people in Florida, and Camille of 18 August 1969 which killed 152 in Mississippi and Louisiana. Camille would have killed many more had not some 80,000 people been evacuated.

Most of this chapter has been about Atlantic hurricanes. Violent and destructive as these are, they are matched in both respects by Pacific typhoons. These are often larger than Atlantic hurricanes, there are more of them, and they frequently occur in comparatively cool weather. When typhoon Vera ravaged central Japan in September 1959, wind, sea and rain left over 5,000 dead, more than 40,000 injured or missing, and completely destroyed over 40,000 houses. Japan's railway system, its lines cut in 827 places, was crippled.

Owing largely to its funnel-like shape, the Bay of Bengal – particularly the Hooghly River area – has experienced the most destructive typhoons in history, chiefly from storm surges. Another factor is that thousands of flimsily built shelters are jammed together near the coast. On 7 October 1737, at the mouth of the Hooghly River near Calcutta, a violent typhoon and its accompanying 40-foot(!) storm surge destroyed 20,000 boats and other vessels and killed 300,000 people.

Stuart Emeny, the *News Chronicle* correspondent, visited Bengal after the typhoon of October 1942. He says that, in order to picture the effect of the tremendous wave which swept over 5,000 square miles, one should try to imagine the sea first receding halfway across the English Channel, then recoiling and rushing back against the southeast coast in an irresistible flood that sweeps over sea walls and rushes for several miles inland.

One of the few men who survived the Bengal floods said that he saw the sea recede for a dozen miles and then come hurtling back as a solid wall of water 30 feet high, driven by a 120-mph wind. He saw it smash over and through a 14-foot-high sea wall; in another place, a massive brick dam was swept away by the overpowering force of the waves.

It is not, therefore, surprising to learn that this area holds the unenviable record for the most devastating storm in world history. In mid-November 1970, a violent typhoon slammed into the Ganges Delta of East Pakistan (now Bangladesh). The sea rose over 30 feet in places, and this, coupled with intense rainfall, caused catastrophic inundation. In a matter of minutes, dry land became a raging sea. No-one will ever know how many perished. The official figure is 300,000. Unofficially, the death-toll has been put at 1 million. Other estimates are: 600,000 dwellings wrecked, 1 million livestock killed, 800,000 tons of rice washed away.

Today the risk from hurricanes, especially along the American coast, is considerably less than it was. Much of the credit for this is due to Willis L. Moore, of the United States Weather Bureau. At the outbreak of the Spanish-American War in April 1898, he went to President McKinley and pointed out that throughout history more ships had been sunk by weather than by war. After examining the evidence, McKinley said: 'I am more afraid of a West Indian hurricane than I am of the entire Spanish Navy. Get this hurricane-warning service inaugurated at the earliest possible moment.'

It is now virtually impossible for a hurricane to come within hundreds of miles of the United States without ample warning unless, of course, it forms near the coast. Weather observations are constantly received from reconnaissance planes, automatic weather stations, radio-equipped balloons, ships, radar stations, Weather Bureau

David's winds also flipped this 15-ton transport plane atop a hangar at Santo Domingo's airport. (Associated Press)

offices, and especially from satellites.

The best-known hurricane joke – it *could* have a basis in fact – concerns a warning:

A man bought a barometer and, when installed, it pointed to 'Hurricane', and continued so to point despite all the ritual knockings with which barometer-owners assault their instruments. The man wrote a letter of complaint to the manufacturer and went out to post it. When he returned, a hurricane had blown his home away.

I also like the heading of the *Miami Herald*'s weather report the day after a hurricane: 'BLEW SKIES'.

Although most hurricanes do not reach the Continental United States, when one forms it is kept under constant watch, and every ship and coastal area likely to be affected is warned. Red flags with black centres are broken out when a hurricane is near, although most people today receive warnings from radio, television and the press.

No warning service is perfect, and hurricanes are notorious for varying their direction and speed, but the watchers and forecasters have caused a drastic reduction in the annual death-toll: it is now some 3% of what it was before the Second World War. When violent Carla of September 1961 was moving towards Texas, sheriffs broadcast: 'Get out or drown.' The result was the greatest mass exodus in American history: half a million people barricaded homes, packed essentials and drove inland. It was as well they did, for Carla was later estimated to possess 90 times as much energy as a 50-megaton explosion! The Texans were wiser than their Louisiana neighbours a few years before. As Audrey approached at the end of September 1957, warnings were given to evacuate; of those who ignored the warnings, some 500 perished.

Atlantic hurricanes are given Christian names, alternating male and female throughout the year; in one year the list begins with a male name, in the next female. For hundreds of years many hurricanes were named, a trifle unfairly, after the saint's day on which they occurred. Later, hurricanes were identified on a latitude and longitude basis, but this was cumbersome. Then, during the Second World War, meteorologists began using girls' names and found it ideal, both in writing and in speaking. This becomes obvious when it is remembered that a single hurricane may be referred to millions of times – on the telephone, television and radio, in telegrams and newspapers and in conversation. When hurricane Ione of September 1955 threatened the eastern United States, the weather numbers in New York City and Washington DC were each called about 400,000 times.

Pacific typhoons are given girls' names, although the naming system is different. Altogether 84 names are listed, and the rota is started again when all these have been used.

Today, the National Weather Service in Washington DC collects data from over 1,000 stations across the country. Further reports come from aircraft, ships, satellites, etc. The information is fed into computers, and the subsequent projections analysed by meteorologists. The remark attributed to Mark Twain, 'Everybody talks about the weather, but nobody does anything about it', is no longer true as far

Mudslide caused by torrential rains of typhoon Olga which swept across Luzon, Philippines, in May 1976. (US Navy)

as forecasting is concerned.

Can a hurricane be prevented from forming, or, once formed, can it be destroyed? Seeding hurricanes with dry ice or silver iodide has been tried on several occasions. The most successful results were achieved with hurricane Debbie of August 1969: a significant reduction in windspeed – and therefore in destructiveness – after seeding. Some meteorologists, however, are sceptical of the long-term benefits of seeding. They consider that the operation does little more than redistribute the hurricane's energies: decreasing the wind speed within the eye may cause an increase at the perimeter.

Mankind's best hope against this meteorological fury may well be to control its direction. Dunn and Miller say:

'It is possible that if a certain portion of a hurricane were seeded, a concentration of energy could develop in one quadrant which might alter the course of the storm in that direction. Of course within a few hours the storm would resume its normal track, but the temporary diversion might take it far enough to one side of a heavily populated area to decrease significantly the damage and loss of life.'

Despite what has been said earlier about the destructive effects of hurricanes, the most modern buildings in threatened areas are now generally more resistant, owing to the use of better cement, steel frames and careful design. Edwin A. Koch, a New York architect, designed a 'hurricane house' which he believed would withstand a hurricane's battering winds. It was built in the form of a giant teardrop

– a good streamlined shape – and rested on flanged wheels. By a simple mechanism it could be rotated in any direction. Should a hurricane approach, the house would be swung around so that the broad end faced the storm. When the winds struck, the broad surface would deflect them smoothly around its curving sides, throwing them harmlessly off at the pointed tip (*Popular Science Monthly*, October 1939).

Strange as it may sound in view of the immense destruction they cause, hurricanes have their blessings for mankind. Science has not yet found an economical way of obtaining large quantities of drinkable water from the seas. Hurricanes do just that, evaporating thousands of millions of tons of sea water and dropping it as salt-free rain. A quarter of Japan's annual rainfall comes from typhoons. The heavy rains accompanying the storms revive crops and replenish supplies of storage water. This benefit is received over a wider area than that ravaged by the winds. After some hurricanes, fruit trees have flowered and borne fruit a second time. If it were not for the loss of life it could be argued that, on balance, hurricanes are a blessing to mankind.

Much thought is given to finding alternative sources of energy, including wind. If ever it became possible to harness a hurricane's winds, the rewards would be tremendous. Unfortunately, the practical difficulties are also tremendous. Even without hurricane-force winds, William E. Heronemus, professor of civil engineering at the University of Massachusetts, considers that the electricity requirements of New England could be met by an elaborate chain of sea-based wind towers (*National Geographic*, December 1975).

After this 1977 Indian typhoon a well-constructed modern building remains unscathed after battering by winds which felled nearby trees. (K. Ottersen, Norwegian Red Cross)

Sometimes hurricanes have affected the course of history. Towards the end of the Second World War, the Allies were made uncomfortably aware of the Japanese word *kamikaze*. Its meaning, 'divine wind', refers to the violent storms which, centuries ago, wrecked the vessels of armies attempting to invade Japan. In 1274, the hitherto all-conquering Kublai Khan sent from Korea a fleet of nearly 1,000 ships containing 40,000 men. The divine wind struck: 200 ships were sunk over 13,000 men drowned. The invasion was abandoned.

In April 1281 Kublai Khan struck again, with one of the greatest fleets known to history: nearly 4,500 ships containing about 145,000 troops. An attack was launched against Kyushu, the most southern of Japan's four main islands. Troops landed but were fiercely resisted. The invaders re-embarked, but in July attacked again. In August, however, a typhoon struck the vast fleet, with devastating results. Torao Mozai, who had made an intensive study of the invasions, says: 'Estimates of the Mongol losses vary, but most accounts set the ships sunk at 4,000. The troop casualties probably exceeded 100,000, including those drowned at sea and others slaughtered by the Japanese on Takashima. The Mongols never seriously threatened Japan again.' Although not technically a hurricane, it was a very similar phenomenon which helped to save England from the Spanish Armada.

Hurricanes affected the rival fleets during the American War of Independence, especially during 1780, one of the worst hurricane years on record. The logbooks of British, French, Spanish and Dutch ships show dramatically this other war – against the elements (William Reid). The Savanna-La-Mar hurricane of the first week of October hit a British fleet some 500 miles east of Florida and damaged most of the ships. It then struck another British fleet patrolling off the Virginia Capes, causing such havoc that an entire squadron had to put into port for repairs. In the middle of the month, an even worse disaster befell a great Spanish fleet of 64 warships and transports assembled in the Gulf of Mexico to reduce the British base at Pensacola, Florida. Solano's hurricane, named after the Spanish admiral, scattered the fleet over the Central Gulf, dismasted some of the ships and severely damaged others. The attack was abandoned. (David M. Ludlum)

The most dramatic example of a hurricane changing history was in 1889. Early that year a German naval force shelled a native village at Apia, Samoa. During the shelling a United States flag, which had been run up to protect property, was torn down and burned, and American property was destroyed. Three American warships were ordered to Samoa, arriving there in March. They steamed into the harbour, where there were already three German warships and one British. The situation was tense, with the three nations on the brink of war. Then a hurricane struck: it swept down the bottleneck of the harbour, and winds and waves surged around the seven warships. War was forgotten in the greater battle against the elements.

The force of the wind was so great that the comparatively feeble engines of the American and German ships were powerless to make headway against the storm, or even to hold their anchorage. All six sank. Six merchant ships which were also in the harbour foundered, and altogether about 150 sailors were drowned. The death-toll would have been higher had not the hurricane made all the belligerents as one, and there were many acts of heroism in the international rescue work: Polynesians saved American and German sailors alike, sometimes at the risk of their own lives.

When the hurricane had passed, there were no ships immediately available to carry on the war; the weather had brought a compulsory armistice. Fortunately, before hostilities could break out again, the dispute was settled amicably, and the Treaty of Berlin in 1889 resulted in the freedom of Samoa being guaranteed for many years.

This, however, was not all. In the harbour when the hurricane struck was the British ship *Calliope*, one of the earliest vessels to be equipped with engines that made her largely independent of canvas. In the teeth of the hurricane, the *Calliope* steamed from the inner harbour for the comparative safety of the open sea. It was a terrific struggle to make headway, taking her an hour to cover less than half a mile, but sound engines and good seamanship eventually brought the *Calliope* out of the harbour and she survived. As she passed one of the American vessels her American crew, although in danger of imminent death themselves, stood and cheered in admiration of the gallant seamanship displayed.

Scene at Darwin, Australia after hurricane Tracy had ravaged the town for over four hours on Christmas Day 1974. Winds reaching 150 m.p.h. reduced 8,000 homes to rubble, forcing the evacuation of almost the whole population. (Australian Information Service)

This episode made a deep impression on naval experts throughout the world. The United States Navy at once laid plans for equipping the fleet with more powerful engines. Thus did a hurricane in the South Pacific change the course of history. (*Report of the Secretary of the [US] Navy*, 1889)

NOTES

1. There are some 40 variant spellings, including harrycain, jimmycane, hurleblast and furicano.

2. The direction of rotation of vortices (hurricanes, tornadoes, etc.) is always expressed as if the observer was looking down on them. The main areas which spawn Atlantic hurricanes are the Gulf of Mexico, the Caribbean and the southwest North Atlantic.

3. December in the new calendar, adopted in 1752.

4. This may be true, for hurricane Carrie, which formed near the North African coast early in September 1957, blew itself out over Cornwall at the end of the month.

5. Writing of hurricane Frederic of 1979 as it hit Mobile, Alabama, Ben Funk says: 'Peak gusts rocked the hotel with battering-ram blows. The floor of my room swayed like the deck of a ship.'

6. The actual Long Island Express was derailed at East Hampton. The track was twisted into loops – but by water, not wind.

BEAUFORT WIND SCALE

Force	Description	Specification for use on land	Specifications for use at sea
0	Calm	Calm; smoke rises vertically.	Sea like a mirror.
1	Light air	Direction of wind shown by smoke drift, but not by wind vanes.	Ripples with the appearance of scales are formed, but without foam crests.
2	Light breeze	Wind felt on face; leaves rustle; ordinary vane moved by wind.	Small wavelets, still short but more pronounced. Crests have a glassy appearance and do not break.
3	Gentle breeze	Leaves and small twigs in constant motion; wind extends light flag.	Large wavelets. Crests begin to break. Foam of glassy appearance. Perhaps scattered white horses.
4	Moderate breeze	Raises dust and loose paper; small branches are moved.	Small waves, becoming longer; fairly frequent white horses.
5	Fresh breeze	Small trees in leaf begin to sway; crested wavelets form on inland waters.	Moderate waves, taking a more pronounced long form; many white horses are formed. Chance of some spray.
6	Strong breeze	Large branches in motion; whistling heard in telegraph wires; umbrellas used with difficulty.	Large waves begin to form; the white foam crests are more extensive everywhere. Probably some spray.
7	Near gale	Whole trees in motion; inconvenience felt when walking against wind.	Sea heaps up and white foam from breaking waves begins to be blown in streaks along the direction of the wind.
8	Gale	Breaks twigs off trees; generally impedes progress.	Moderately high waves of greater length; edges of crests begin to break into the spindrift. The foam is blown in well-marked streaks along the direction of the wind.
9	Strong gale	Slight structural damage occurs (chimney pots and slates removed).	High waves. Dense streaks of foam along the direction of the wind. Crests of waves begin to topple, tumble and roll over. Spray may affect visibility.

10	Storm	Seldom experienced inland; trees uprooted; considerable structural damage occurs.	Very high waves with long overhanging crests. The resulting foam, in great patches, is blown in dense white streaks along the direction of the wind. On the whole the surface of the sea takes a white appearance. The 'tumbling' of the sea becomes heavy and shock-like. Visibility affected.
11	Violent storm	Very rarely experienced; accompanied by widespread damage.	Exceptionally high waves (small and medium-sized ships might be for a time lost to view behind the waves). The sea is completely covered with long white patches of foam lying along the direction of the wind. Everywhere the edges of the wave crests are blown into froth. Visibility affected.
12	Hurricane	—	The air is filled with foam and spray. Sea completely white with driving spray; visibility very seriously affected.

Source: the British *Observer's Handbook* (HMSO, 1975).

| Force | Specification for coastal use | Equivalent speed at 10 m above ground | | | | | |
| | | Knots | | Miles per hour | | Metres per second | |
		Mean	Limits	Mean	Limits	Mean	Limits
0	Calm.	0	<1	0	<1	0.0	0.0–0.2
1	Fishing smack* just has steerage way.	2	1–3	2	1–3	0.8	0.3–1.5
2	Wind fills the sails of smacks which then travel at about 1–2 kt.	5	4–6	5	4–7	2.4	1.6–3.3
3	Smacks begin to careen and travel at about 3–4 kt.	9	7–10	10	8–12	4.3	3.4–5.4
4	Good working breeze, smacks carry all canvas with good list.	13	11–16	15	13–18	6.7	5.5–7.9
5	Smacks shorten sail.	19	17–21	21	19–24	9.3	8.0–10.7
6	Smacks have double reef in mainsail. Care required when fishing.	24	22–27	28	25–31	12.3	10.8–13.8
7	Smacks remain in harbour and those at sea lie-to.	30	28–33	35	32–38	15.5	13.9–17.1
8	All smacks make for harbour, if near.	37	34–40	42	39–46	18.9	17.2–20.7
9	—	44	41–47	50	47–54	22.6	20.8–24.4
10	—	52	48–55	59	55–63	26.4	24.5–28.4
11	—	60	56–63	68	64–72	30.5	28.5–32.6
12	—	—	≥64	—	≥73	—	≥32.7

* The fishing smack in this table may be taken as representing a trawler of average type and trim. For larger or smaller boats and for special circumstances allowance must be made.

[< means less than, ≥ means equal to or greater than.]

TORNADOES

A tornado is the most violent of all windstorms. Its behaviour is often so fantastic as to border on the incredible. Nevertheless, extraordinary tornadic phenomena have been described by reliable observers – and sometimes photographed – and their reality is fully established. Tornadoes occur in all continents but the most violent develop in the United States, where about one tornado in 50 causes 90% of the damage and deaths.

Despite considerable research into all aspects of these violent storms, a complete answer to what causes them still cannot be given. It is, however, certain that tornadoes are always associated with convection, that is the rising of warm and falling of cooler air. G. T. Meaden, an expert on tornadoes, has given me the following description of their formation:

'Tornadoes most commonly form within well-developed thunderstorm cells on cold fronts, at the boundary where advancing cold air is overrunning and displacing much warmer, very humid air. In every cell a strong persistent updraught of warm moist air is maintained as air enters the forward right flank of the cell at low altitudes. The rising air is forced to turn as it ascends due to the variation of wind force with height (this is called wind shear) and due to the proximity of a downdraught of much drier, cold air. In this way, the strong updraught acquires an initial small rotation in an anticlockwise sense. Gradually, the spiralling effect extends along the whole updraught, increasing the speed of rotation of the updraught as its diameter diminishes. Just as water runs more rapidly from a bath by spiralling down the plug-hole, so the rising moist air is carried more effectively through the cloud when it is a spiralling updraught. As the spiralling column extends beneath the cloud-base, it is made into a visible funnel cloud when water vapour condenses within it because of the decreasing pressure and temperature inside. Finally, if the rate of spin is sufficient, the tornado funnel cloud lengthens until it reaches the ground, bringing with it its devastating winds.'

The violent whirling action of the winds – inward and upward – is the main characteristic of a tornado, and accounts for its popular name 'twister'. Within the main funnel of large tornadoes there are miniature twisters, 'suction vortices' as Theodore Fujita calls them, small fast-spinning columns of air usually fewer than 30 feet in diameter. A large tornado sometimes has half a dozen such vortices.

A tornado is the most localised of all windstorms, travelling in a destructive path which is generally short and narrow – 'a furious buzz-saw that gouges, chops, chews and spews its way across the earth'. Sometimes tornadoes form in 'families', whose paths may envelop an area several miles wide. Louis J. Battan considers that the average duration of tornadoes in the United States is about four minutes and the path 2 miles; average funnel width is about 150 feet, but some of over 1 mile have been reported. According to Kendrick Frazier, one of the tornadoes in the outbreak of 3/4 April 1974 (see page 54) swept a 121-mile path across Indiana, and another cut a destructive path 5 miles wide in Kentucky.

There are several accounts of people standing within 150 feet of the funnel and feeling no violent wind. Sometimes the destruction in one place is complete, with every building, tree and fence levelled to the ground, while a few feet away the lightest object is undisturbed.

The Great Plains, stretching from the Gulf of Mexico to Canada, have more severe tornadoes than anywhere else on earth. The area comprising Texas, Oklahoma, Kansas and Missouri has been called 'Tornado Alley'. Washington DC has been hit four times this century, by far the worst blow coming on 17 November 1927 when damage amounted to nearly 700,000 dollars. There is no record of any damaging tornado ever hitting New York City.

The conditions preceding the birth of a violent tornado have been described by many eye-witnesses. Some while before the clouds appear, the atmosphere becomes sultry and peculiarly oppressive. 'It seemed as if the lightest garments that I could put on were a burden to me', and 'The air at times came in puffs as from a heated furnace', are two typical comments.

John G. Albright says: 'The temperatures preceding tornadoes are higher than usual, but soon after they fall very rapidly. The relative humidity is unusually high, making the air very oppressive and sultry for hours or even days before the tornado.' Sometimes it is as though night had descended prematurely as strange-coloured clouds mill wildly about. Jet-black, greenish, purple, or of 'a strange lividness', often mingled with steam-like greys and whites, are some of the descriptions of the colours of tornado-forming clouds.

Many observers tell of seeing two cloud masses meet, one moving from the southwest and the other from the northwest. 'They came together with a terrific crash, as if thrown from the mouths of cannons' says one eye-witness. As the clouds meet they break up in a wild turmoil; sometimes they dart towards the earth, then shoot up high into the sky like gigantic rockets.

In the midst of this confused medley portions of cloud begin to roll about each other in a well-developed whirl until a funnel is formed. Occasionally, however, there is a windstorm with all the other characteristics of a tornado but without a funnel, and in some tornadoes clouds do not appear to merge into the funnel at all. Whether or not a funnel is visible depends on the degree of moisture in the air: the more moisture, the more prominent the funnel. Some tornado funnels are obscured by heavy rain.

The funnel frequently looks like a gigantic elephant's trunk, sometimes 1 mile high, dangling from the heavens. Both shape and colour vary according to atmospheric conditions and the viewpoint of the observer. Typical descriptions are: 'balloon-like', 'the tail of an enormous kite', and 'a wide and solid-looking funnel' (the most dangerous). The same tornado may change its shape from time to time. The axis of the funnel may be straight or contorted, vertical or considerably inclined.

The colour is generally grey, owing to condensation of the water

Page 36 *A dust-devil whirls across a barren field near Phoenix, Arizona. They are caused when surface heat forces air to rise rapidly. Dust-devils lack the violence of tornadoes but a pilot told me he saw a small plane flipped over when caught in one about 1,000 feet tall.* (Sherwood B. Idso)

vapour. In air with a fairly low moisture content the funnel may be invisible. When it touches the ground and begins its work of destruction, the colour may be considerably modified by dust and debris. A tornado in Utah passed over a snowfield and turned almost white.

When a tornado is fully formed it scythes across the countryside at speeds averaging 35 mph, although speeds of from 5 mph to 70 mph have been reported. Sometimes a tornado remains almost stationary for a few minutes, occasionally for much longer. One may double back on itself, or travel in circles.

The funnel often rises from the earth and dips again a little farther on. Although it generally moves in a fairly straight line, it sways from side to side and frequently writhes and twists. It changes form and shape, and bounces up and down – hindering the escape efforts of those caught in its path.

The noise from the most violent tornadoes is heard several miles away. As the tornado approaches, there is a peculiar whistling sound that rapidly changes to an intense roar, reaching a deafening crescendo as it strikes. The screeching of the whirling winds is then so loud that the fall of wrecked buildings, the crashing of trees and the destruction of other objects are seldom heard. The 'bellowing of a million mad bulls'; 'the roar of ten thousand freight trains'; 'like that of a million cannons'; 'the buzzing of a million bees' (when the tornado is high in the air); and 'the roar of jet aeroplanes' – these are some of the phrases used by those who have experienced a tornado. Joseph E. Minor comments: 'It is noteworthy that in some instances eyewitnesses standing very close to very intense tornadoes have noticed no noise at all.'

A tornado's awesome effect is frequently heightened by an accompanying thunderstorm, with deluges of rain and hail. Sometimes very heavy stones fall, weighing a pound or more, and lightning may play about the funnel. George Raveling, an observer of the United States Weather Bureau, says of one tornado: 'From the sides of the boiling, dust-laden cloud a fiery stream poured out like water through a sieve, breaking into spheres of irregular shape as they descended.' It is not, therefore, surprising to learn that strange sulphurous odours (ozone?)

Below right   The classic photograph of a tornado, taken near Jasper, Minnesota, on 8 July 1927. (Lucille Handberg)

Below   A rare twin-funnel tornado caught by the photographer as it nears Elkhart, Indiana on 11 April 1965. Debris sucked up by the tornado's updraughts spills out from the left-hand funnel. (Paul Huffman, Elkhart Truth)

are sometimes emitted by tornadoes, probably caused by the lightning.

One of the most impressive displays of lightning was seen at the time of the great St Louis, Missouri, tornado of 27 May 1896. A Weather Bureau official reported:

'The electrical display during the storm was of exceeding brilliancy. The whole west and northwest sky was in a continuous blaze of light. Intensely vivid flashes of forked lightning were frequent, being outlined in green, blue, purple, and bright yellow colours against the dull yellow background of the never-ceasing sheet lightning.' (Quoted by H. T. Harrison)

In view of the awesome accompaniments of a tornado, it is understandable that, in a less sophisticated age, the sight and sound of a twister made men think that the end of the world and the Day of Judgement were at hand. Indeed, a tornado *has* been the end of the world for many people. Consider this account, taken not from a novel or popular work, but from a scientific textbook, Snowden D. Flora's *Tornadoes of the United States*. He is writing of the tremendous tornado which struck Irving, Kansas, on 30 May 1879:

'There appeared in the west a cloud of inky blackness and enormous dimensions. It presented a square front of blackness almost two miles wide, with the front almost perpendicular. Many people actually believed that Judgement Day had come and offered up fervent prayers and loud appeals for preservation.

'With a roar "like that of a thousand cannons", the cloud covered the little town. In an instant everything was swept away from the earth in ruin, and death was experienced in its most dreadful forms. In the twinkling of an eye, according to persons who experienced it, all was gone. Life, property, and happiness were crushed and annihilated. The power of the storm was sufficient to accomplish in a few moments what disease and accident had not done in years.

'Persons who lived through the storm to tell the tale said that the air was filled with fumes like sulphurous smoke, the sky had a reddish tinge bordering on purple, and the ground was rocked as if by an earthquake. What seemed to them vast waterspouts reached the ground in several places, swinging to and fro in the gale like elephants' trunks, seizing and taking up into the whirling vortexes everything that stood in their way.'

The air composing a tornado whirls at high speed, but varies greatly from one tornado to another. Chester W. Newton of the United States National Center for Atmospheric Research says 'more than half have winds less than 100 m.p.h.' (Sybil P. Parker). To the speed of the whirling wind there has to be added the speed of the tornado as it moves across country, and some travel as fast as 70 mph.

Maximum tornado wind speed has never been measured directly, because no instrument has so far proved capable of withstanding the terrific buffeting. The highest wind speed ever recorded by an anemometer was a gust of 231 mph (see p. 14), but this was not in a tornado. Winds in large tornadoes certainly reach greater speeds: they blow anemometers away!

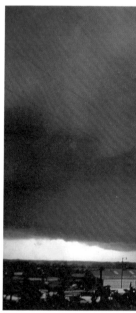

Top *A canopy of cumulus mammatus clouds overhangs the Kansas countryside at sunset. These pendulous cloud formations often presage tornadoes.* (David Hoadley)

Above *Not quite a tornado. Such menacing clouds sometimes breed tornadoes but this Oklahoma storm, photographed on 23 May 1974, produced only a 'shelf-line squall'.* (David Hoadley)

In the past, greatly exaggerated speeds have been claimed. John P. Finley, a 19th-century student of tornadoes, says that 'theoretical velocities of over 2,000 m.p.h., based upon certain assumed atmospheric conditions, have been deduced'. He wryly adds: 'Such velocities are mathematically possible, but not meteorologically probable.'

American meteorologists, using tornado speedometers based on radar, have recorded wind speeds of over 200 mph. Another method of estimating the speed is by analysing films of the motion of cloud wisps and debris as they swirl about the funnel; the maximum figure thus obtained was about 250 mph, a long way from some earlier claims!

Several estimates of the wind speed have been made from the effects produced. These are certainly remarkable. Willis L. Moore, then chief of the Weather Bureau, visited St Louis, Missouri, the day after the 1896 tornado. He says that he saw a piece of pine 'shot through five-eighths [inch] of solid iron on the Eads Bridge, the pine stick protruding several feet, exemplifying the old principle of shooting a candle through a board . . . Such was the fearful velocity of the wind as it gyrated about the small center of the tornado.'

John A. Shanahan, an engineer who has made a detailed study of the effects on various structures of violent tornadoes, says that in the Brandenburg, Kentucky, tornado of 3 April 1974 a cemetery was hit and tombstones were moved. One 'monument was notched into the base stone and therefore did not slide off. The stone was rotated 180 degrees on the ground indicating that it tumbled by an overturning movement.' Shanahan calculates that the wind speed necessary to do this was 325 mph.

It is virtually certain that 325 mph is near the absolute maximum wind speed for a tornado. The United States Atomic Energy Commission, responsible for nuclear establishments is, however, taking no chances: such buildings have to be built to resist winds of up to 360 mph. I asked Shanahan the specification for such a building. He replied: 'Depending on size of walls and roof, specially designed metal siding or reinforced concrete ranging from 6 to 18 inches thickness provides protection against maximum wind and most missiles.'

In Great Britain nuclear establishments are built to withstand winds of varying speeds, depending on the site. The maximum speed envisaged is 153 mph, which is faster than the highest officially-recorded (conventional) wind-speed for Great Britain – 144 mph – and is estimated to occur only once in 10,000 years. Such a safety measure seems reasonable enough – until tornadoes are considered. Meaden tells me that winds of 250 mph have occurred in British tornadoes, and that the frequency of such winds is around once a century. Tornado winds of 180 mph probably occur about once every ten years and 160 mph winds once every two years.

Remember that in proportion to area, this country is one of the most tornado-prone in the world. 'When 102 tornadoes sweep across England in one day (23 November 1981), who can stand by the official wind-speed estimates (which ignore tornadoes)?' True the vast majority are not exceptionally violent but in view of the immense risks involved Meaden considers 'buildings at British nuclear power stations should be designed to withstand 230–250 mph winds'. As mentioned, the comparable figure for American nuclear buildings is 360 mph.

41

I don't want to alarm unnecessarily but it is a fact that very few structures could withstand a wind of 160 mph – let alone 250 mph! – which would, of course, include battering by heavy objects picked up by the wind. In their report on the Severn Bridge, consulting engineers Mott, Hay and Anderson say that in its present state the bridge 'may not survive a wind-speed of 100 mph' (*The Sunday Times*, 13 November 1983). At the slightest hint of a tornado in the vicinity of such vulnerable structures, all traffic should be prevented immediately from crossing them.

The destruction wrought by tornadoes is caused by pressure, updraught and vacuum (reduced atmospheric pressure).

PRESSURE

The pressure of wind increases alarmingly with increase of speed. A tornado striking at 300 mph is not ten times but *100 times* more destructive than a 30-mph wind. The winds of a great tornado sometimes exert pressures as high as 230 pounds per square foot. They turn normally harmless objects into dangerous missiles. Sand and gravel are whipped along with such force that they enter human bodies like shotgun pellets.

After the St Louis tornado of 1896, some wheat straws were found embedded over 1 inch deep in a tree trunk. Even more remarkable was an incident which occurred during a tornado at Scottsbluff, Nebraska, on 30 May 1951: an egg was found with its shell uncracked, but with a neat hole through which a bean had been forced 1 inch into the yolk. It has even been claimed that after one tornado a *flower* was found in a plank of wood (Flora)!

Minor tells me: 'Physicists have examined the "straw into the fence post phenomenon" by firing straws of different types and found that penetrations of broom straws into soft woods are not a phenomenon which takes very large speeds. The "straw into the fence post" reports, therefore, are entirely believable at rather low wind speeds.'

Tornadoes have been known to wrench large iron bridges from their foundations and drop them in a heap of crumpled metal. In one incident a 200-pound steel beam, $13\frac{1}{2}$ feet long, was fastened down at each end with two half-inch bolts; the tornado hurled this beam an eighth of a mile, then drove it endwise through the heart of a cottonwood tree 15 inches in diameter at the point where it struck, 20 feet above the ground. On 12 June 1957, a tornado struck a steel airport hangar in Dallas County, Texas, and tore the concrete piers from the ground (Laura V. Wolford).

One of the most vivid illustrations of the tremendous power of a tornado's winds occurred on 11 May 1970 at Lubbock, Texas. A 45-ton switching locomotive, *with its brakes on*, was pushed about 150 feet along the track by the pressure of the tornado's winds. It was during this same tornado that an 18-ton cylindrical liquid fertiliser tank, 40 feet long and 11 feet in diameter, was pushed by the wind for just over half a mile (Shanahan).

The airborne missiles carried by a violent tornado are, of course, extremely dangerous. Shanahan tells of a 2-ton station waggon that was picked up by the furious winds, carried a fifth of a mile, and then crashed onto the roof of a house. He believes that 1-ton cars can be hurled through the air at speeds of up to 125 mph.

UPDRAUGHT

One of the most powerful effects of a tornado's winds is the creation within the funnel of updraughts of high velocity; estimates in large tornadoes range as high as 225 mph. When fully formed, the suction power performs feats which, to those unacquainted with tornadic phenomena, seem incredible. Occasionally trees over 1 foot in diameter are wrenched from the ground, roots and all, and carried hundreds of feet.

W. J. Humphreys (1937), of the United States Weather Bureau, says that a man once walked into one of their offices and asked: 'What I want to know is: can the thing happen that I saw happen?' The man may be forgiven for doubting his own eyesight, for he thought he had seen a tornado pick up a railway engine from one track, turn it around in mid-air, and set it down on a neighbouring parallel track facing the other way! Humphreys comments: 'What our observer saw happen could have happened.' Modern tornado experts, however, are more inclined to side with the man's scepticism of his own eyesight than Humphreys' confidence in it. Minor, quite rightly of course, comments to me: 'This often-cited incident has not been documented as to locomotive size, weight, etc.'

Nevertheless, there is no question that large tornadoes *have* lifted

Scooped-up debris darkens this tornado's funnel as it races across the Oklahoma countryside on the evening of 5 August 1965. Streaks within the funnel show an inner core. (Wayne C. Carlson)

heavy locomotives from their tracks and carried them a fair distance. V. C. Hanna, an experienced engineer, writing of the great tornado which struck St Louis, Missouri, on 8 March 1871, says: '. . . a locomotive weighing some 25 tons was lifted bodily and thrown on its back at the foot of an embankment 15 feet high without disturbing the track or the embankment in its flight'; and in the same tornado '. . . a heavy sleeping car was taken from the tracks and thrown across a body of water against a bank 75 feet away'. Flora, who records several encounters between trains and tornadoes, says that on 27 May 1931, near Moorhead, Minnesota, the *Empire Builder* was hit when travelling at 60 mph; five 60-ton coaches were lifted from the track, one being carried 80 feet.

The following are some of the miscellaneous objects which have been levitated by 'this giant vacuum cleaner of the skies' as Humphreys calls the tornado. Each incident is recorded by a reliable authority. An 800-pound ice chest was transported over 3 miles; the spire of a church, complete with weathercock, was carried 15 miles through the air; a wooden house was blown 2 miles, and the roof of another 12 miles. Some legal documents were carried 50 miles and dropped on the top of a mountain, and an insurance policy was taken for a 75-mile ride. Joseph H. Golden tells me: 'After the giant destructive tornado at Wichita Falls, Texas, on 10 April, 1979, many cheques, bits of newspapers and utility bills etc. were carried aloft as far as Tulsa, Oklahoma (200 miles) and dropped along the way!'

The most strongly built modern aircraft stands little chance if caught in the winds of a 'prairie twister'. It is possible that some unexplained disappearances of aeroplanes, when no trace of machine or load has been found, may be due to their having been caught in the violent winds of tornadoes. On 6 October 1981, an aeroplane flying at 3,000 feet near Rotterdam was caught in a tornado and destroyed, all on board perishing (*Meteorological Magazine*, February 1983).

Many times animals have been whisked away and carried through the air. One tornado dipped into a corral, lifted a cow and deposited it several hundred feet away. A bull was similarly levitated and carried 40 yards. A horse that was snatched from the ground was flung 200 yards and torn in two. When I was in Oklahoma I was told of a horse that had been picked up and set down astride a barn.

The Great Plains were the favourite resort of the vast herds of bison, numbering tens of millions, which roamed North America before the coming of the white man. There is no parallel on earth today of the appalling scenes which must, at times, have been witnessed by the Plains Indians when the long, dark funnel swept across the closely packed ranks of these great animals. Bison would have been hurled to the ground, as the tornado cut a swath of dead and dying animals perhaps miles long and hundreds of yards wide. Some bison would be lifted skyward, carried for a distance, then smashed to the ground. There are a few observations which give a glimpse of such fantastic happenings. Ely Moore says that two bison were found completely stripped of hair and with every bone broken; and Robert P. Davies-Jones tells me that, after the Benger, Oklahoma tornado of 22 May 1981, a few dead steers were found in trees 10 feet or so above the ground.

Sir Graham Sutton tells of a Kansas story 'of a herd of cows

Opposite *The unusual colour of this tornado is due to the dark reddish dust it sucked up as it spiralled across open country near Northam, Western Australia. It is estimated that windspeeds reached some 200 m.p.h. but fortunately the only damage was to trees, even large ones being torn out of the ground, roots and all.* (P.J. May and C.J. Crane)

Cars reduced to scrap metal by the furious winds of the great Flint, Michigan, tornado of 8 June 1953. The most violent tornadoes can pick up a one-ton car and hurl it through the air at 125 m.p.h. (Flint Journal, Michigan)

emulating the nursery rhyme and taking off for the moon "looking like gigantic birds in the sky"'. I wrote to the Weather Bureau district office at Kansas City about this legend. Donald C. House, the meteorologist in charge, replied: 'We have been unable to verify the legend you refer to in your letter, but we believe that it is within the realm of the possible.' He added that if a herd of cows did thus become airborne they would probably refer to it as 'the herd shot round the world'.

Under the heading *Tornado on a Wild Goose Chase*, the *Journal of Meteorology* (England, October 1978) reported the remarkable effect the British tornado of 3 January 1978 had on geese in Norfolk. Dead geese rained down from the skies along a track some 25 miles in length; 57 were found 'in a heap' in a field, and the total counted was 136.

Human beings are certainly carried aloft by tornadoes. A spectacular tragedy was reported in the *Yorkshire Observer* for 25 February 1911. A sudden gust of wind picked up a schoolgirl from the playground and carried her upwards. At the inquest, a witness said that he saw the girl parallel with the school balcony 20 feet above the ground, her skirt blown out like a balloon, before she crashed to her death.

Finley tells of a man who was picked up by a tornado and, while travelling skyward, stretched out his hand which came in contact with the tail or mane of a horse (his indefiniteness may be pardoned in the circumstances). He grasped this firmly but, during his aerial excursion, he became separated from the horse. When he eventually landed he was grasping a handful of horse's hair in one hand and his hat in the other. . . .

This is one of the more spectacular stories found in old accounts of people and animals being levitated and set down virtually unharmed. Modern tornado experts, however, do not accept these tales. They point out that bodies carried aloft by a tornado will later be thrown out by centrifugal force and crash back to earth at considerable speed. Davies-Jones, writing of the experiences of himself and his colleagues of the United States National Severe Storms Laboratory, tells me: 'In all our tornado studies we have not seen any piece of debris fall gently to earth.'

VACUUM (reduced atmospheric pressure)

People who have had a tornado sweep over them and lived to tell their tale speak of a bursting sensation in their ears and chest. This feeling is due to the partial vacuum in the tornado's funnel, associated with the centrifugal forces of the whirl. Few barometers – or the walls to which they are attached! – are likely to withstand the shock of a big tornado. Nevertheless, there are a few records of barometer readings taken at the time a tornado passed, or passed nearby, which show a dramatic drop in pressure.

Normal air pressure is 14.7 pounds per square inch. No-one knows by how much pressure drops in the funnel of a great tornado. Estimates range up to about 4 pounds per square inch. While this is almost certainly an exaggeration, even half this figure is an extremely drastic drop. Expressed in terms of the air in a small building $10 \times 10 \times 10$ feet in dimensions, it means that the drop in air pressure outside causes a sudden upward force on the ceiling of about 13 tons, and an outward force on each of the walls of the same amount. The two movements of the air, upward and outward, seem necessary to explain some of the incidents which occur in tornadoes. Moreover, the structure against which the forces are applied has probably already been battered by the tornado's violent winds.

When anything containing air is encompassed by the tornado's funnel, the reduction in the surrounding pressure causes the internal air to burst outward with explosive violence. When the funnel encompasses a house, air sometimes cannot escape quickly enough and occasionally houses literally explode – destroyed by the outrush of the entrapped air. Charles Sanford remembered this when he heard a tornado warning: he went through his house and broke every window and opened every door – and his was the only house on the block that wasn't severely damaged (Frazier).

The passing of the funnel pulls corks out of bottles; splits kegs wide open; explodes chests, scattering their contents far and wide; explodes automobile tyres; strips harnesses off horses — and clothes off human beings, sometimes leaving them completely naked.

One of the weirdest effects of a tornado's passing is sometimes witnessed in a farmyard; the twister leaves behind a number of naked or near-naked chickens. A woman in Oklahoma told me that she had known a tornado deplume a chicken and drive its feathers into trees. Flora says that, after a tornado near Lansing, Michigan, on 1 June 1943, 30 nude chickens were found in the poultry house: they were all sitting stiffly to attention — dead. There is controversy about the exact mechanism of the depluming. Flora suggests that the hollow quills suddenly expand, or explode, in the funnel's vacuum. Another suggestion is that the feathers are blown out. Maybe it is a mixture of both mechanisms.

Guy Murchie reports that a pilot once had a bird's eye view of the remarkable vacuum effect of a tornado. The pilot was flying over Waco, Texas, on 11 May 1953 when a tornado struck:

'Plate-glass windows on both sides burst outward into the street in progressive waves, then opposing brick walls met each other as they crashed on top of the lanes of slow-moving cars, roofs falling into the wall-less interiors of the stores. A theatre and a six-storey furniture mart burst at the seams like slow bombs, both immediately collapsing into twisted heaps of wreckage.'

Writing of the vacuum effect, Frazier says: 'Most tornado researchers now feel this effect has been greatly over-emphasized. Instead, the worst effect of a tornado on a building is due to the blast of wind.' In the same way that air flowing swiftly over the curved upper surface of an aeroplane's wings provides the uplift which carries it off the ground, so the blast of a tornado's wind along a rooftop sometimes tears the house from its foundations.

Pressure, updraught and vacuum have been dealt with separately but obviously all three effects are present in any tornado, and some results are probably caused by a combination of all three. Anything in the direct path of a tornado experiences a fourfold attack: pressure from the first winds, vacuum and updraught from the funnel, and then pressure again from the second winds (the back wall of the tornado).

These various wind effects help to account for some of the strange incidents recounted in tornado lore. There is nothing intrinsically impossible in these stories, highly improbable though they must appear to those unacquainted with tornadoes.

During the violent tornado of 7 August 1979 which ripped across southern Ontario, Canada, eye-witnesses saw houses explode as though hit by a bomb; and farm animals, furniture, cars and uprooted trees picked up 'as if they were feathers' and carried through the air (John Toll). Humphreys says that in a small town in Oklahoma one building only – the unoccupied one-storey wooden jail – was untouched by the tornado of 2 May 1920, yet 30 feet away a *concrete* store was utterly wrecked. A tornado sometimes runs along a wire fence, pulling up the supporting posts and rolling up the wire as if it were knitting yarn; the resulting ball may be 50 feet in diameter. During the tornado on 30 June 1912 at Regina, Saskatchewan, a telephone pole was seen travelling vertically along a street.

Margaret Dvorken, who was an eye-witness of the violent tornado which hit Wichita Falls, Texas, on 10 April 1979, says:

'Our storm was freakish: it tossed gasoline tank trucks about like balloons, but left a china cabinet in place and undamaged; it picked up a car with four men in it, carried it about a mile and set it down without a bump – but every inch of the metal had been dented and there was no paint left on it.'

She adds that she once asked a friend, who had experienced both earthquake and tornado, which was worse. He said: 'Tornado, because

nothing is left.' After an earthquake at least the rubble is left more or less *in situ*; after a tornado it's 'gone with the wind'. (*The Illustrated London News*, July 1979)

Often the tornado's destructive funnel skims over the ground, 20 or 30 feet high, and sometimes it shears off the upper storeys of buildings, leaving the lower parts practically unscathed.

Tornadoes have various effects on trees. Owing to the whirling winds, trees often fall on opposite sides of the path and also at opposite angles. Sometimes a tornado just plucks off the tops of trees; at other times it twists them clean out of the ground. A violent tornado carries trees aloft, and they sail through the air like huge mis-shapen birds. On 18 June 1927, at Elfros, Saskatchewan, a tornado cleared a strip of bush country 7 miles long by 200 yards wide: thousands of trees were piled on each side of the strip, some heaps being 50 feet high (A. B. Lowe and G. A. McKay).

A tornado's habit of skipping was responsible for one of the most remarkable observations ever made. In the afternoon of 22 June 1928, Will Keller, a Kansas farmer, was out in a field when he saw a tornado heading in his direction. He ran to his cyclone cellar, but just as he was about to close the door he turned for a last look as the destroyer swept down on him. Here is his account of what he saw, as quoted by Alonzo A. Justice:

Steel girders twisted like shoestrings by one of the tornadoes which ravaged the central United States on 3 April 1974. The girders supported a 40-foot billboard near Louisville, Kentucky.
(Copyright © 1974, *The Courier-Journal and Louisville Times* Co. Reprinted with permission.)

'As I paused to look I saw that the lower end which had been sweeping the ground was beginning to rise. I knew what that meant, so I kept my position. I knew that I was comparatively safe and I knew that if the tornado again dipped I could drop down and close the door before any harm could be done.

'Steadily the tornado came on, the end gradually rising above the ground. I could have stood there only a few seconds but so impressed was I with what was going on that it seemed a long time. At last the great shaggy end of the funnel hung directly overhead. Everything was as still as death. There was a strong gassy odor and it seemed that I could not breathe. There was a screaming, hissing sound coming directly from the end of the funnel. I looked up and to my astonishment I saw right up into the heart of the tornado. There was a circular opening in the center of the funnel, about 50 or 100 feet in diameter, and extending straight upward for a distance of at least one half mile, as best I could judge under the circumstances. The walls of this opening were of rotating clouds and the whole was made brilliantly visible by constant flashes of lightning which zig-zagged from side to side. Had it not been for the lightning I could not have seen the opening, not any distance up into it anyway.

'Around the lower rim of the great vortex small tornadoes were constantly forming and breaking away. These looked like tails as they writhed their way around the end of the funnel. It was these that made the hissing noise.

'I noticed that the direction of rotation of the great whirl was anticlockwise, but the small twisters rotated both ways – some one way and some another.

'The opening was entirely hollow except for something which I could not exactly make out, but suppose that it was a detached wind cloud. This thing was in the center and was moving up and down.'

Tornadoes were described by early Greek writers although, being a maritime people, they were more concerned with waterspouts. Some meteorologists consider that there are references to tornadoes in the Old Testament. Was the fiery whirlwind that snatched Elijah up to heaven a lightning-filled tornado? Ezekiel's strange description in Chapter 1 of 'the likeness of four living creatures' may be the attempt of a writer, more familiar with religion and its symbols than with meteorology, to describe strange events in the heavens. Verse 4 at the beginning of Ezekiel's description reads:

'And I looked, and, behold, a whirlwind came out of the north, a great cloud, and a fire infolding itself, and a brightness *was* about it, and out of the midst thereof as the colour of amber, out of the midst of the fire.'

It needs no great imagination to see here a sand-filled ('amber') tornado with lightning playing about the cloud. G. B. Bathurst, who analyses the whole description, wonders if this is the earliest fully reported tornado: the date would be about 600 BC.

Tornado-like whirlwinds sometimes form when great heat is generated, as in volcanoes and fires. The heat sends hot air rushing upward, and this starts the typical tornadic whirling action. Writing of the Mexican volcano Paricutin, Frederick H. Pough says that he saw a great rush of gas from the crater which formed a miniature tornado some 20 feet in diameter and roared away 'as if it had irresistible force'. Sir Charles Lyell reports that, during the far greater eruption of the Indonesian volcano Tambora in April 1815, 'tornadoes' tore large trees from the ground, covered the surrounding seas with debris, and tossed houses, men and cattle into the air.

On that black day, 1 September 1923, when the Tokyo-Yokohama area of Japan was devastated by earthquake, fire and flood, the final horror came from the 'dragon twists' – fire-induced whirlwinds. The immense heat of burning Tokyo sent hot air rushing upward at some 150 mph, to form an immense pile of artificial cumulus cloud that bulked larger and taller than Mount Everest. Terrified survivors of the earthquake and fire saw writhing pillars of black smoke, skyscraper-tall and as wide as office blocks, bearing down on them. In one area alone a whirlwind was estimated to have killed 40,000 people (Noel F. Busch).

These artificially induced whirlwinds also occur in forest fires. Howard E. Graham of the Fire Weather Service, Portland, Oregon, and a companion watched a forest fire on 23 August 1951 at Vincent Creek:

'From our vantage point about 200 yards away it was evident that violent whirling surface winds existed near the fire over a diameter of some 100 to 200 feet. In the middle of this circulation was a dark tornado-like tube extending upward, whose top was obscured by drift smoke above approximately 1,000 feet. The winds in this tube were so extreme that a green Douglas-fir tree, which at breast height was about 40 inches in diameter, was quickly twisted and broken off about 20 feet above the ground. Near the whirlwind the fire flames leaped several times higher than those in surrounding areas. A large treetop burst into flame like the flash of a powder keg when the whirl

passed by. Within the tube, gases and debris were moving upward at a high velocity. The whirling column remained nearly stationary during its activity, moving little more than 50 yards; had that not been the case, extremely rapid fire spread might have resulted. The whirlwind rapidly disappeared and as rapidly re-formed a moment later, repeating this procedure at least three times during a 10-minute interval.'

Sir Napier Shaw states that it was suggested during the First World War that tornadoes be created artificially for the discomfiture of the enemy. One ingenious inventor claimed that shells fired vertically in rapid succession would produce a vortex and start the tornadic process. Apparently the thought did not occur to him that, in the unlikely event of the success of his scheme, the tornado might sweep against his own lines.

Tornado-like whirlwinds occurred in the Second World War as a result of fire-bombing. The normal fire raids, terrible as they were, could be dealt with, but occasionally these raids turned into the dreaded firestorms, against which all human effort was useless. The first occurred in Hamburg, during the large bomber raid on the night of 27 July 1943. There had been a heat wave and the night was sultry. This doomed Hamburg. The rain of high explosives and incendiaries, and the fires which they started, turned sultriness into violent heat. The resultant firestorm burnt out 8 square miles of the city. David Irving writes:

Part of Louisville, Kentucky after it was hit by one of the tornadoes of 3 April 1974. Winds reaching 250 m.p.h. destroyed 900 homes in 20 minutes.
(Robert Steinau)

'As a result of the sudden linking of a number of fires, the air above heated to such an extent that a violent updraught occurred which, in turn, caused the surrounding fresh air to be sucked in from all sides to the centre of the fire area. This tremendous suction caused movements of air of far greater force than normal winds. In meteorology the differences of temperature involved are of the order of 20 to 30°C [actually nearer 5–10°C: F.W.L.]. In this fire-storm they were of the order of 600, 800 or even 1,000°C. This explained the colossal force of the fire-storm winds.'

In typical tornado fashion, the funnels twisted large trees out of the ground and tossed them as giant torches into the air; tore the clothes off people fleeing for shelter; and overturned cars and trucks. Nor was this all: the oxygen at ground level was burnt up and thousands suffocated in the shelters. A contemporary German account says that what happened on this night went 'beyond all human imagination' (Sir Arthur Harris). A whirlwind also formed after the atomic bombing of Hiroshima, and was strong enough to uproot large trees.

A township can be wiped out by a tornado. Look what happened when a twister ripped across Udal, Kansas, on the night of 25 May 1955. Out of a population of 610, 80 died and 270 were injured. Of the 187 houses, 170 were smashed to rubble, 16 damaged beyond repair – and one escaped unscathed. *Time* magazine (6 June 1955) reported:

'Old Railroader Fred Dye was snatched out of his shoes, whirled outdoors and thrown alive up a tree. Barber Henry Norris went to bed, woke up unhurt in the street: "I don't know how I got there." Will Sweet and his wife cowered in a back bedroom until it was over, then opened the door and found the rest of the house gone. Norman Lanning huddled with his wife and three children against the kitchen wall by the refrigerator, which skidded away; the wall was the only thing left standing in the area, and it saved them. "Oh God," said Lanning. "How lucky we were."'

They certainly were. Urban J. Linehan, in his study of tornado deaths, says that ten people were killed in one house during a tornado in Colorado.

What is the first known American tornado? According to David Ludlum, an authority on early American weather, it was one that struck a meeting house in Massachusetts in 1643. He adds that, although an Indian was killed, the tornado 'was regarded more as a curiosity than a significant event'. Later generations of Americans were to learn differently.

Ludlum has also drawn my attention to a vivid description of a tornado given by George Milligen-Johnston in his *A short description of the Province of South Carolina*. It struck Charleston on 4 May 1761. 'A terrible phenomenon resembling a large column of smoke and vapour. Its prodigious velocity gave it such a surprising momentum as to plough Ashley River to the bottom, and to lay the channel bare.' It went on to hit warships offshore, sinking five and dismasting several more. The tornado then struck southwest, leaving a wide swath of destruction 'tearing up trees, houses and everything that opposed it; great quantities of leaves, branches of trees, even large limbs, were seen furiously driven about, and agitated in the body of the column as it passed along'. (I have abbreviated and modernised the account.)

The most destructive tornado known in American history, and probably in world history, occurred on 18 March 1925. It formed about 1 p.m. in southeast Missouri, and in a little over three hours had blasted an almost straight and continuous path of 219 miles across southern Illinois, finally blowing itself out about 30 miles inside Indiana. During its course the storm cloud varied in width between a quarter of a mile and 1 mile, and in speed between 56 mph and 73 mph. In length of path, width of cloud and speed of travel this tornado was,

Farm machinery and cars scattered from buildings which were demolished by a tornado. (J.C. Allen and Son)

therefore, exceptional, being very much above average in all three. 'Very few people reported seeing anything like a funnel-shaped vortex cloud in the course of this storm. Apparently the storm cloud was so close to the earth there was no room for a pendant cloud.' (Flora)

The toll of this great tri-state tornado was: 689 people killed, over 2,000 injured, and property losses of some 17 million dollars. About 3,000 houses were destroyed or damaged, and four small towns practically wiped out. The saddest feature of this terrible disaster was that, although the tornado lasted for over three hours and travelled 250 miles, nobody gave warning. Such an elementary lack of foresight is virtually impossible today (*Weatherwise*, April 1966).

This was proved on 3/4 April 1974, when an even worse outbreak of tornadoes occurred. Thirteen mid-continent states were involved in 148 tornadoes, lasting 24 hours, which raked across 2,600 miles. In Tennessee a tornado swept down a 1,000 foot-deep canyon and climbed out again. In Georgia a tornado skimmed over 3,300-foot-high Betty Mountain. Some 10,000 homes and buildings were wrecked. Yet such was the efficiency of the tornado-warning services that the death-toll (315) of this greatest of all tornado outbreaks was less than half that of the 1925 tornadoes, which travelled less than one-tenth the distance (Frazier, and T. T. Fujita, 1976).

Although the most severe tornadoes occur in the United States, that country is not, relative to its size, the most tornado-prone. That dubious honour belongs, surprisingly, to Great Britain. G. T. Meaden tells me:

'The country with the highest annual density of tornadoes is Britain.[1] This has become clear since the formation of the Tornado and Storm Research Organisation in 1974, and is due to Britain's sea-board position near one of the primary cyclone tracks of the world. This means that tornado-producing cold fronts and line squalls occur at relatively high frequency in all months of the year, whereas the majority of United States ones are limited to the hotter months. In 1981 Britain was known to have over 150 tornadoes, of which just over 100 are known to have hit North Wales, central and eastern England during a terrifying six-hour spell on Monday 23rd November.'

In a lecture to the Royal Meteorological Society in 1975, Meaden said that he had records of nearly 750 British tornadoes. By 1982 this total had doubled!

The earliest British tornado of which there is authentic record appears to be the 'whirlwind' which William of Malmesbury says hit London on 17 October 1091, demolishing over 600 houses and damaging many churches. At St Mary le Bow it raised the roof of the church and killed two men.

'Timbers and beams were carried through the air ... Four rafters, 26 feet long, were driven into the earth with such force that barely four feet protruded. And it was a remarkable sight how they penetrated the hard surface of the street, in the same position in which they had been placed by human skill in the roof, until, being an obstacle to passers-by, they were cut off at ground-level, since they could not be pulled out.'

The second earliest recorded British tornado was described by John of Worcester. In May 1140, at Welsburn (now Wellesbourne), Warwickshire, 'a very violent whirlwind sprang up, a hideous darkness extended from the earth to the sky and the house of a priest was violently shaken, and all of his outbuildings were thrown down and broken to pieces'. He adds that the church roof was carried away, some 40 houses severely damaged and large hailstones fell, one of which killed a woman. Undoubtedly many tornadoes went unrecorded in those distant days, as the country was sparsely populated and scribes were few. Both M. W. Rowe and G. T. Meaden have written about historic British tornadoes.

Between 1900 and 1981 London was hit 30 times by tornadoes. The worst, on 8 December 1954 in West London, was rated as the fifth most violent tornado in Gt. Britain this century. The trunks of several full-grown trees were twisted off several feet above the ground. Nobody was killed, but 12 people were injured.

As far as I know, the first British tornado to be studied in thorough and scientific detail occurred on the evening of 27 October 1913. It swept 100 miles along the boundary of England and Wales from Barry to Chester. At Treforest, the iron chimney stack of the generating station was blown down and the whole western side of the building, made of corrugated-iron sheets, collapsed. A few miles away the tornado completely wrenched off the corrugated-iron roof of a store; later, such a piece of metal was found over half a mile away, firmly wrapped around a fallen telegraph pole.

The tornado moved on. It lifted the roofs off houses; wrecked a church, piling up the pews against the west wall; picked up cows, carried them over a high hedge and dropped them in a field, killing three; uprooted trees, blowing one 80 yards; twisted the tops off other trees, leaving only the trunks standing; picked up one large tree and dropped it in the middle of a field. Before the day was done, this tornado had claimed five lives. It was the subject of a government report (H. Billet).

In the afternoon of 21 May 1950, three tornadoes occurred which have been more thoroughly investigated than any others in British history. The path of the main tornado stretched, with some breaks, from Wendover in Buckinghamshire to Ely in Cambridgeshire, 65 miles away, in about two-and-a-half hours – one of the longest paths ever recorded for a tornado in the British Isles or in Continental Europe. The tornado varied considerably in width and wind speed, maxima being 80 yards and about 120 mph. It was accompanied by heavy rain, lightning and hail, some stones being about 2 inches in diameter (H. H. Lamb).

L. C. W. Bonacina quotes the following eye-witness description by people who saw the tornado near Wendover:

'All of a sudden it became as dark as night, and before we had time to wonder what was about to happen there was a terrific crash of thunder followed by an avalanche of large hail, which devastated all the telegraph wires along the road and lay inches deep on it. Then when all this had abated sufficiently we ventured to look at the sky, to see the black clouds literally spinning like a top and scores of tree tops being snatched off their trunks and hurtling through the air.'

Damage and destruction to trees was particularly severe. In one place an orchard was uprooted and nearby a swath, some 15 yards wide, was torn through a wood. Full-grown oak trees were felled, and the branches and most of the 1-yard-diameter trunk of an oak were twisted off. At Linslade, Buckinghamshire, 50 houses were unroofed; a brick-built bakery demolished; and cars, and a horsebox complete with horse, were lifted and tossed about. The *mild* British climate?

One of the most macabre tragedies in the whole violent saga of tornadoes occurred in an English village. It created such a sensation that several tracts were written about it. The village schoolmaster also composed a poem about the tragedy which was painted on boards and has been seen by thousands of visitors.

The tornado struck on Sunday 21 October 1638 at Widecombe-in-the-Moor on the southern flank of Dartmoor. The congregation was gathered in the church, and the vicar had just begun the service, when suddenly everything went black and the building was hit by wind and lightning of the utmost violence. A ball of fire moved through the church and then burst with a thunderous explosion, 'which so much affrighted the whole Congregation that the most part of them fell downe into their seates, and some upon their knees, some on their faces, and some one upon another, with a great cry of burning and scalding, they all giving up themselves for dead'. If a bomb had exploded in the church, the damage and carnage could hardly have been worse: the roof and tower were wrecked, stone and masonry showering down both inside and outside the building.

The tornado and lightning ball killed and maimed scores of men and women, and a dog. People were snatched from the pews and whirled about. Some were set down completely unharmed, others were dashed against walls and pillars. A man's head 'was cloven, his skull rent into three pieces, and his braines throwne upon the ground whole, and the haire of his head, through the violence of the blow at first given him, did sticke fast unto the pillar or wall of the church; so that hee perished

Just so! (David Hoadley)

there most lamentably'. And look what befell Mistress Ditford: 'Her gowne, two wastcoates, and linnen next her body, burned cleane off; and her back also very grievously downe to her waste burned and scalded, and so exceedingly afflicted thereby, shee could neither stand nor goe without helpe, being lead out of the church.' The tracts tell that many other people were 'burned and scalded in divers places of their bodies'. Altogether about 60 were killed or injured.

All this took place within a few seconds and, while those who were left alive were still numb with uncomprehending horror, the church was filled with 'a very thick mist,[2] with smother, smoake and smell'. The latter, reminiscent of brimstone, came from the lightning and the bursting fireball. To the 17th-century worshippers, however, it was the signature of the Devil himself. Many believed, understandably enough, that the Last Judgement had come and that they were in the very flames of Hell. Centuries later, a child in a Devonshire school was asked: 'What do you know of your ghostly enemy?' He replied: 'If you please, ma'am, he lives to Widecombe.'

The tracts end with a familiar prayer, charged with a new and terrible meaning:

'From lightening and tempest, from Plague, Pestilence and Famine, from Battell and murder, and from suddaine death, Good Lord deliver us.' (L. C. W. Bonacina, E. C. Wood, and J. B. Rowe)

In view of the danger and damage from tornadoes, some meteorologists have wondered if it is possible to prevent them. The total masses of air involved are, however, so vast that nothing short of a huge nuclear explosion could influence them – so better the disease than the cure!

In the United States much attention has been given to the broadcasting of advance tornado warnings. One result has been that more tornadoes have been found! In 1958 Morris Tepper wrote that since about 1920 the average number of tornadoes reported annually had risen more than fivefold. This can only mean that many tornadoes used to go unreported.

In Kansas City, Missouri, there is a Severe Local Storm Warning Center which tries to forecast areas – covering some 30,000 square miles – where tornadoes are likely, and then sends out appropriate warnings. The forecasts are based on information received from ground observations, weather balloons, radar and satellites. It has been suggested that rockets equipped with television cameras could be used to view storm areas.

The National Severe Storms Laboratory in Norman, Oklahoma, has a Tornado Intercept Project, consisting of teams which 'chase' tornadoes. Equipped with tape recorders, still and movie cameras, meteorological instruments, radio telephones, etc., they collect valuable information on various aspects of tornadoes and the damage they cause (Davies-Jones, 1981).

Anyone witnessing a tornado should send full details, and any films or photographs, to the nearest meteorological office. In Great Britain, details should be sent to G. T. Meaden, 54 Frome Road, Bradford-on-Avon, Wiltshire BA15 1LD. This is also the address of *The Journal of Meteorology*, which specialises in the reporting and study of severe storms, tornadoes and all types of unusual weather.

Flora, who for 47 years was a meteorologist of the Weather Bureau in tornado-prone Kansas, considered that a modern reinforced steel and concrete[3] building should be relatively safe even if directly in the path of the worst tornado. The violent tornado of 10 February 1940 in Albany, Georgia, which destroyed 32 city blocks, offers proof. Right in the path of the storm was the Hotel Gordon, six storeys of steel and concrete. On each side of the hotel buildings were lifted into the air and demolished yet, apart from extensive damage to its windows, the hotel suffered hardly at all. Incidentally, the safest place in a building is a small interior room on the lowest floor.

Further confirmation of Flora's views came when the great tornado of 8 June 1966 hit Topeka, Kansas, causing damage estimated at 100 million dollars. Steel and concrete buildings escaped with only superficial damage. Photographs clearly show these modern buildings standing erect amid the surrounding devastation. Samuel O. Grimm, Jr, of the Weather Bureau tells me: 'A study of the damage to the Washburn University buildings definitely shows that, while the old buildings were severely damaged, adjacent modern reinforced concrete buildings suffered damage only to the windows.'

What does one do if caught in the open and a tornado approaches? If the tornado is seen in the distance, and appears to be standing still but grows wider and noisier, then it is probably moving directly towards you. If, however, it is seen to be moving, it will probably bypass you. As the forward speed of a tornado averages under 30 mph, people in cars should be able to outdistance it fairly easily, providing they move at right angles to its track (and aren't in a traffic jam!). Anyone caught in a car about to be hit has two choices, both unpleasant: (1) stay in the car and have some protection from flying debris, but risk being crushed if the car becomes airborne and reduced to mangled metal; or (2) get out and risk the flying debris, but hope for nearby shelter. Tornado safety experts favour the second course of action.

If it is impossible to escape a tornado, lie on the ground, face down, preferably in a ditch or gully, as far as possible from trees and telegraph poles. If any covering is available, such as blankets or car cushions, use them to protect the body, especially the face. Sand, gravel and splinters fill the air when a tornado is passing.

In tornado-prone regions of the United States, storm or cyclone cellars are built. Sometimes they are reinforced basements, sometimes underground rooms separate from the house. Moore, writing from a very wide knowledge of tornadoes, says that he had never known anybody to be killed by a tornado while sheltering in the cellar of a wooden house.

Far flimsier structures have, at times, provided shelter. One summer, a man was driving his car in Kansas when he saw an ominous cloud approaching. Fearing that it might be a tornado, the motorist abandoned his car (why he did not make full speed for the horizon I do not know) and ran for cover in a nearby school. The door was locked, so he dived into the coal shed at the rear of the building. A moment later the tornado struck: the car was blown off the road, the school was wrecked, but the coal shed and the motorist were unhurt.

It is right that this chapter on the most violent of the earth's windstorms should end on an optimistic note. A letter written to me by

Opposite above
The best place to be when a tornado is near. 'Cyclone cellars' are sometimes built separately from houses, others are reinforced basements. Either afford adequate protection from the most violent tornado. (David Hoadley)

Left *What the black box is to aeroplanes this white cylinder is to tornadoes. Ordinary meteorological instruments are blown away by violent winds, so scientists have constructed this portable 400-pound shatter-proof weather station made of aluminium and iron. When a tornado is sighted the cylinder is loaded onto a truck whose two-man crew place it directly in the path of the oncoming twister – then bolt for safety!* (By Howard B. Bluestein)

Minor, who is Director of The Institute for Disaster Research at Texas Tech University, included the following:

'We have concluded that our societies can live with and design for these acts of nature. Natural events (tornadoes, hurricanes, earthquakes, etc.) *are* violent, as you say. However, their effects are both understood and bounded. We can do much to live with these hazards. However, convincing people that we can, for example, design a tornado-proof shelter for schools becomes more difficult if the myths of unmanageable violence are perpetuated.'

NOTES

1. The United States has 32 times the area of Great Britain, but only ten times the number of tornadoes. They form in changeable weather, of which Great Britain has a good deal more than the United States.

2. Eric Crew comments: 'The mist was probably caused by a very sudden fall in the atmospheric pressure, causing condensation in the humid air.'

3. Both are necessary: stone and concrete structures without steel reinforcement have been destroyed by tornadoes.

THE MEADEN-TORRO TORNADO INTENSITY SCALE

Force	Name	Characteristic Damage on Tornado Scale
FC	FUNNEL CLOUD or INCIPIENT TORNADO	No damage to structures, unless to tops of tallest towers, or to radiosondes, balloons, and aircraft. No damage in the country, except possibly agitation to highest treetops and effect on birds and smoke. Record FC when tornado spout seen aloft but not known to have reached ground level. A whistling or rushing sound aloft may be noticed.
0	LIGHT TORNADO	A. Loose, light litter raised from the ground in spirals. B. Temporary structures like marquees seriously affected. C. Slight dislodging of the least secure and most exposed tiles, slates, chimney pots or TV aerials may occur. D. Trees severely disturbed, some twigs snapped off. Bushes may be damaged. Hay, straw, and some growing plants and flowers raised in spirals.
1	MILD TORNADO	A. Heavier matter levitated includes planks, corrugated iron, deckchairs, light garden furniture, etc. B. Minor damage to sheds, outhouses, lock-up sheds, and other wooden structures such as henhouses. Wooden fences flattened. C. Some dislodging of tiles, slates and chimney-pots. D. Hayricks seriously disarranged, shrubs and trees may be uprooted, damage to hedgerows, crops, trees, etc.
2	MODERATE TORNADO	A. Exposed, heavy mobile homes displaced; caravans damaged/blown over. B. Major damage to sheds, outhouses, lock-up garages, etc. C. Considerable damage to slates, tiles and chimney stacks.

		D. General damage to trees, big branches torn off, some trees uprooted. Tornado track easily followed by severe damage to hedgerows, trees, etc.
3	STRONG TORNADO	A. Mobile homes displaced, damaged or overturned; caravans badly damaged or destroyed. B. Sheds, lock-up garages, outbuildings torn from supports/foundations. C. Severe roof damage to houses, exposing much of roof timbers, thatched roofs stripped. Some serious window and door damage. Gable-ends may give way. D. Considerable damage (including twisted tops) to strong trees. A few strong trees uprooted or snapped.
4	SEVERE TORNADO	A. Mobile homes destroyed or gravely damaged. B. Sheds and similar debris carried through air. C. Entire roofs torn off some frame/wooden houses and small/medium brick or stone houses and light industrial buildings leaving strong upright walls. D. Large well-rooted trees uprooted, snapped, or twisted apart.
5	INTENSE TORNADO	A. Vehicles lifted off the ground. C. More extensive failure of roofs than for force 4, yet with house walls remaining. Small weak buildings, as in some rural areas (or as existed in mediaeval towns), may collapse. D. Trees carried through the air.
6	MODERATELY DEVASTATING TORNADO	A. Motor vehicles over 1 ton lifted well off the ground. C. Most residences lose roofs and some a wall or two; also some heavier roofs torn off (public and industrial buildings, churches). More of the less-strong buildings collapsed, some totally ruined. D. Across the breadth of the tornado track, every tree in mature woodland or forest uprooted, snapped, twisted, or debranched, some being carried big distances.
7	STRONGLY DEVASTATING TORNADO	C. Walls of frame/wooden houses and buildings torn away; some walls of stone or brick houses and buildings collapse or are partly beaten down. Steel-framed industrial buildings buckled. Locomotives and trains thrown over. D. Some debarking of trees by small flying debris.
8	SEVERELY DEVASTATING TORNADO	C. Entire frame houses levelled; most other houses collapse in part or whole. Some steel structures quite badly damaged. Motor cars hurled great distances.
9	INTENSELY DEVASTATING TORNADO	C. Many steel structures badly damaged. Locomotives and trains hurled and rolled some distances.
10	SUPER TORNADOES	C. Entire frame/wooden houses hurled into air and carried considerable distances. Steel-reinforced concrete buildings may be severely damaged.

WATERSPOUTS

A waterspout is one of the most remarkable spectacles that any ocean-traveller can behold. From the dawn of recorded history men have set down their experiences of this freak creation of wind, weather and sea. Lucretius, writing in the first century BC, says: 'It happens at times that a kind of column let down from the sky comes down into the sea, around which the waters boil, stirred up by the heavy blast of the winds; and if any ships are caught in that tumult they are tossed about and come into great peril.'

Other ancient writers regarded a waterspout as a gigantic serpent, sea dragon or other monster. The Arabians considered it a manifestation of a Jinnee: a spirit capable of assuming various forms and exercising special power. It is thus referred to in the *Arabian Nights*.

W. E. Hurd, an early American authority on waterspouts, quotes the following picturesque description from an ancient commentator:

'A great black dragon is seen to come from the cloud and put its head into the water, and its tail seems as though it were fixed in the sky; and this dragon drinks up the waters so greedily, that it swallows up along with them any ships that may come in the way, along with their crews and cargo, be they ever so heavy.'

I also like Roger of Wendover's description of what were undoubtedly two waterspouts, observed in June 1233 off the south coast of England: 'Two huge snakes were seen by many along the coast, fiercely battling in the air, and after a long struggle one overcame the other, and drove it into the depths.' G. T. Meaden suggests that waterspouts may account for some of the sightings of the Loch Ness Monster.

Small wonder that readers of such perfervid descriptions regarded a waterspout as a creature to be avoided at all costs. Various suggestions were made about propitiating or scaring away the all-devouring sea monster. Sprinkling the spout with vinegar (how?) was one nostrum, while other advisers favoured loud noises. Drums and gongs were beaten, swords clashed, and seamen shouted and stamped on the deck in attempts to scare the fearsome monster away. Even today some seamen think that gunfire will break a spout, but Hurd says that he knows of no instance where one was destroyed either by atmospheric shock following gunfire, or through shot actually hitting it.

To the onlooker, the formation of a waterspout is an awesome spectacle. From the sky, which is generally cloudy, a funnel-shaped mass descends towards the sea. The sea itself is disturbed, and immediately beneath the dipping funnel the water may foam and turn white. As the funnel comes lower, spray rises to meet it. At last the rising cone of water and the low-swinging, writhing tube of air meet, and the waterspout is fully formed. Around the base is the 'cascade', or circular whirl of spray, which is considerably wider than the spout.

When the characteristic whirling motion starts, the rotating air in

Opposite Spanning *sea and sky and dwarfing pier and lighthouse, a waterspout spins in bright sunlight near Gerona, Costa Brava, Spain. Whirling winds lift sea-spray to form a huge misty curtain at the base of the funnel.* (Jean-Pierre Willauer)

Overleaf Two *further views of the spectacular Costa Brava waterspout.* (Ricardo Pla Maranges)

the vortex cools by expansion, and the consequent condensation of the water vapour forms the funnel-shaped cloud. In most waterspouts this cloud is only a filmy screen through which distant objects can be plainly seen, although where the spout touches the water a large amount of spray is swept up into the vortex. Like tornadoes, waterspouts sometimes occur in association with hurricanes.

Golden, who has made a detailed study of the waterspout-prone region of the Florida Keys, says that waterspouts undergo a life cycle of five stages. The first is characterised by a light-coloured disc on the sea surface. The spout then develops through the typical spiral stage, to the mature stage accompanied by spray. The decay stage is often abrupt: the waterspout dissipates as it is overtaken by cool down-draughts from a nearby rain shower.

Waterspouts have been seen moving across the sea at only 1–2 mph; others rush along at torpedo speed, 50 mph or more. The average appears to be between 15 mph and 20 mph. The duration of a spout varies between three minutes and an hour, both extremes being exceptional.

Through tricks of light and shade, waterspouts appear to vary considerably in colour. One was described as 'a solid column of dense, black cloud', but most are so semi-transparent that the interior of the tube can be seen. Charles F. Holder has a picture of a luminous waterspout; the glow was caused by a multitude of tiny luminous organisms which the spout sucked up. To see such a waterspout coursing over the ocean at night, its whole length outlined in phosphorescent light against the darkness, must be a magnificent spectacle.

Various waterspout noises have been recorded: sighings, hissings and sucking sounds, as well as roarings and crashings. Waterspouts appear in various shapes and sizes: one was about 1,000 feet high but fewer than 20 feet in diameter; another was 2,000 feet high and 500 feet wide. The highest waterspout reliably reported occurred off Eden, New South Wales, on 16 May 1898: it was 5,014 feet high by theodolite measurement.

Many waterspouts are shaped like an hourglass: two cones with the waist midway between sea and sky. Double- and even triple-walled spouts have been reported. Waterspouts frequently occur in families, three or four appearing in the same general area at once; occasionally as many as 15 – very occasionally even more – have been reported.

Waterspouts form in various conditions: in near calms and gales; in warm and cold weather; at night and by day; and in summer and winter. They may travel with or against the surface winds. They are sometimes harmless, but are often dangerous to small boats and aeroplanes. Waterspouts are not confined to the high seas, and occasionally form on freshwater lakes and rivers. There have been many on Lake Erie in North America where seven were seen in one morning.

Most textbooks state that the funnel of a waterspout is composed of condensed water vapour from the air, and is not, as is sometimes thought, a huge column of water. It appears, however, that spray can be drawn up to a considerable height. In the Cottage City waterspout which appeared off the coast of Massachusetts on 19 August 1896, the height of the cascade was estimated to be over 400 feet. A violent tornado can lift a railway engine, so it should not be difficult for a large

spout, although admittedly less powerful than a tornado, to lift sea-water droplets to a considerable altitude.

How fast does the air in a waterspout whirl? It is obvious that the speed of rotation must be high, otherwise the funnel of air could not form at all or, if it did, it could not be maintained as a vaporous entity. Hurd says that the whirling winds of one waterspout extended upward to heavy clouds, through which they bored a hole to the blue sky beyond. Analysis of ciné films indicates that the wind in a large waterspout sometimes whirls at about 200 mph (Golden, 1974).

In tidewater regions, such as southeast Virginia, a tornado some-times changes into a waterspout and back again several times as it crosses bays and rivers. J. J. Murphy says that, on 5 September 1935, a tornado formed near Norfolk, Virginia, and destroyed trees and sheds. It crossed a creek and, as a waterspout, lifted small boats[1] on to the shore, ripped off part of a heavy pier and – as a tornado once again – destroyed several buildings. Crossing Hampton Roads, it turned into a waterspout again, then into a tornado which flung rolling stock off the tracks in a railroad yard. It became a waterspout as it crossed another creek and, as a tornado, damaged some aeroplane hangars on shore. When last seen in was heading up Chesapeake Bay as a waterspout.

Golden (1973) describes the alarming experience of Bill Wright and his wife when hit by a waterspout on 27 May 1969. They were on their 27-foot trimaran, which was tied to one of the four pillars on a wood and metal shelter at Boca Grande Key, Florida. They saw a waterspout approaching, ran to the shelter, lay on the ground and grasped the concrete pillars supporting the shelter.

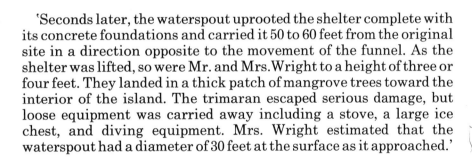

'Seconds later, the waterspout uprooted the shelter complete with its concrete foundations and carried it 50 to 60 feet from the original site in a direction opposite to the movement of the funnel. As the shelter was lifted, so were Mr. and Mrs.Wright to a height of three or four feet. They landed in a thick patch of mangrove trees toward the interior of the island. The trimaran escaped serious damage, but loose equipment was carried away including a stove, a large ice chest, and diving equipment. Mrs. Wright estimated that the waterspout had a diameter of 30 feet at the surface as it approached.'

An even more alarming experience befell Donald Goodwin on Lake Altoona, Georgia. He was in his cabin cruiser, which was securely tied to a 100-foot-long floating dock, when a powerful tornado struck. It lifted both dock and cruiser and dumped them on an adjacent dock (John A. Shanahan).

Waterspouts are often referred to as water tornadoes. While there are undoubted similarities between the two, there are also differences. Joseph H. Golden (1974) says of the waterspouts of the eastern seaboards of the United States: 'Waterspout production occurs in lines of active clouds with most of the cells in the cumulus or early mature stage in their life cycle.' Tornadoes occur when the clouds are fully formed and most violent. The vast majority of waterspouts, although not silent, do not have the accompaniment of the thunderous roars so characteristic of tornadoes. No waterspout has the widespread de-structive violence of the greatest tornadoes. A waterspout with such

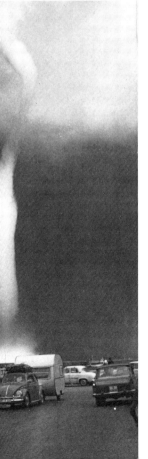

awesome power would devastate even the most modern liner, probably killing everybody on deck.

Rarely, waterspouts – the most violent kind – are formed from meteorological conditions akin to those which spawn tornadoes. Chester W. Newton says: 'Many of the larger and more violent spouts are true tornadoes, formed in association with thunderstorms over land and passing out to sea.' Sometimes the reverse is true. Many of the damaging tornadoes affecting the central and eastern Gulf Coast during the late autumn and early spring originate over the northern Gulf of Mexico as intense waterspouts.

There is a detailed record of such a waterspout/tornado which formed over the eastern Mediterranean. During the afternoon of 22 December 1969, a series of waterspouts was observed off the southern coast of Cyprus. Two of these crossed the Akrotiri peninsula, causing damage and killing four people. R. N. Hardy says that one of these tornadoes was 'the most intense in living memory in southern Cyprus'. It demolished several mud-brick houses and removed the top half of a brick-built minaret; then it scythed across country in a path 300 yards wide for about 4 miles. Buildings were damaged, cars overturned and water tanks, weighing 250 pounds, were lifted and carried away. The noise of the tornado's passage was described as equal to that of 'several jet aircraft flying low overhead'. The tornado finally died when it encountered a steep escarpment, but not before it had damaged a monastery at an altitude of 600 feet.

Waterspouts cannot be ignored, even by a modern liner. Damage is caused primarily by the whirling winds, and to a lesser degree by the sudden reduction in atmospheric pressure and by the deluge of water. The explosive effects of tornadoes, however, are absent or less pronounced. Hurd gives the following examples of encounters between ships and waterspouts.

At night on 30 March 1923, in mid-Atlantic, the White Star liner *Pittsburgh* was struck by a huge waterspout. Her bridge was wrecked, the chart room badly damaged, electrical connections destroyed, the officers' cabins flooded, and the crow's nest filled with water. The liner had to stop her engines for an hour while the worst damage was repaired. The deck officers estimated that the mass of water in the spout was between 40 and 50 feet wide and over 70 feet high.

Most records of waterspout damage relate to sailing ships, which are obviously more vulnerable. Small sailing ships have become total wrecks when hit by large spouts; some have capsized, others have had masts torn away and hulls tossed violently about. While in the South Atlantic, the barque *Lilian Morris* encountered a giant waterspout said to measure nearly 500 feet in diameter at its base. Although the barque collided only with the edge of the spout, the terrific whirl of wind struck her like a giant fist: her fore topgallant mast, the mizzen topmasts, and all her canvas were torn away; one of the crew was swept overboard and drowned. The master of the ship 'was blown round the poop like a piece of paper . . . sky and sea seemed one, resembling a smoking furnace'. Eventually the ship was brought safely to harbour under jury rig.

One other instance of a waterspout's fury occurred on 4 April 1902. The American steamship *Hestia* was steaming off Cape Hatteras at sunset when a large waterspout was observed travelling straight for the ship. The Captain found it impossible to avoid collision and ordered all hands below. He remained on deck until the last moment. The oncoming spout was about 50 feet wide, with an almost black core about 2 feet across. As it struck amidships the captain dived below. There was a deafening roar, strong gusts and a sudden shock as the spout passed over. After the attack the captain came on deck again. Two large hatch tarpaulins, and a plank of wood 8 feet long by 10 inches wide, were high in the air; the log line from the taffrail, complete with weighted spinner, was suspended in space like an imitation of the Indian rope trick!

Guy Mountfort tells me that during the Second World War he was in an aeroplane which hit a waterspout in the Bay of Bengal. The aeroplane was partly turned over and, when examined afterwards, one side was buckled. This must, I think, have been a large and comparatively violent waterspout. Golden has flown through small waterspouts many times, using a specially adapted and instrumented aeroplane. As a result of such flights much has been learnt, by direct measurement, of the winds, temperatures and pressures of waterspouts (Verne H. Leverson, Peter C. Sinclair and Joseph H. Golden).

Perhaps the most interesting phenomenon connected with waterspouts is the so-called 'rains' of fishes and other objects. That live fish, frogs and similar small fry should suddenly descend from the sky is so extraordinary that it is not surprising that many have refused to believe it. That fine British 18th-century naturalist, the Reverend Gilbert White, referred to 'that foolish opinion of [frogs] dropping from the clouds in rain': he considered that it was the refreshing showers that brought frogs out of their hiding places, which is undoubtedly true, and that this sudden appearance gave rise to the story of the clouds 'raining frogs'.

In our day, Bergen Evans, famed debunker of pseudo-science, is sceptical of the 'rains'. In June 1946, *Science* published an exchange of letters between Evans and E. W. Gudger of the American Museum of Natural History. It was Gudger who, in a series of papers published between 1921 and 1946, made scientists realise that the falls were to be taken seriously. He collected over 80 reports from five continents, including various islands, extending over 2,350 years, and set out some of the evidence in his letter to *Science*. In his reply Evans seemed to rely chiefly on the assertion, which is probably true, that 'no trained observer has yet seen quantities of fish coming down out of the sky'. It is fair to add, however, that in *The Natural History of Nonsense* (1947) he admits that the waterspout theory is 'possible though not probable'.

To me such scepticism borders on obscurantism, and implies an inability to evaluate evidence properly. It was the same attitude that motivated the French Academy in the 18th century to deny, in the face of the strongest anecdotal evidence, that stones (meteorites) fell from the sky.

The following item appeared in *The Times* (London) for 17 June 1939. The superintendent of the municipal swimming pool in Trowbridge, Wiltshire, reported that in the afternoon of the 14th there was a heavy shower. He ran for shelter and, as he did so, he heard what he thought were lumps of mud falling behind him:

'I turned and was amazed to see hundreds of tiny frogs falling on to

One of the numerous waterspouts that spiral across Florida waters every summer, sometimes three at once. Notice inner core in funnel and rotational effect of wind on sea's surface. (Joseph Golden)

the concrete path surrounding the bath. It was all over in a few seconds, but there must have been thousands of these tiny frogs, each about the size of the top of one's finger. I swept them up and shovelled them into a bucket.'

Many other frogs were found on nearby grass.

A typical *Times* correspondence followed this report, letters continuing until 11 July 1939. One correspondent recalled that Samuel Pepys wrote in his diary for 23 May 1661 that Elias Ashmole, the antiquary, 'did assure me that frogs and many insects do often fall from the sky, ready formed'. I believe that the earliest reference to the phenomenon is by Athanaseus in his *De Pluvia Piscium*, written some 2,000 years ago.

Two military correspondents wrote of rains they had witnessed in India. Lieutenant-Colonel R. C. R. Owen said that, when he was in Bareilly, he rode across the parade ground immediately after a heavy storm and cloudburst: he found three or four acres covered with small fish about the size of whitebait or small sardines. General Beauvoir de Lisle reported that, after a heavy shower at Lucknow in 1908, his lawn was covered with fish about $1\frac{1}{2}$ inches long, two or three to the square yard and some alive: it seemed impossible for them to have come from anywhere but the sky. To make certain the general inspected the flat roof of his bungalow, where he found several more fish.

One of the strangest falls occurred on the afternoon of 28 May 1881, when a shower of periwinkles fell on Worcester, England. The incident was thoroughly investigated at the time, and was the subject of a leader and long correspondence in the *Worcester Daily Times* (30 May to 11 June 1881). The storm which bore the periwinkles apparently came via the west coast of Scotland and Anglesey, so that the *nearest* place of origin of the winkles was about 100 miles away. According to eye-witnesses, the periwinkles fell between one and two hours before the lightning and rain reached Worcester.

News of the miraculous shower soon spread, and men, women and children went collecting: in one lane, 30 children were seen all busy

Probably the rarest waterspout photograph so far taken – a twin and single spout caught in one shot. (Humble Oil and Refining Co., Houston, Texas)

winkle-picking. The periwinkles were found in hedgerows, gardens, fields and on roads. One man reckoned that two sackfuls fell in his garden. Some were buried 1–2 inches deep in sand, and many were still alive when picked up. The total weight that fell was estimated to be about half a ton.

Weather for December 1983 reported a fall of 'several thousand seashells' in Staffordshire on 21 March 1983. It also recorded that on 5 June 1983 a crab nearly 10 inches across fell within 7 feet of a man at Brighton, Sussex; at the same time waterspouts were observed at sea, some 2 miles away.

None of the above reports was by a scientist. The biologist, A. D. Bajkov, however, wrote a detailed account of a fall that occurred on 23 October 1947 at Marksville, Louisiana. Between 7 a.m. and 8 a.m., over an area approximately 1,000 feet long and 80 feet wide, fish rained down on streets, gardens and rooftops. Bajkov was having breakfast in a restaurant when the waitress excitedly told him 'fish are falling from the sky!' He immediately collected some. He spoke to two people who had actually been struck by falling fish. Over half a dozen species were involved, ranging from a $9\frac{1}{4}$-inch-long large-mouth black bass to minnows; all the species are found in local waters. Bajkov says that a fish weighing over 6 pounds was reported to have fallen in India – a world record for 'fish from the skies'.

Waterspouts may not be the only winds involved in such falls. There are updraughts in whirlwinds, as well as especially powerful ones in heavy thunderstorms and, of course, in tornadoes.

Animals are by no means the only objects to fall from the skies. There are records of the following showering from above: hay, leaves, algae, lichen, nuts, seeds, grain, seaweed – and cannonballs! It is virtually certain that some falls of pwdre ser (see pages 147–50) are due to wind.

William R. Corliss (1977), who has made a wide-ranging study of the literature, questions whether the conventional explanation – wind – is adequate to account for all falls. Among the points he mentions are falls of fish which inhabit deep waters, fish which are dry – and sometimes headless – and falls of immense numbers of animals. He cites the rain of live snakes which descended on Memphis, Tennessee, in 1877. The *Scientific American* reported:

'Thousands of little reptiles, ranging from a foot to 18 inches, were distributed all over the southern part of the city. They probably were carried aloft by a hurricane [*sic*] and wafted through the atmosphere for a long distance; but in what locality snakes exist in such abundance is yet a mystery.'

Nevertheless a levitating wind must have crossed snake-infested fields before reaching the city. What comes down must have gone up. And a funnel of air which can lift tons of spray 400 feet would have no difficulty in similarly raising a horde of rattlesnakes – or periwinkles. The airborne freight is carried for miles and then, when the funnel dissolves, is showered down on an unsuspecting countryside.

NOTE
1. Golden tells me: 'Waterspouts *can* lift heavy objects, as in the five-ton houseboat at Miami's Dinner Key, 1968.'

HAIL

There are several forms of hail. This chapter deals with large hailstones, nearly as dense as pure ice, which are formed almost exclusively in severe thunderstorms during hot weather.

Ordinary hailstorms seldom last for more than half an hour, or for more than a few minutes at any one place. On rare occasions, however, violent storms – supercells – occur. These may be 10 miles across, last for 12 hours and travel 500 miles at speeds up to 1 mile a minute. A hail-bearing thundercloud sometimes towers over 10 miles high, with air currents continuously rushing to the top, carrying with them water vapour.

In the higher, colder regions of the cloud some droplets freeze, sometimes spontaneously, sometimes by coalescing onto a tiny particle which forms the nucleus. As it becomes heavier the incipient hailstone begins to fall, collecting more water droplets which freeze onto the kernel. Powerful updraughts prevent it from reaching the earth and it receives more coatings. This process continues until the hailstone becomes too heavy for the updraughts and falls to earth.

If a hailstone is cut in half, it is generally found to consist of onion-like layers. These are created as the incipient hailstone passes through regions of high water content, when a layer of clear ice is usually formed. When there is not so much liquid available the layer is opaque, owing to entrapped air.

If the upcurrents of air are relatively weak, only small hailstones form. If, however, there are very strong updraughts – exceptionally 100 mph or more – remarkably large stones may form. Sometimes these have only three or four concentric layers, which are relatively thick. At other times a large number of thin layers are formed: 25 were counted in one stone.

Large hailstones often grow without numerous journeys. When they have acquired a coating of ice, they grow by accretion in the part of the cloud bearing large amounts of supercooled water. A very strong updraught is, however, essential to hold the hailstone in the cloud for a lengthy period. The very largest hailstones probably grow in a steadily increasing updraught which travels along with the storm.

In suitable conditions huge hailstones form. Records of stones the size of hens' eggs are comparatively common in meteorological literature, while others the size and weight of cricket balls are sometimes reported. On 6 July 1928, at Potter, Nebraska, H. Stevens, the Weather Bureau's observer, reported: 'Monster chunks of ice could be heard hissing through the air, and when they hit in ploughed or soft ground completely buried themselves, and sank halfway in on prairie ground.' These stones, as large as grapefruit, fell 10 to 15 feet apart. One was measured, weighed and photographed immediately after falling: circumference 17 inches, diameter nearly $5\frac{1}{2}$ inches, weight $1\frac{1}{2}$ pounds. When cut open it was found to consist of the typical layer structure, thus proving that it was a single stone and not several stuck together.

The largest hailstone reliably reported fell on 3 September 1970 at

Hail plummets from a thundercloud over a plain in Colorado. A hail-bearing cloud sometimes towers ten miles high and travels 500 miles at speeds up to a mile a minute. (Bob Stone)

Coffeyville, Kansas. It weighed 1.67 pounds[1] and had a circumference of $17\frac{1}{4}$ inches. Its terminal speed was estimated at about 100 mph, but the vertical updraught speed aloft was nearer 120 mph.

Although the Coffeyville monster is the heaviest authentic hailstone, it is certain that heavier ones have fallen. F. H. Ludlam quotes weights of 5 and $7\frac{1}{2}$ pounds for hailstones which fell in storms over the state of Hyderabad, India, in March 1939 (see also page 78). He adds, however: 'The largest stones mentioned anywhere in the meteorological literature were reported to have fallen at Yüwu in the Chinese province of Shansi, in the summer of 1902.' An English missionary said that two of these weighed $7\frac{1}{2}$ 'catties' each, about 9 pounds. 'Roofs of the house and chapel were beaten almost to powder, bricks in the courtyard split into two halves.'

I should imagine that such extreme weight referred to two or more stones stuck together on landing, but Ludlam comments: 'Although the largest sizes quoted may seem incredible, they should not be dismissed lightly.' He says that such huge hailstones imply a fall speed of 180 mph, which means that, in storms which spawned such monstrous stones, updraughts must have blown at speeds approaching 200 mph, otherwise the stones would have fallen before reaching such enormous weights.

Large hailstones sometimes explode with a sharp crack. W. G. Brown writes of 'a fall of large hailstones, which on coming in contact with the windows or walls or pavement in many instances exploded with a sharp report, so loud as to be mistaken for breaking window panes or a pistol shot. As the hail fell, the fragments sprang up from the ground and flew in all directions, looking like a mass of "popping corn" on a large scale.'

There is evidence from radar that very powerful updraughts do occur in thunderstorms. On page 83 I have recorded the experience of a pilot descending by parachute in a thunderstorm; at times he was sent *upward*, and a descent which would normally have taken 15 minutes took nearly three times as long. Another pilot said: 'I was flying a plane over western New Jersey when I got in the front part of a thunderstorm. Before I knew it I had gained 4,000 feet. I shut my engine

Section of hailstone photographed under polarised light. Rings grow around a central core, often a tiny ice particle. Generally the longer a hailstone stays in the thundercloud the greater the number of rings – 25 have been counted in one stone. Colours reveal the underlying ice crystal texture within the hailstorm.
(Charles Knight)

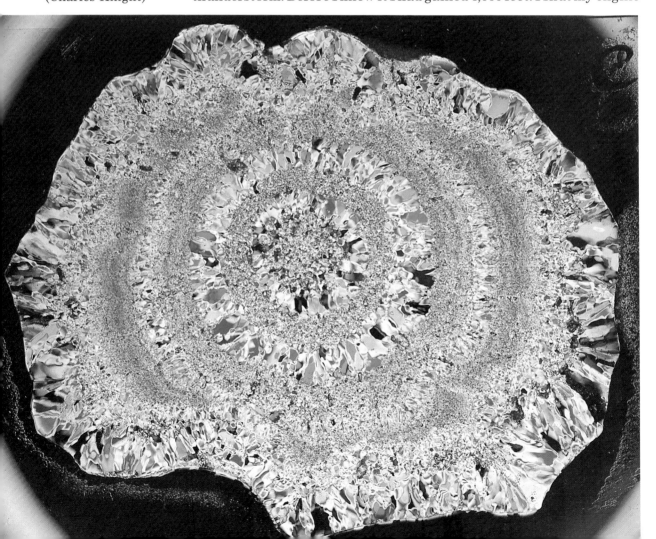

off and dived at *100* mph – and I was still going up!' (quoted by Frederick G. Vosburgh).

It is not unusual for a severe storm to hurl down some 500 hailstones on each square foot of its passage, which sometimes covers 1,000 square miles. In such a storm the number of stones is in the region of 10 million million, give or take a million million or so! Most of these are small; giant stones fall in small concentrations.

Although most hailstones are spheroidal, very different shapes sometimes occur: conical, pear-shaped, oblong, doughnut-shaped (with or without hole), as well as stones with many irregularities and protuberances. Others are covered with icy spikes from $\frac{1}{4}$ inch to nearly 1 inch long projecting from a central core. These unusual shapes are caused by varying conditions of water and temperature in the cloud, air currents in the upper atmosphere, and the way the hailstone is formed – and sometimes split. Some hailstones are soft and mushy, containing a large proportion of unfrozen water.

Nancy C. and Charles A. Knight have published a paper on 'Some Observations on Foreign Material in Hailstones'. They examined a stone in which the nucleus was a small insect (a chalcid). Much larger objects – stones, twigs, nuts, etc. – have been reported in hailstones, although some of these may have adhered to the ice as it lay on the ground. The speed of the updraught of air in a violent hailstorm, and the known power of waterspouts and tornadoes to lift various objects and later shower them down upon the earth, render such incidents credible. J. R. Norman, a British ichthyologist, says that there is a record of a hailstone as large as a hen's egg which fell during a heavy storm at Essen, Germany and that inside was a $1\frac{1}{2}$-inch carp.

The *Monthly Weather Review* reported that after a severe hailstorm on 11 May 1894 over Bovina, Mississippi, a large 'hailstone' measuring about 8×6 inches was found to be a gopher turtle entirely encased in ice.

I have not read of a bird becoming embedded in a hailstone, but such an occurrence is not impossible. Charles F. Brooks says that during a storm at Worcester, Massachusetts, there was a fall of iced ducks. Had a very strong updraught been blowing, it is possible that these ducks would have received several more layers of ice before they finally descended. They could then have been described as ducks in hailstones – although with rather a large nucleus! Did a local journalist caption his story 'Fowl Weather'?

That this is no far-fetched report was proved in 1930 when five German glider pilots soared into a thundercloud over the Rhön Mountains. The men, afraid that the violent winds would tear their gliders apart, bailed out. The powerful updraughts evidently caught the billowing parachutes and carried the pilots into the region of supercooled water drops, the raw material of hailstones. The men formed gigantic nuclei, rising and falling like outsized yo-yos until they eventually landed entirely covered with ice and frozen to death – except one, who miraculously survived. Seff Kunz, of the German Aero Club, tells me that a somewhat similar tragedy occurred among gliders at Rhön in 1938, one pilot being killed.

Hailstones are a hazard to aeroplanes. They have damaged planes flying as high as 45,000 feet (9 miles). Robert Buck, a veteran airline pilot says:

'Flying through hail is probably the most nerve-racking experience in the sky. The clatter is overpowering. Some hailstones are bigger than tennis balls, and thousands of these, rock-hard and [with the aircraft] coming at over 180 miles an hour, can damage an aircraft badly.[2]

'Years ago a friend of mine flew into severe hail. He decided to turn and get out. The hail had already broken the windshield, beaten the front of the wing, and smashed out the landing lights. As he banked the aircraft to circle back, the fuselage was turned broadside to the hail, which quickly broke every window on the exposed side.'

Severe hailstorms occur only rarely in Great Britain. One at Barton, Lincolnshire, is commemorated in a monument, surely one of the strangest ever erected:

'In memory of the great hailstorm at Barton, July 3, 1883, 10.30 to 11 p.m. Ice 5 inches long, 3 inches wide – 15 tons of glass broken – ice weighed $2\frac{1}{2}$ ozs.'

The monument is of bricks which were being made at the time of the storm. Some of the large hailstones made deep indentations in the hardening bricks, which thus preserve a record of the storm for posterity.

A violent hailstorm occurred on 5 September 1958 at Horsham, Sussex. Some stones were tennis-ball size, one weighing $6\frac{3}{4}$ ounces. In their report of this storm, F. H. Ludlam and W. C. Macklin say:

'In most places shortly before the onset of the hail and rain there was a sudden squall from between west and northwest, strong

Left   *Largest known hailstone compared with chicken's egg. The hailstone, which fell at Coffeyville, Kansas on 3 September 1970, weighed 1.67 pounds and was 17.25 inches in circumference. (National Center for Atmospheric Research, Boulder, Colorado)*

Right *Large hail wrecks a light plane . . .* (Marty Haedtler)

Above *and batters a heavy one.* (Braniff Airways)

enough to break down tree branches and sometimes to uproot trees. People hastening to close windows were driven back to shelter by a bombardment of hailstones, which arriving at a shallow angle broke many panes with such violence that glass splinters were flung against the opposite walls. The larger stones broke roof tiles and carried away the lead frames of small window panes. Car drivers were brought to a standstill by road-flooding, loss of vision in the torrential rain and swirling foliage, and by the felling of large trees across the road; some cars were covered with dents from the impacts of the hailstones.'

The severest hailstorms occur in regions of great land masses and with warm, though not tropical, climates. The frequency of storms varies greatly throughout the world. Whereas some areas, such as deserts, never have a hailstorm, other areas have them frequently. Athens, Greece, has hail on average once every six days during January and February. Probably the most hail-prone area in the world is Kericho in the Nandi Hills, Kenya, where hail falls on an average of 132 days throughout the year, mostly between April and October. The reason for this appears to be the meeting of rising moist air from Lake Victoria with winds over the Nandi Hills (Alexander L. Alusa).

To anyone who has not experienced it, the havoc caused by a violent hailstorm is almost unbelievable. In his well-known autobiography, Benvenuto Cellini, the 16th-century Italian sculptor and goldsmith, says that in the summer of 1545, while out riding with some companions, he was caught in a violent storm: '. . . the heavens made a noise so great and horrible that I thought the last day had come.' Then came the hail, small at first but later 'the size of big lemons'. He and his friends took refuge in a wood. A huge hailstone shattered a thick branch of the

pine tree under which he was sheltering.

'The storm raged for some while, but at last it stopped; and we, who were pounded black and blue, scrambled as well as we could upon our horses. Pursuing the way to our lodging for the night, we showed our scratches and bruises to each other; but about a mile farther on we came upon a scene of devastation which surpassed what we had suffered, and defies description. All the trees were stripped of their leaves and battered; the beasts in the fields lay dead; many of the herdsmen had also been killed; we observed large quantities of hailstones which could not have been grasped with two hands.'

Exaggeration by a medieval layman writing for effect? Four hundred years later on, an American scientist described the hailstorm of 14 July 1953 which swept over the Canadian province of Alberta, covering a path some 140 miles long and 5 miles wide. Some hailstones were as large as golf balls, a few even larger. The storm was accompanied by winds of up to 75 mph. Allen G. Smith, biologist of the United States Fish and Wildlife Service, says:

'A close investigation of the hail damage on the ground presented a picture of unbelievable devastation. Grasses and herbs were shredded beyond recognition and beaten into the earth. Trees and shrubs were stripped of all leaves and small branches and the bark on one side of the larger trees had been torn away or deeply gouged

76

by hailstones. Plants growing in waters of the potholes and lakes were reduced to nondescript pulp. Emergent vegetation had disappeared, destroyed and beaten under the water's surface by the weight of the hail. Ponds that had been choked with grasses, sedges, cattails, and bulrush since June, were stripped of all evidence of former plant growth.'

Songbirds, hawks, owls and wildfowl were killed by the thousand. Examination of hundreds of ducks showed that many had had their skulls crushed. The post-mortems revealed the gruesome fact that the upper mandible had been torn from many adult ducks, leaving only the lower mandible and the tongue. The number killed was estimated with reasonable accuracy because the hailstorm occurred in an area where there are regular aerial surveys of wildfowl. These showed at least 36,000 ducks and ducklings killed, in addition to thousands of other birds. On 18 July another severe hailstorm occurred in the same area, this time killing an estimated 28,000 ducks and ducklings. Within the space of five days, therefore, over 60,000 ducks were killed in an area of 700 square miles.

It is not only birds which suffer from large hail. In the Alberta hailstorm a 600-pound hog, caught out in the open, was battered to death. During a hailstorm in Nebraska on 8 August 1917, piglets and calves were fatally injured and scores of rabbits were killed in the fields. Horses and cattle which were caught in open pasture were found after the storm covered with blood and with big lumps on their bodies. On 15 July 1978, more than 200 sheep were killed in Montana by 'baseball-sized hail' (Kendrick Frazier). In the discussion following Bilham and Relf's paper on hail, given before the Royal Meteorological Society in 1937, Sir George Simpson said that, when in India, he had received a report that buffaloes over a large area had been completely wiped out by a hailstorm. If the stones were the size of grapefruit and were pelting down at 100 mph or more, I suppose that this was possible – just!

Readers of the Bible, unacquainted with the size that hailstones sometimes attain, may have been puzzled by the ravages said to have been caused by hail during one of the plagues of Egypt (Exodus 9: 19 and 25) and by the statement in the Book of Joshua (10: 11) about the battle with the Amorites: '. . . *they were* more which died with hailstones than *they* whom the children of Israel slew with a sword.' The Amorites were caught on a steep mountain path and many probably fell to their death. It is, however, known that very large hailstones sometimes fall in Palestine: Douglas V. Duff says that he has seen cattle brained by a Palestinian hailstorm.

There are other records of people being killed by violent hailstorms. This is not surprising when it is remembered that the impact of a giant hailstone is greater than that from a cricket ball hit for six, or a home-run hit at baseball. On 1 May 1928, six children were killed and ten other persons injured by hailstones the size of hens' eggs which fell at Klausenberg, Romania. On 10 July 1923, at Rostov, Russia, hailstones reported to have weighed 1–2 pounds killed 23 people and many cattle; most of the human fatalities were peasants who had run into the fields to save their cattle. On 13 June 1930, in the Siatista district of Greece, hailstones killed 22 people (Talman, 1931; and Flora).

The farmer's foe, large hail, wrecks a field of maize. Known in North America as the 'White Plague' a single hailstorm sometimes causes losses of several million dollars. Damage resulting from the devastating hailstorm in Calgary, Canada on 28 July 1981 was estimated at 100 million dollars!
(J.C. Allen and Son)

There are more records of death from hailstones in India than from any other country. The *Report of the British Association* for 1855 says that a hailstorm on 12 May 1853 at Peshawar killed 84 people and 3,000 oxen; some of the stones were $3\frac{1}{4}$ inches in diameter, cricket-ball size. The most deadly hailstorm of which there is authentic record burst over the Moradabad and Beheri districts of India on 20 April 1888: 246 people were killed. Some were pounded to death but the majority were knocked down by stones and wind, buried under drifts and died of cold and exposure. J. S. MacIntosh, who was an eye-witness, says:

'A terrific storm of hail [broke] all the windows and glass doors. The verandas were blown away by the wind. A great part of the roof fell in, and the massive pucca portico was blown down. The walls shook. It was nearly dark outside, and hailstones of an enormous size were dashed down with a force which I have never seen anything to equal ... The really destructive hail seems to have been confined to a very small area, about six or seven miles around Moradabad ... Men caught in the open and without shelter were simply pounded to death by the hail. Fourteen bodies were found in the racecourse. The police report that 1,600 head of cattle, sheep and goats were killed.' (Quoted by A. W. Greely)

Other accounts of human deaths from hail are mentioned by Frazier.

Very occasionally large chunks of ice which are not true hail fall, often from a clear sky. There is a simple explanation for some of these falls: J. Hallet tells me that one large chunk contained tea leaves, presumably waste from the kitchen outlet of an aeroplane.

There are reliable accounts of ice-falls before the Wright brothers. Consider what happened on Mr Moffat's farm at Balavulich, Ross-shire, Scotland, one evening in 1849. First there was a tremendous thunderclap, then a great mass of ice, nearly 20 feet in circumference, thudded on to the ground. Examination showed that it was transparent except for a small part apparently consisting of large hailstones frozen together. 'No appearance whatever of either hail or snow was discernible in the surrounding district.' An idle press report? No. It was reported in the sober pages of the *Edinburgh New Philosophical Journal*.

One of the most remarkable ice-falls was witnessed by R. F. Griffiths, a professional scientist. On the evening of 2 April 1973, at Manchester, there was a violent flash of lightning and about ten minutes later a large lump of ice fell within 10 feet of him. Griffiths picked up the largest fragment, which was later examined in the cold room of the University of Manchester Institute of Science and Technology. The ice was extensively layered, composed of cloud water, was nearly 6 inches long and weighed about 20 ounces. It was estimated that the original weight of the ice was about 3 pounds. After numerous enquiries Griffiths concluded that it was not a hailstone and that it was most unlikely to have fallen from an aeroplane (*Meteorological Magazine*, England, September 1975).

An aeroplane was suggested as the explanation of the *ton* of ice which crashed down on American Avenue, Long Beach, California, on 5 June 1953. For about two minutes an estimated 50 chunks of ice, some weighing 150 pounds, 'fell like bombs'. There were no casualties but

Hail cannon and shed for storing its gunpowder. In Europe, at the turn of the century, thousands of these cannons bombarded the heavens in attempts to shatter the damaging large hail before it fell on farmers' crops. Some

the hoods of two cars were crushed. The Civil Aeronautics Authority speculated that the ice was shed from an aeroplane flying at 35,000 feet, but Paul Light, a special investigator of the American Air Force, was 'extremely doubtful' if such large ice chunks could form on the wings of even the largest plane (*Long Beach Press-Telegram*, 5 June 1953).

To readers of that doughty collector of the strange and rare, Charles Fort, ice blocks from the heavens will come as no surprise. According to astronomers there is ice in space, notably in the head of some comets, but hardly 'vast fields of aerial ice from which pieces occasionally break away' and shower down on the unsuspecting earth!

Today these wayward chunks of ice have been christened ice meteors. They are one of the unexplained mysteries of meteorology. Several articles and letters on the subject appeared in *The Journal of Meteorology* (England), in 1977.

Probably no country in the world suffers greater financial loss from hailstorms than the United States: nearly twice that from lightning and tornadoes combined. A single hailstorm frequently causes damage of 2 million dollars or more. David M. Ludlum says that the storm of 23 June 1951, which swept across parts of Kansas and Missouri, caused property damage alone (not counting crop losses) of $12\frac{3}{4}$ million dollars. The hailstorm of 28 July 1981 in Calgary, Canada, caused damage of 100 million dollars!

To farmers, especially, hail is well named the 'White Plague'. Many have had the bitter experience of owning fields of flourishing crops one day, fields of worthless vegetable debris the next. No wonder hail insurance is a multi-million dollar business in the United States. And the rest of the world? According to the World Meteorological Organisation 'worldwide losses from hail damage are in excess of two thousand million dollars'. And that is *per year*.

J. A. P. Laurie has described the tests carried out by the South African National Building Research Institute to discover the effects of hail bombardment on various materials. Artificial hailstones were formed from clear ice, most of them $2\frac{1}{2}$ inches in diameter and weighing 4–5 ounces. These projectiles were then fired from a hailgun powered by compressed air at speeds up to 100 mph. The results showed that galvanised corrugated steel was dented, corrugated aluminium was punctured, and $\frac{1}{2}$-inch-thick slates cracked.

Throughout the centuries various rituals have been used in attempts to prevent hail from falling on vulnerable areas, or to prevent it from falling at all. The ancient Greeks used to sacrifice a lamb or pullet when hail threatened. In the present century peasants in rural Italy have practised such rites as ringing silver bells, hanging amulets on trees, and sprinkling bits of charred wood from the Yule log on the fields in vain attempts to prevent hail from ruining their vineyards and crops.

Endeavours have also been made to ward off hail by mechanical means. At one time church bells were rung when a storm threatened, presumably because it was thought that the vibration might prevent the hail from forming, but by far the most famous of early attempts was the 'hail cannon'. At the turn of the century, funnel-shaped cannons or mortars proliferated among the agricultural communities of France, Italy and Austria, which suffered grievous losses from hailstorms. The cannons fired blank charges which, it was thought, prevented the

hail cannons were nearly 30 feet long and weighed eight tons. The effect on the hail was negligible but accidental explosions caused hundreds of injuries and some deaths. (Illinois State Water Survey)

formation of the large damaging hail. Some believed that the noise accomplished this beneficial effect; others put their faith in the 'vortex rings' of the discharge, or the effect of the smoke rings, or a combination of these factors.

The enthusiasm for the cannons was fantastic. Several international congresses on 'Hail Shooting' were held. In November 1900, in Padua, Italy, 60 different models were displayed, the largest of which was nearly 30 feet long and weighed some 8 tons. In 1900, in the vineyards of upper Italy, the skies were rattled by some 10 million firings from 10,000 cannons. Whatever these firings did to the hail, they were certainly dangerous to the farmers: in Venice and Brescia alone, seven deaths and 78 injuries were reported.

The psychological effect of being able to 'shoot at the enemy' doubtless provided some comfort, but the truth is that this enormous expenditure of effort was valueless in preventing the formation of large hail. Following an international conference in July 1902, the Austrian and Italian governments carried out careful tests in two hail-prone areas. B. C. V. Oddie says: 'Both were well provided with weapons and manpower, and able to put up a barrage far more intense than [usual]. Within two years both areas had been visited several times by heavy and destructive hail storms, and the hail cannon was completely discredited.' Nevertheless, some European enthusiasts were still battering the heavens with hail cannons in 1983 (Stanley A. Changnon Jr, and J. Loreena Ivens).

Since the Second World War more scientific measures have been used. They all have the same principle: to supply more nuclei similar to the ice on which hailstones develop. The hope is that this will lead to more, but smaller stones. The extra nuclei are released into the hail-forming cloud in several ways. One method, used chiefly in France and Switzerland, is to generate smoke on the ground, which wafts millions of particles into the clouds. Soviet scientists have used rockets to try to deliver nuclei into regions which have been identified by radar as having a high liquid content.

In many countries aeroplanes have been used to 'seed' hail clouds, chiefly with silver iodide or common salt, but many meteorologists are not satisfied that such measures have the effects claimed for them. J. C. Thams, a Swiss authority on hail, tells me: 'The last experiment from 1957–63 with silver iodide gave no significant results that the formation of hail can be prevented by seeding the clouds with silver iodide. I think till now there is no evidence that we can influence the formation of hail.' Unfortunately, despite more recent experiments in various countries, Thames' conclusion is still valid.

Some scientists are sceptical of all attempts at weather modification. Dean E. Mann said at the 1978 meeting of the American Association for the Advancement of Science: 'The lightning suppression programme is virtually dead, hail suppression has undergone retrenchment, major efforts at hurricane modification have been delayed.' He added that for those scientists still trying to moderate the violent storms that maul the earth 'the frustration level is high'.

Attempts have been made, notably in the United States, to forecast the occurrence and location of hail-bearing storms. The first forecasts, in February 1950 at Tinker Air Force Base, Oklahoma, were for the benefit of military aircraft. Today there are regular hail-warning systems for both the military and civilians. Balloons carry packages of meteorological instruments (radiosondes) which transmit to ground stations information on weather conditions in the high atmosphere (up to 20 miles); further information is obtained by orbiting satellites. Radar is used extensively to detect the characteristic echoes of hailstorms.

Like hurricanes, severe hailstorms have played an important part in history. In the morning of 13 July 1788, two great hailstorms began in southwest France and swept in parallel bands, about 12 miles apart, nearly 500 miles to the northeast. The hail affected 1,039 communes, caused great damage to crops and ruined the harvest. The consequent food shortage helped to bring about the French Revolution in the following year.

After this, it is surprising to learn that a violent hailstorm once brought peace to France. In May 1360, Edward III was with his army between Paris and Chartres, preparing to renew the war with France. On 8 May there was such a violent storm that, according to Sir John Froissart, the famous chronicler of the times: 'It seemed as if the world were come to an end. Giant hailstones killed men and horses, and even the most courageous were terrified.' The king was so affected that 'he vowed to the Virgin that he would conclude a peace'. The treaty of Brétigny followed.

NOTES

1. Authorities are not agreed on the weight of the heaviest recorded British hailstone. The Horsham stone of 6¾ ounces (see page 74) is authentic, but I do not doubt that heavier hailstones have fallen on Great Britain.

2. If this is a literal description of a bombardment, the wonder is that the aircraft survived!

Wing-tip rockets scatter silver-iodide crystals towards clouds heavy with potentially crop-damaging hail. Such cloud-seeding is widely used in attempts to prevent large hailstones from forming but many meteorologists are doubtful whether the results are worth the effort. (Jim Bradenburg)

LIGHTNING

To the ancients lightning was supernatural. The blinding light and tremendous roaring surely could come from no lesser source than the gods, but were Jove's bolts a punishment or a warning? For many centuries lightning divination was part of Roman statecraft, and about 300 BC the College of Augurs was entrusted with this task. A thunderstorm was the signal for a furious outbreak of bell-ringing. Medieval bells were frequently inscribed *Fulgura frango* – 'I break the lightning'. Many bell-ringers were killed as a result of strikes on church towers.

The true cause of lightning was not known until the middle of the 18th century. Before then various picturesque theories had been held concerning its origin, such as clouds rubbing together, an atmospheric explosion of 'nitrous and sulphurous vapours' or an emanation from the earth. It was not until the experiments of such men as Benjamin Franklin that the true origin of lightning was established.

Lightning is the electrical discharge from a thundercloud, but the precise mechanism is still debated. This is hardly surprising. Richard E. Orville says: 'The transient, unpredictable nature of the lightning flash makes it one of the most difficult atmospheric phenomena to study. The discharge strikes without warning, carries currents from a few tens to a few hundred thousand amperes, and has components that emit light with intensities varying over several orders of magnitude.' Lightning is the fastest of all natural phenomena, some strokes travelling at nearly half the speed of light. Yet, by the use of special cameras, spectroscopic techniques and electrical measuring devices, it is now possible to give a fair description of what happens when lightning strikes.

Generally, the electrification which produces lightning is thought to be caused by the interaction of wind, water and ice in a thundercloud (cumulonimbus). Lightning also occurs, however, in snowstorms, sandstorms and in the ash clouds over erupting volcanoes. Thunder is the noise caused by the effect of the discharge – the *spat-spat* of a gigantic spark plug.

Since the end of the Second World War thunderstorms have been investigated by radar, rocket, balloon and aeroplane. There are two types: local storms which last an hour or two and produce moderate lightning, and groups of storms which last many hours, travel tens or hundreds of miles and produce the most violent lightning.

A thunderstorm generally forms when an updraught of warm, moist air (which provides the energy) rises into cold air. In an extreme tropical storm the resulting thunderclouds sometimes tower 13 miles above the earth, cover an area of 500 square miles, and contain more than a million tons of water. The cloud looks like a huge cauliflower or an enormous white anvil, and is topped by a 'cirrus umbrella' composed of countless millions of ice crystals. These giant cloud masses are cells of turbulent energy whose electrical potential is millions of volts, in a great storm hundreds of millions. The rising air gathers momentum;

frequently there are currents shooting upward at 50 mph, and occasionally at 100 mph or so. There are also downcurrents, but they are less violent. As the moist air rises it cools and usually, although not always, ice crystals form. The stage is set for lightning.

So much for the technical description. Thanks, however, to one man's extraordinary experience, we have an account of what it is like to be caught in a thunderstorm miles above the earth. When US Marine Corps jet pilot, William Rankin, was at an altitude of 47,000 feet (9 miles, or $1\frac{1}{2}$ times the height of Everest), his engine failed and he bailed out. His pre-set parachute did not open until he had fallen to 10,000 feet. Normally he should have reached the ground in about 13 minutes but, caught in the thunderstorm's turbulent air and tremendous updraughts, the nightmare journey took him nearly three-quarters of an hour. At times Rankin was actually going up.

'I was blown up and down as much as 6,000 feet at a time. It went on for a long time, like being on a very fast elevator, with strong blasts of compressed air hitting you. Once when a violent blast of air sent me careering up into the chute and I could feel the cold, wet nylon collapsing about me, I was sure the chute would never blossom again. But, by some miracle, I fell back and the chute *did* recover its billow.

'The wind had savage allies. The first clap of thunder came as a deafening explosion that literally shook my teeth. I didn't *hear* the thunder, I actually *felt* it – an almost unbearable physical experience. If it had not been for my closely fitted helmet, the explosions might have shattered my eardrums.

'I saw lightning all around me in every shape imaginable. When very close, it appeared mainly as a huge, bluish sheet several feet thick. It was raining so torrentially that I thought I would drown in midair. Several times I held my breath, fearing that otherwise I might inhale quarts of water.' (*Time*, August 17 1959)

Broadly, the top of the thundercloud is charged with positive electricity, the bottom with negative; in many thunderstorms there is also a small charge of positive electricity near the bottom of the cloud. But how is the normally insulating air transformed in a fraction of a second into a white-hot conductor?

On the earth directly below the cloud, positive charge is induced.[1] As the cloud drifts over the earth the positive charge follows it like a shadow, climbing any prominences, such as church steeples and chimneys, which will bring it nearer to the cloud. Enormous differences of electrical potential – typically 50 million volts – between earth and cloud are built up. Something has to give. Suddenly from the base of the thundercloud a spark, called the stepped leader, shoots towards the earth. It travels in a step of about 50 yards in less than a thousandth of a second, followed after a pause of 50 millionths of a second by another similar step towards the ground. The process is repeated step by step until there is an electrically conductive channel reaching from the cloud to very near the earth or an earthed object.

A leader in reverse now leaps up from the earth. It makes contact with the downward leader and then the main lightning stroke soars *upward*. D. J. Malan told me that the highest return-stroke speed he

Overleaf Lightning splits the skies over Kitt Peak National Observatory, Arizona. During the time exposure the strokes at extreme right and left were nearest to the camera. The film was thus over-exposed, resulting in an exaggeration of the width of the strokes. (Gary Ladd)

and his colleagues have measured is 87,000 miles per second – nearly half the speed of light! There are usually a series of such return strokes in less than a second. As the main flash ascends, it energises and lights up the branches made by the leaders. These branches, of course, point downward and this explains why photographs of lightning often give the impression that the main flash is directed towards the earth.

The bright central core of the main flash is surrounded by a corona envelope (glow discharge) with a diameter varying from about 3 feet to 20 feet or so. The diameter is exaggerated in photographs because of halation – the reflection and dispersion of the intense light on the negative. The core of the flash is very narrow, ranging from about one-tenth of an inch to 2 inches.

Where does the 'light' in lightning come from? The tremendous blast of the stroke – sometimes 1 million horse-power – causes the surrounding air atoms and ions to glow. A similar process is seen on a miniature scale in the light produced in an old-fashioned arc-discharge lamp.

The lightning causes a drop in the electrical charge in the thundercloud. It recharges in some tens of seconds and is then ready for another flash. People who have been in the midst of a violent thunderstorm have experienced this 'recharging' for themselves. Ann Strong, who was caught on a mountainside in British Columbia during such a storm, says of the lightning:

'After each strike we moved in silence for a while, with only the tearing wind and slashing rain. Then the rocks would begin a shrill humming, each on a slightly different note. The humming grew louder and louder. You could feel a charge building up in your body. Our hair stood on end. The charge increased, and the humming swelled, until everything reached an unbearable climax. Then the lightning would strike again – with a crack like a gigantic rifle shot. The strike broke the tension. For a while we would grope forward in silence. Then the humming would begin again.' (Quoted by Colin Fletcher)

Some series of discharges last for a second, during which there are many successive strokes: 31 have been photographed in three-fifths of a second. Incidentally, lightning does sometimes strike twice in the same place; the Empire State Building in New York is often struck a dozen or so times during a single storm. Some people have been struck more than once, and lived to tell two – or more – tales. One man has been struck seven times!

Throughout the world there are an estimated 16 million thunderstorms a year, and at any given moment about 1,800 are taking place. The humid tropics have more than any other region, many places having over 100 thunderstorm days a year. Bogor, on the mountainous island of Java, averages 320, a world record.

For comparison, the average number of thunderstorm days in Great Britain varies from five (central Scotland) to 20 (southeast England). In the United States, the west coast has about three, the central states about 45, and Florida about 90 thunderstorm days a year. It has been estimated that throughout the world there are between 100 and 150 lightning strokes every second.

There may be thousands of flashes, both horizontal and vertical, in a storm. During the great thunderstorm in July 1923, 6,924 were recorded over London, at one point 47 flashes in one minute. On 25 December 1923, at Pretoria, South Africa, 360 flashes occurred in three minutes, and for about an hour 100 flashes a minute were recorded. And Cicely M. Botley told me that during a thunderstorm in southeast England on 5 September 1958: 'From Tunbridge Wells at one time the whole northwest horizon was ablaze. The strokes were too rapid to be distinguished.'

Lightning activity of this order belongs to what Bernard Vonnegut and Charles B. Moore have called 'giant electrical storms'. The clouds of these storms rise higher than those of ordinary thunderstorms, the updraughts are faster, and the electrical activity is more violent and continuous. These giant storms are associated with the most powerful type of tornado, such as the one which wrecked part of Worcester, Massachusetts, on 9 June 1953.

While the vast majority of thunderstorms seldom last for more than a few hours, some last for days. F. H. Ludlam says that the most prolonged thunderstorm mentioned in the meteorological literature appears to be one which drenched the Saint Malo area of France. It began at about 8 p.m. on 15 September 1929 and did not rain itself out until about 4 p.m. on the 17th; about 10 inches of rain fell during these 44 hours.

The length of a lightning stroke varies quite considerably. In the cloud-to-earth discharge it is rarely more than 1 mile, although flashes 4 miles long have been reported. The longest occur when lightning discharges from one part of a cloud to another, or from one cloud to another: in the first a length of 10 miles has been recorded; in the second over 100 miles (as proved by radar observation). Rarely, one of these long horizontal flashes finally turns earthward, striking the earth from a blue sky, hence the probable origin of the phrase 'bolt from the blue'. There are far more horizontal than vertical strokes, the proportion varying in different areas of the world. In Great Britain and

Below *Lightning over Pretoria, South Africa.* (G. Held)

Below right *Lightning over Lugano, Switzerland.* (Hugo Binz)

The most frequent form of lightning – horizontal. In Great Britain and North America there are about four horizontal strokes for every vertical one. Radar observations prove that some horizontal strokes are over 100 miles long.
(Daphne Kinzler)

North America the ratio is about four to one. Horizontal flashes are generally less powerful than vertical ones.

The colour of a lightning flash varies considerably. The most usual is white, the combination of the spectra of nitrogen and oxygen. Red and yellow flashes are often seen in South Africa when the air is very dusty. A red or pink discharge occurs when air rich in water vapour is ionised and adds the spectrum of hydrogen to that of nitrogen and oxygen. Every colour in the spectrum has been reported but, after white, the main colours are yellow, pink and red. E. L. Hawke told me that, in England, blue lightning is a common feature of exceptionally violent thunderstorms.

The German meteorologist, Walter Knoche, while travelling down the Rio Paraguay in South America, encountered one of the weirdest lightning displays ever reported by a reliable observer. There were dazzling white flashes resembling strings of glowing pearls, rapidly moving orange-coloured discharges, flashes that revolved like Catherine wheels and hundreds of luminous arcs that were so brilliant that Knoche had to close his eyes. For several hours of this fantastic display there was no thunder. 'A ghastly quiet prevailed: not a breath of air stirred.' (C. F. Talman)

Before dealing further with lightning, it is necessary to explain the accompanying thunder. Some picturesque theories have been advanced to account for this, the loudest of all the common sounds of Nature: a cloud bursting; ice and hail crashing together; and two clouds bumping against each other. In the 19th century there were many advocates of the 'vacuum theory': lightning caused a vacuum,

and thunder was the result of the divided atmosphere coming together with a bang.

Lightning streams down over Mountain Home, Indiana on 4 August 1983. This storm started over 20 fires in an hour. (David McCoy)

The real cause is the intense heat of the lightning stroke, ranging up to 30,000°C, five times the surface temperature of the sun! The air along the path of the discharge expands with the violence of an explosion, radiating pressure waves through the atmosphere. Thunder seldom reaches the ears as a single clap. If it does the lightning is uncomfortably close and the sound is a sharp and terrific crack, like a field gun a few feet away. This sound comes from the *shock wave* of the white-hot expanding channel; it is supersonic but attenuates rapidly with distance. At a distance of about 500 feet the more familiar sound of thunder (caused by the pressure waves) is heard. As sound travels at about 1,000 feet per second, the distance of the lightning can be estimated from the interval elapsing between seeing the flash and hearing the thunder, counting 1 mile for every five seconds.

Thunder can normally be heard at up to 7 miles, but occasionally freak atmospheric and ground conditions enable it to be heard 40 miles away. Such thunder comes only from extremely powerful earth-to-cloud strokes.

About 1/400th of the total energy dissipated in a lightning stroke goes into the production of thunder. This may not seem much until it is realised that this means that thousands of horse-power are momentarily expended in some thunderclaps.

Thunder is not the only sound associated with lightning. Other sounds reported by those who have been very near lightning strokes vary from 'a mild hissing' or 'the swishing of a long whip' to 'a sudden

Lightning streaks the sky over Tuscon, Arizona, during a ten-second exposure. As many as 1,500 strokes have been recorded during one storm in the Tuscon area. (Thomas Ives)

rush of wind' or 'a tearing noise as of canvas being ripped violently'.

Only two types of lightning are popularly referred to: *fork*, a multi-branched vertical flash; and *sheet*, a discharge between clouds, the diffuse illumination giving them momentarily the appearance of a white sheet. Several other types of lightning, however, are mentioned in the technical literature.

Streak or *fork* lightning appears as one or more vivid lines or streaks. It is the form most often seen, the straightforward cloud-to-earth and return strokes or cloud-to-cloud strokes. The earth-to-cloud strokes are the most powerful form and cause the loudest thunder.

Ribbon lightning is streak lightning occurring in a very strong wind which moves the conducting channel (the ionised path) so that the individual strokes are sometimes seen separately.

Heat lightning sometimes plays along the horizon on summer evenings during hot weather. It is too distant for thunder to be heard and often no thunderstorms are visible. It is generally explained as the reflection of lightning flashes occurring below the horizon, although some meteorologists believe that it is the result of glow-like discharges in the sky.

Beaded, pinched or *pearl* lightning appears as a flash broken into more or less evenly spaced dashes. This 'pearl-necklace' effect lasts for a second or so. It has been suggested that this form of lightning is related to ball lightning (see below).

Rocket lightning is a very rare and unexplained form which is slow enough for its movement to be visible, as with a rocket.

Ball lightning is controversial and is dealt with later.

Dark or *black* lightning, as it is called, is merely a photographic freak resulting from the reversal of the image and has nothing to do with true lightning.

On rare occasions, after the main storm has passed, an extremely violent flash of lightning occurs, the so-called 'parting shot'. It is so vivid that even in daylight it appears as a blinding flash. The accompanying thunder is also far louder than ordinary claps. Charles F. Brooks says:

> 'The cloud from which this lightning comes is the rear portion of the far-flung spreading top of a storm of great intensity, the center of which may be miles away. It is characteristic of heavy thunderclouds that they mushroom out like a vast-spreading umbrella. When their electrical charges are powerful they may let loose a bolt which will reach the earth, though it must jump a gap of four or five miles. Such a bolt is, of necessity, of particularly destructive force, for the difference in potential between cloud and earth must be enormous, even when compared with that of the usual jump of a mile. The thunder may be heard 20 miles away.'

Very rarely giant lightning strokes occur which greatly exceed those normally experienced. Optical sensors on orbital satellites, installed to record nuclear explosions, have detected lightning 1,000 times more powerful (brighter) than average. 'The powerful discharges were found to attain optical peak powers of 10^{13} watts and total radiant energies exceeding 10^9 joules.' (*Journal of Meteorology*, England, December 1977)

LIGHTNING

The destruction caused by lightning is due almost entirely to the sudden and intense heating which occurs along the path of the discharge. In a fraction of a second trees burst; the sap is volatised and explodes. Sometimes a tree just disappears, fragments flying for hundreds of yards. Rock is shattered in a similar way; if there is a deep crack containing moisture – ice or water – the lightning can turn it into superheated steam which explodes like a charge of dynamite, smashing the rock. Chimneys have been destroyed when lightning suddenly volatised the moisture in the bricks. Windows have vanished because lightning evaporated the glass, and very rarely a small and flimsily built house is wrecked completely, as if by an earthquake.

In the days of wooden sailing ships, lightning was a major hazard of the sea. In 1838 the 800-pound topgallant mast of HMS *Rodney* was struck and instantly converted into shavings; the sea looked as if the carpenters had swept their shavings overboard. Sometimes, when a mast was struck, the violence of the explosion was so great that the heavy iron bands encircling it were broken.

Lightning has totally destroyed some wooden ships and may have caused the otherwise inexplicable disappearances of others. The *Royal Charlotte* was struck in her powder magazine and blown to pieces, and HMS *Resistance* was similarly blown up by a flash which reached her magazine. Between 1799 and 1815, lightning damaged 150 ships of the Royal Navy: 18 were set on fire, 70 seamen were killed and 130 seriously hurt. Not until 1849, when lightning rods were fitted to practically all warships, was the hazard from lightning virtually eliminated (William

Snow Harris). Yet, on 28 October 1975, a Greek oil tanker was destroyed by lightning at Jurong, Singapore.

One of the most terrible disasters caused by lightning occurred in 1769, when the state arsenal at Brescia, Italy, was hit and over 100 tons of gunpowder exploded; a sixth of the city was destroyed and 3,000 people died. The explosion was probably initiated by the lightning igniting powder suspended in the air, forming a highly dangerous mixture. This disaster was paralleled in the United States on 10 July 1926, when an ammunition dump in New Jersey was struck. The series of explosions which followed destroyed all buildings within half a mile and killed 16 people; debris was hurled to an extreme distance of 22 miles.

Where a lightning stroke encounters high electrical resistance the result is an 'explosion', as if TNT were ignited. This fact helps to render credible some 'lightning stories' which otherwise would be hard to credit.

Hard stone is sometimes reduced to powder. Many instances have been reported in which lightning has knocked holes in stone or brick walls, which may look as if a shell had been fired through them. When the belfry of a church was struck, a lump of stone weighing over 200 pounds was flung on to the roof of the apse 60 yards away. One of the pinnacles of a church in Cornwall was demolished by lightning: a stone nearly 350 pounds in weight was hurled 60 yards over the roof, and another was flung nearly a quarter of a mile.

The freakish action of lightning sometimes has beneficent effects: once a powerful stroke instantaneously gouged out a well which it would have taken many man-hours to dig. The well, in a pasture field, was about 1 foot in diameter and 30 feet deep (*Scientific American*, 5 July 1856). Then there were the thunderstruck potatoes. Lightning struck a field of potatoes and burnt the stalks to cinders, but the potatoes underneath were cooked to a turn just as if they had been cooked beneath hot ashes! I asked R. H. Golde, a British authority on lightning, if this story was credible. He said that if the soil was dry it could have happened. R. Gordon Wasson, in a paper on *Lightning-bolt and Mushrooms: An Essay in Early Cultural Exploration*, says that in the Province of Kwangsi, China, there are three species of mushroom linked with thunder. They have Chinese names which, when translated, read: 'Thunder mushroom', 'Thunder-peal mushroom' and 'Thunder-aroused mushroom'. This sounds so extraordinary that a Chinaman in England was shown the Chinese characters, but not told anything about the context: he at once translated them as I have here.

Under the heading *The Spoor of a Thunderbolt*, Sterling B. Talmage relates how he traced the passage of a lightning stroke. It first shattered a tree, then ploughed a furrow for 16 feet, and then struck and half uprooted a 6-foot pine tree. Next it passed to some rocks and one large block, weighing over a ton, was moved 4 inches and apparently broken in the process. The lightning ploughed on through soil thick with grass and moss, and folded back this sod carpet over an area measuring 3×5 feet. Altogether the lightning passed over or through rock, wood and soil for 85 feet from the base of the tree it first struck until it was fully discharged.

When lightning strikes the earth it sometimes burns a channel with radiating furrows. If the lightning discharges into sand, it forms tubes

Above   *Not a lightning tornado but a multiple stroke at Lake Maggiore, Switzerland. Experts who have examined the negative believe the photograph was the result of camera shake while the lens was open.*
(A. Baumann)

Left   *Lightning flashes through the five-mile high ash clouds above Surtsey on 1 December 1963. The photographer was ten miles from the volcano and left the camera shutter open for two minutes.* (Sigurgeir Jónasson)

of fused silica (melting point 1,710°C) to which the name 'fulgurite' is given. These vary greatly in size and length. The largest known appears to be one found many years ago near Drigg in Cumberland, England, which had a maximum diameter of 2½ inches and was over 40 feet long. A curious effect of lightning is occasionally seen when a haystack is struck: the silica from the grass melts, and welds together into a large lump. S. E. Ashmore told me: 'It is usually in fragments because it breaks up when the stack collapses.'

No-one can examine the records of lightning without being impressed by its freakish actions. The French astronomer, Camille Flammarion, collected numerous examples, including the following. A farmer's labourer was carrying a pitchfork over his shoulder when lightning hurled it 50 yards, twisting the tines into corkscrews. Lightning struck a room where a girl was sitting at her sewing machine, holding a pair of scissors; there was a brilliant flash of light, the scissors were spirited away, and the girl found herself sitting *on* the sewing machine. In another instance, two ladies had their knitting needles snatched out of their hands.

Lightning can play odd tricks with people's clothing. The sudden intense heating of the air in the fabric causes it to expand so violently that clothes and footwear are blasted off. Men struck by lightning have sometimes been found completely naked, their clothes scattered in fragments over a wide area. Two girls were standing by a reaping machine when lightning struck; they were stripped naked and their boots torn from their feet. The girls were unharmed, only embarrassed.

Lightning once struck a chainmaker's shop. It welded all the links in a yard-long chain, and another chain became a bar of iron. The United States National Safety Council's Report for 1943 states that a soldier was welded into his sleeping bag when lightning struck the zipper.

Yet another strange effect of lightning is the way in which it magnetises various metal objects, often with bizarre results. A shoemaker's tools were once affected in this way, so that his hammer, pincers, knife, nails and other metal implements were constantly sticking together. Lightning sometimes magnetises objects so powerfully that they are capable of sustaining three times their own weight.

To conclude this section on the freakish behaviour of lightning, here is a passage from Guy Murchie's *Song of the Sky*:

'I heard of one house that was saved by the same lightning that set it afire. After passing through the building and igniting some woodwork, this bolt with a conscience "leaped to a near-by fire-alarm box, set it off, and summoned the engines!" There is a story in Minneapolis of lightning throwing a typewriter up from a table so hard it was imbedded in the ceiling, a case of lightning at sea burning the gold braid off an unpopular mate's uniform, in Argentina of melting a farmer's bedsprings at night so deftly that he sagged to the floor without waking up. And you may have heard of the brewery that got hit in such a skilful manner that the beer was aged and flavoured faster than ever before – undoubtedly the earliest case in recorded history of a storm actually brewing.'

A minor legend in American folklore concerns the stools supplied to forest-fire watchtowers. The stools stand high off the ground to

Above *Pinched or beaded lightning photographed during a severe thunderstorm at Los Alamos, New Mexico. Such lightning has almost certainly been the cause of some alleged UFO sightings.* (B.T. Matthias and S.J. Buchsbaum)

Right *Ball
lightning
photographed
during a violent
thunderstorm in
Nebraska on 30
August 1930. See
pages 98–9 for
details.* (J.C.
Jensen)

provide a refuge for the fire warden if attacked by a ball of lightning. The theory is that the ball will snap around the legs like a terrier and then, frustrated, depart through a door or window. Fantastic nonsense? Anyone unacquainted with one of the most intriguing byways of lightning lore may be forgiven for thinking so, yet the legend may be based on fact.

Ball lightning must be taken seriously. Flammarion says that a girl seated at a table in a room noticed a large ball of fire moving slowly towards her across the floor; it rose and spiralled around her before darting to the chimney, up which it travelled to the open air.

It is natural to dismiss such an incident as the result of an adolescent girl's excited imagination. Yet here are the words of B. L. Goodlet, taken from a lecture delivered at the British Institution of Electrical Engineers in 1937:

'They [i.e. fireballs] are attracted towards closed spaces which they enter through the open window or door, sometimes even through small cracks; the chimney is a favourite path, so that the fireballs frequently appear in the kitchen from out of the fireplace. After circling round the room several times, the fireball leaves by some air path, often the one by which it entered.'

After reading the first British edition of *The Elements Rage*, A. Edward Hobbs wrote to me as follows:

'About 40 years ago [1905] in the course of a heavy thunderstorm

at Wargrave-on-Thames, I – in company with a professional fisher-
man – saw a remarkable example of this freak of Nature [i.e. ball
lightning]. We were perfectly sober and sane, and had no doubt
about the quality of our eyesight!

'We were in a punt endeavouring to get from a high bank some
shelter from driving rain. The ball descended to the opposite bank
and apparently was 2 to $2\frac{1}{2}$ feet in diameter: it ran along the sedgy
surface for about 60 yards, then immediately in front of some timber
camp-sheathing – which it appeared to impact – exploded with a
terrific rolling bang, after which the atmosphere became delightful-
ly fresh and carried an ozonic-chemical smell. The ball was flame
colour, but the explosion produced a mixture of colours.'

William R. Corliss (1982) has combed the scientific literature of the
past 150 years and quotes various encounters with ball lightning. From
these and other accounts, it appears that the balls nearly always
appear towards the end of a storm and vary in diameter from an inch to
several feet (some reports indicate many feet). They generally last for
periods of one second to three minutes. Donald J. Ritchie, however,
says that 'one large ball was observed to hang near the base of a cloud
for 15 minutes'. He also says that the calculated surface temperature
can be as high as 5,000°C; and that one ball 'cut a very clean hole
through a wall of an apartment house.' There are several accounts,
some accompanied by photographs, of almost circular holes burnt in
glass windows by alleged ball lightning (Ingrid Holford). On 8 June
1972, one such hole – 1.9×1.8 inches – was burnt in a window at
Edinburgh University; appropriately, it was in the Department of
Meteorology.

The colours of lightning balls are reported as lavender or pale red,
but other colours have been recorded. Their appearance is often
accompanied by a hissing noise.[1] The balls sometimes follow air
currents, sometimes move against the wind. Several observers have
commented on a ball's rapid rotation compared with its slow progression, reminiscent of a spinning top. Most shine steadily but some
pulsate.

Some alleged UFO sightings may well have been of ball or beaded
lightning. Consider the experience which befell Robert Taylor in a
forest clearing at Livingston, Scotland, at about 10.00 hours on the
morning of 9 November 1979. Rounding a bend in the forest track, he
saw, hovering in a small clearing, what appeared to be the upper half of
a sphere with a diameter of some 18 feet. It was dark grey and noiseless.
As he watched, two small balls rushed towards him. Steuart Campbell,
who recounts the incident, says:

'The BLs stopped one each side of him, in such a position that a
protrusion from each became attached to his trousers, just below the
pocket. Immediately he felt himself being drawn towards the
primary. As the BLs reached him he was overwhelmed by an acrid
choking smell which he likened to burning brake linings. Struggling
for breath and trying to resist the pull of the spheres, he lost
consciousness and collapsed forwards.'

When he recovered consciousness some 20 minutes later, the spheres had vanished. Subsequent examination of the area showed tracks and holes exposing fresh earth. Taylor's trousers were torn below each pocket. Campbell points out that black ball lightning has been reported before. Philip J. Klass has also written on the relationship between ball lightning and alleged UFO sightings.

If reports are to be credited, ball lightning can be highly dangerous. Flammarion lists some 50 instances of its occurrence in France, among them several which had fatal results. One of the worst was on 27 July 1789 at Feltri: a glowing sphere 'about the size of a cannon ball' fell into a hall containing 600 people; its subsequent explosion killed ten and wounded many others. I have already mentioned (pages 56–7) the fireball which exploded in a British church.

To judge by an experience related by W. Morris in the London *Daily Mail* for 3 October 1936, the best way to deal with a fireball is to drown it! At Dorstone, Hereford, Morris saw 'a red-hot ball the size of a large orange' cut a telephone wire, burn a window frame, and then dive into a butt containing 4 gallons of water, causing the water to boil for several minutes. When Morris investigated, he could find nothing: the ball had completely disappeared. After 20 minutes the water was still too hot to be touched.

Scientists are cautious, sometimes too cautious (see page 140), of accepting lay accounts of unusual phenomena, but there are several eye-witness accounts of ball lightning by scientists. The most impressive of these are by J. Durward, one-time Deputy Director of the British Meteorological Office.

In the summer of 1934 Durward was in Scotland with his son when they were caught in a thunderstorm. Durward saw, among some pine trees by a road, a ball of fire about 1 foot across. It moved towards them and struck an iron gatepost just as the boy had his hand on the latch. There was no noise from the impact, but the boy yelled in pain and for several hours afterwards he was unable to lower his arm.

That was impressive enough, but four years later and 1,000 miles away, at a height of $1\frac{1}{2}$ miles above the earth, Durward had an even more spectacular demonstration of the reality of ball lightning. He was in a flying boat near Toulouse, France, at 8,500 feet in dense nimbostratus cloud (very dark raincloud), when what appeared to be a ball of fire entered the aeroplane through the cockpit window, which the captain had opened because of poor visibility.

The ball passed so near to the captain that it singed off his eyebrows and some of his hair, then burned holes in his safety belt and dispatch case. Leaving the cockpit the ball passed through a small compartment, on through the forward passenger cabin to the rear cabin, where it burst with a loud explosion (E. Gold).

The evidence for the existence of ball lightning, although anecdotal, appears to be overwhelming, yet some meteorologists and electrical experts deny this. Karl Berger of Switzerland, a leading authority on lightning, has summarised his views for me:

'I have spent [many] years of panorama-photography of lightning at night, covering an area of at least 10-kilometre [about 6-mile] radius, on Mount San Salvatore, near Lugano-Paradiso. During the whole of that time I have not seen the least sign of inexplicable

lightning phenomena, nor have the trained technical observers working with me. This result is confirmed by many hundreds of photographs showing thousands of lightning strokes.

'Furthermore, during 30 years of research into lightning we never obtained a photograph – nor saw one that anybody else had taken – which I considered could be regarded as proof of the so-called "ball lightning." It is not possible today to prove either the existence or non-existence of something called "ball lightning." In all cases where people have claimed to have seen the so-called "ball lightning" and I have been able to question them closely, it has been possible to explain what they saw in a simple physical manner. Unfortunately, it is not possible so to question those who tell fantastic stories from the past.'

W. J. Humphreys, also a sceptic, concluded that many alleged sightings were optical illusions, probably caused by over-exposure of the eyes to a nearby lightning stroke. The vision of aeroplane pilots has been afflicted for as long as ten minutes after a lightning stroke, and nearby lightning at night sometimes temporarily blinds seamen.

The sceptics maintain that some of the observations could probably be referred to St Elmo's fire, a more or less continuous discharge of weak electricity. In thundery weather, this pale fire (generally blue or green) sometimes clings to trees, aeroplanes, metal spikes and ships' masts, hence its name (St Elmo is one of the patron saints of sailors). It has also been seen on climbers on mountain tops. It has been suggested that St Elmo's fire was responsible for the bush that burned but was not consumed, which so greatly impressed Moses (Exodus 3: 2).

Golde told me of an experience which helps to explain the caution of scientists in accepting ball lightning as a valid phenomenon. During a heavy thunderstorm in Bulawayo, Rhodesia, one stroke was followed immediately by a ball of fire which slowly collapsed. Enquiries revealed, however, that at the time a powerline had been struck. 'What I had seen was clearly the light produced by the power-follow current which can give rise to spectacular lengths of electric arcing extending over many tens of feet.'

Of the evidence for ball lightning from photographs sceptics say that these are in fact of such objects as fireworks, street lamps,[3] etc. and that sometimes camera movement produces strange effects. Many photographs of alleged ball lightning have been taken, but none has been generally accepted by lightning experts. The late J. C. Jensen, Professor in the Department of Physics of Nebraska Wesleyan University, published some of his own photographs, with full details, in *Scientific Monthly* for August 1933 and in *Physics* for October 1933. I have corresponded with his son, Robert R. Jensen, who assisted him at the time.

At about 9.45 p.m. on 30 August 1930, J. C. Jensen, using two cameras, was taking photographs during a violent storm near the university. After one flash, several bright masses were seen and estimated to be between a quarter and half a mile away. One mass floated slowly towards the earth; others seemed to roll along a pair of electric power-lines for about 100 feet, and then fell to the ground, disappearing with a loud report. One mass was estimated to be 28 feet in diameter.

The photographs have aroused great interest, and controversy. One sceptic suggested to Jensen that the result was caused by a flaw in the photographic emulsion. What! Identical flaws on seven negatives, taken with *two* cameras using *two* kinds of film – highly improbable. The most widespread theory of the sceptics is that the professor was the victim of a prank by some of his students, who let off fireworks during the storm, but: (a) the students were on holiday; (b) no-one could have foreseen the storm, or that Jensen would be photographing it, or the direction in which his camera would be pointing; and (c) some of the balls lasted for at least three minutes, a much longer duration than would be expected of any fireworks that students could obtain.

Finally, Jensen says: 'On another occasion during the course of our researches, balls of similar magnitude were seen at a distance of $2\frac{1}{2}$ miles but no photographic record was obtained. In this case also the balls collapsed with a sharp, loud report.'

Undoubtedly a large number of observations can legitimately be dismissed in various ways, but there is still a strong case for the existence of ball lightning. Impaired vision does not affect the ears, so what is to be said of the loud bang when the ball explodes? It would seem to be stretching coincidence rather far to say that on every single occasion that an alleged ball has disintegrated there was a nearby thunderclap, or a car backfiring. Impaired vision cannot heat a bucket of water, let alone burn off a pair of eyebrows!

Various theories have, of course, been propounded to account for ball lightning but Peter Ryder of the British Meteorological Office says: 'There is no known theory to explain how a luminous sphere capable of a lifetime of several seconds can move rather slowly horizontally and vertically, apparently of its own volition, and disappear either silently or explosively.'

The most comprehensive study of ball lightning known to me is James Dale Barry's *Ball Lightning and Bead Lightning* (1980). It is a book of some 300 pages, nearly one-third of which are taken up with a bibliography of 1,600 entries. After a thorough survey of the evidence, both for and against, Barry concludes: 'I believe that the atmospheric luminous phenomena denoted as ball lightning and bead lightning exist.'

Since I wrote the above an incident occurred which, I believe, finally proves that ball lightning is an objective fact: a visit by this luminous phenomenon to one of the most prestigious scientific laboratories in the world. In *Nature*, 19 August 1982, Sir Brian Pippard wrote as follows:

Ball of fire?

SIR – On Tuesday, 3 August, shortly after 4.00 p.m., the Cavendish Laboratory and the surroundings were struck by lightning several times during an exceptionally intense storm. No structural damage ensued, but immediately after one of the discharges a ball of light was seen by a number of observers. Their descriptions are not entirely consistent but certain features are agreed upon well enough to enable a broad description to be given. The discharge apparently responsible struck near the centre of the Bragg Building, which runs east-west. An observer on the ground floor of the Mott Building, whose back was to the window, saw his room momentarily

A very rare photograph. The camera, on time exposure and from a distance of 200 feet, catches the split-second when lightning struck this 23-foot tall ash tree near Lugano, Switzerland. The tree suffered no external damage.
(Richard E. Orville)

lit as if by a very bright object moving past rapidly towards the west, between the Bragg and Mott buildings. Another observer on the first floor saw the space between the buildings filled with a luminous haze at least to the first floor level, and on looking to the west noticed a blue-white light that he thought at first was a warning light on a distant tower. He apparently noticed no motion, but his companion in the same room must have seen it an instant earlier for she had the impression that it was moving past and away, and possibly expanding as it went, being about the size of a grapefruit when first seen. Three people who saw it after that, as it moved over the ground to the west, agreed it looked about the size of the moon, was blue-white in colour, very bright, and was visible for some 4–5 seconds before suddenly vanishing.

To this reasonably well attested observation must be added that while an assistant in the duplicating room, on the ground floor, was closing a small window she was startled by a noise that made her think the window had been knocked in; a bright sparkling object, resembling the lights thrown out by expensive rockets, entered by her head, rebounded from a machine and left as it came. The window was in fact undamaged, and when examined next morning entirely unmarked. Both assistants who were there at the time are convinced something came into the room. Brian Pippard, Department of Physics, University of Cambridge, U.K. (Reprinted by permission from *Nature*, Vol. 298, No. 5876, page 702. Copyright © 1982 Macmillan Journals Limited)

The extreme currents of lightning make it a very efficient killer. Sheep and cattle are particularly vulnerable. They live outdoors and their four legs cover more ground, thus receiving a greater shock, than two-legged humans. Moreover, during storms they tend to cluster and the lightning charge may pass from animal to animal. During July and August 1977, 118 cattle are known to have been killed by lightning in the United States. On 22 July 1918, 504 sheep were killed by one discharge in the Nasatch National Forest, Utah.

Sometimes the bodies of beasts killed by lightning are inedible, because the bones are shattered and their splinters are intermingled with the flesh. Other bodies have been split in two, as though cleft by a giant axe. Birds have been killed by lightning while in flight; they have been seen to fall from the sky, and when examined were found to be partly roasted. Fish, too, can be killed when lightning strikes; a very small shock is sufficient.

Despite the potentially deadly power of lightning, the number of human deaths it causes directly[4] each year is small. Today, the annual deaths from lightning average ten in Great Britain and 110 in the United States. Judging by police statistics in both countries, the probability of death by lightning is much less than that by murder. Even so, for many years in the United States lightning was the main weather-related killer; it is only since the 1970s that floods have killed more people (see page 125). The largest number of people killed by a single lightning flash is 21: on 23 December 1975, while they were sheltering in a hut near Umtali, Zimbabwe.

Lightning is the major source of interference in telecommunications, disrupting telephone-, telegraph- and power-lines. In the United

Opposite Oak tree shattered by lightning. The sudden intense heat of the stroke volatizes the sap which explodes like dynamite. (Ray Bird)

States it is rated as the sixth most frequent cause of fire, and is responsible for nearly half of all the fires occurring in the national forests. Loeb tells me that in California lightning causes 70% of all forest fires.

At Saint-Privat d'Allier in France, experiments have been carried out on the artificial release of lightning. A rocket-propelled wire was fired towards a thundercloud and acted as an elongated lightning conductor. The greatest height reached was about one-third of a mile. Of 134 shots, 71 produced lightning discharges.

Lightning is a danger to aeroplanes. The official report on the crash of a *Boeing 707* in Maryland on 8 December 1963 said that the probable cause was lightning igniting the fuel-air mixture in a reserve tank (Civil Aeronautics Board Report, 3 March 1965). This is not an isolated example of such an accident. Incidentally, when the Apollo 12 spacecraft was launched on 14 November 1969, it was struck by lightning when passing through clouds above Cape Kennedy, although no serious damage was done.

Eric Crew has pointed out another possible danger to aircraft from a by-product of lightning. There is evidence that lightning sometimes causes powerful blasts of hot air to travel several miles. Could these be one of the causes of air turbulence which strikes with no warning and is believed to have torn aircraft apart?

Investigations at the University of Dayton Research Institute since 1979 have established that heavy rain, as in thunderstorms, is a great danger to aircraft. It is probable that some plane crashes hitherto attributed to lightning or violent wind were actually caused by torrential rain. James K. Luers tells me: 'The roughness of water splashing on the wings of a plane can change the airflow properties around the wing and destroy much of the lift capability of the aircraft. We believe several serious aircraft accidents have resulted from attempted landings in very heavy rain.' Such rain, in effect, drowns the engines.

Another electrical phenomenon, St Elmo's fire, has none of the violence of lightning but it sometimes occurs on aeroplanes and can be very frightening. First, the plane begins to glow with pale light, and sparks play across the glass. From inside the cockpit the display looks like miniature lightning. The sparks then become larger and there is a constant flickering off the nose. Meanwhile radio reception is impossible; all that the pilot can hear is a high-pitched squeal. Very occasionally a large nerve-jarring flash and explosion follows: the aircraft has discharged the build-up of electricity in the form of a lightning stroke. Nearly always the only real damage is to human nerves. It has, however, been suggested that the explosion which wrecked the airship *Hindenburg* in 1937 was caused by St Elmo's fire igniting a mixture of air and hydrogen.

The turbulent winds in thunderstorms are a danger to anything that flies. Planes have been wrecked by flying from an updraught into an adjoining downdraught. The aeroplane is carried wildly aloft – it can be several miles – and before the pilot can regain control it is caught in an equally powerful downdraught and smashed into the ground. Even 300-ton jetliners are easily flung about the sky by the violent winds of a thunderstorm. The report of the investigation into the crash of a *Boeing 707* on Mount Fuji in Japan on 5 March 1966, in which 124

Above left
Lightning holes in one. It struck the fibreglass flagpole and then spread outwards to form the branched pattern of burned grass, extending some 35 feet. (Philip Krider)

Below left
Not lightning but an elongated lightning conductor. French scientists have fired rocket-propelled wires towards thunderclouds to initiate lightning discharges. The greatest height reached was one-third of a mile. Of 134 shots, 71 produced discharges. (Electricité de France)

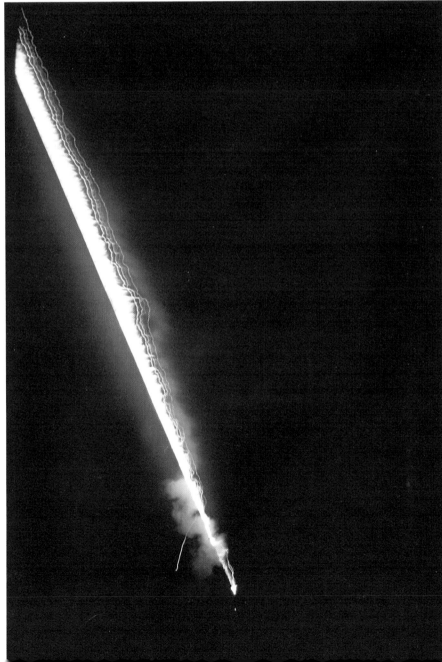

people were killed, states that it was caused by tremendous wind currents which ripped the plane apart. A downburst, as these avalanches of air are called, is believed to have caused the crash of a *Boeing 727* at Kennedy Airport in June 1975.

Codes for protection against lightning are published in the United States by the National Fire Protection Association and in Great Britain by the British Standards Institution.

If one is indoors during a thunderstorm, it is best to avoid the fireplace. The chimney, being the highest point of the house, is the most likely target for lightning; if it is hit the current will flow earthward down the chimney, unless a better conductor is found on the way. In a storm it is wise to stay away from walls, fireplaces, radio and television sets, telephones, radiators and any large metal objects. Do not use anything connected to the electricity supply. In violent nearby storms, go to a basement, if one exists, and wait there until the worst is over. The centre is the safest part of a room providing it does not place you between a conductor leading from the roof and another opposite leading to the ground. Standing between a fireplace and a radiator would be hazardous if lightning struck down the chimney. Do not take a bath, go for a swim or indulge in any form of watersport.

Other safety hints are: avoid high ground, open spaces, tents, small sheds and lone trees. About 25% of all lightning fatalities are due to people sheltering under trees. Keep well away from wire fences, otherwise you may get a shock from a bolt that strikes half a mile away; even when the storm is over, a fence is sometimes lethal to touch.

If caught in a storm when out shooting, fishing or playing golf, drop all metal objects. Take off your shoes if they have any metal on the soles. If swimming or out in a boat, head for shore at once. If you can, make for a dense wood and stand near trees which are shorter than the average. You are relatively safe in a deep valley. A car or coach is relatively also safe as, if hit, the lightning is directed straight to earth.

When lightning is very severe and close, it is safest to crouch on the balls of both feet with arms clasped around the shins, i.e. make your body into a ball with the minimum of contact with the ground. Stay in that position until the storm has passed – better be soaked than shocked! Remember the saying, which is 99% true: 'If you heard the thunder the lightning didn't strike you. If you saw the lightning it missed you. And if it did hit, you're not likely to know it now.' That is, however, no reason for not attempting resuscitation: prompt mouth-to-mouth breathing, cardiac massage and long artificial respiration have often revived a lightning victim, even when there was no sign of life.

Opposite Not ordeal by spaghetti but a laboratory test with artificial lightning. It is safe to be in a car during a thunderstorm as any lightning strokes are directed straight to earth. (Siemens Werkbild)

NOTES

1. Normally the earth has a negative charge, but a thundercloud causes the ground beneath it to develop a positive charge. This applies to nearly all lightning strokes, but there are exceptions.

2. 'I cannot help noticing a strong similarity between the description of the descent of the Holy Spirit at the beginning of Acts and the descriptions of ball lightning.' (M. L. Cartwright). Herbert Thurston, in his authoritative *The Physical Phenomena of Mysticism*, records 'a ball of fire' descending on a prioress. A Tass report on 13 January 1984 said that a lightning ball entered a Soviet aircraft and 'slowly flew about the heads of the stunned passengers'.

3. This is the explanation suggested by D. W. Davies and R. B. Standler for the well-known Roy Jennings' colour photograph of alleged ball lightning.

4. Additional deaths, however, are caused by lightning-induced fires.

AVALANCHES

'Hast thou entered into the treasures of the snow?' The question is as old as the Book of Job, but it is only during the last 100 years that the full wonder of a snow crystal has been revealed through photo-micrography. Since it is trillions of these crystals which, in violent motion, make the snow avalanche, it is necessary to know what they are and how they behave.

Snow is the crystallisation of water vapour in the air into geometrical forms, nearly always hexagonal. The popular notion that snow comes from rain is therefore incorrect; the product of frozen rain is ice pellets. Snow crystals form on tiny particles of solid matter, the nuclei. Over industrial and civilised areas there is an abundance of such material in the form of smoke and dust. In areas remote from civilisation the nuclei are provided by a wide variety of natural airborne substances, such as pollen and other vegetable matter and tiny ice particles.

Balloonists have sometimes found themselves surrounded by incipient snow crystals, so tiny that they were made visible only by the sunlight glinting on them. Further deposits of water vapour increase the size of the crystals, which vary in diameter from about three-thousandths of an inch (about twice the size of a fog particle) to two-tenths of an inch. In plate-like forms the thickness is one-fiftieth or less of the width.

There are at least 80 different types of snow crystals, varying according to atmospheric conditions. Generally, the simpler types form at high altitudes when water vapour is scarce and temperatures are low, the more complex types at low altitudes when there is an abundance of water vapour and temperatures are high.

When snow first falls, the snow cover contains a large proportion of air. Frequently, about 12 inches of newly fallen snow contain only as much water as 1 inch of rain, although atmospheric conditions obviously cause wide variations. The specific gravity of fresh snow varies from about 0.06 to 0.10, but the figure for the ice of which it is composed is just over 0.9 (the specific gravity of water is 1.0). These figures emphasise the great amount of air present in newly fallen snow. Rarely, falling snow is composed of one part ice and 250 parts air. These facts explain why men who have been buried for 48 hours in snowdrifts have not always suffocated.

The number of snow crystals which fall during a heavy storm is astronomical. Vincent J. Schaefer estimates that during one ten-hour storm about 10^{15} (1,000 million million) flakes fell on 1 acre.

In $27\frac{1}{2}$ hours during 14–15 April 1921, 87 inches of snow fell at 10,000-feet-high Silver Lake, Colorado: the most intense snowfall for the United States since records began. The greatest known seasonal snowfall in the United States, and almost certainly for the world, occurred during the winter of 1971/72, when 1,224 inches (102 feet) fell at the Paradise Ranger Station, 5,500 feet up on the southwest flank of Mount Rainier, Washington.

Opposite
Avalanche path cut through a stand of hemlock trees. A very large avalanche sometimes uproots trees and sends them careering through the air like rockets. (Parks, Canada: taken in Glacier National Park, British Columbia, Canada)

It is massed snow which causes the most familiar form of avalanche. Snow avalanches used to be divided into two categories: the *ground* avalanche of wet snow which slides over the ground and carries quantities of earth, stones and other debris with it; and the *powder* avalanche consisting of dry powdery snow, great clouds of which fill the air as the avalanche descends. This twofold division is an over-simplification. Some avalanches are a combination of two, or even three types, and others are too complex for any classification. (The subject is dealt with in detail by M. de Quervain *et al.*) The most common type, and the most potent source of danger, is the slab avalanche. This consists of layers of consolidated snow which carry considerable distances, sometimes extending a short way up the slope of the opposite valley.

An avalanche occurs when part of the snow cover on a slope hurtles down. Irregularities formed by rocks or mounds act as anchoring points and tend to arrest any tendency to avalanche, as do large trees standing close together. Most fatal avalanches are started by the victims themselves: it is very easy for a skier to set off an avalanche that is 'ready to go'. Comparatively few accidents are caused by naturally released snow falling on unsuspecting skiers.

An avalanche goes through three phases before coming to rest: gathering speed, travel at maximum speed, and reduction of speed. The maximum speed varies considerably. The slowest avalanches are those composed of damp snow (although very wet snow avalanches can travel at great speed) and the fastest are those composed of dry powder snow. The angle of the slope on which the avalanche occurs is an important factor in causing variations of speed.

Some avalanches, chiefly of wet snow, travel at speeds which would enable a fast skier with a fair start to outrun them, but top speed can exceed 200 mph. On 6 March 1898, at Glärnisch, Switzerland, an enormous airborne powder-snow avalanche travelled at an average speed of about 225 mph.

Avalanches vary greatly in width, from 10 feet to about 1 mile. The distance they travel necessarily varies greatly. Sometimes, after descending a slope, one may run for a mile or so across level ground. One ice avalanche crossed a valley and then ran up the opposite slope. Snow avalanches sometimes do the same, especially in deep, narrow, V-shaped valleys; survivors have reported that the snow 'came up from below'.

The volume and weight of snow in a big avalanche are enormous. A wet snow avalanche which fell in the Italian Alps in 1885 was estimated to contain 4 million cubic yards; its weight would have been about $2\frac{1}{2}$ million tons. Even this colossal weight may be exceeded in the Himalayas where some of the greatest avalanches occur, but these are rarely observed.

The movement of an avalanche is a combination of sliding, flowing and bouncing. This action sometimes pulverises the snow into such fine particles that it penetrates cracks around closed doors and windows.

Avalanches exert great pressure. Wet snow avalanches often carry a mass of debris, scraped from the ground as they pass. Avalanche defences at Fionnay, Switzerland, designed to resist pressures of 8,000 pounds per square foot, were destroyed by an avalanche of wet snow

Plunging from a Swiss mountainside an avalanche races across a snowfield. Some avalanches contain over a million tons, travel at 200 m.p.h. (D. Gnos, Avalanche Research Station, Davos, Switzerland)

and rock. A medium-sized avalanche falling in a laterally restricted space, such as a gully, exerts pressures of up to 22,000 pounds (nearly 10 tons) per square foot. In Japan monster avalanches have registered about 14 tons per square foot (*National Geographic*, September 1982).

No measurement has yet been made of the pressures exerted by a large avalanche falling in a confined space: as with tornadoes, the measuring device is swept away. A small avalanche has lifted a 120-ton locomotive from the track and slammed it against the station buildings.

Estimates have been made of the horse-power of avalanches. A wet loose-snow avalanche of about 150,000 tons falling 6,500 feet involves some 20 million horse-power. A giant one can generate ten or more times this figure: the 1885 avalanche in Italy generated an estimated 300 million horse-power. The fall of a large powder-snow avalanche is a majestic and awesome sight: an irresistible mass, glinting in bright sunlight, sweeping down a mountainside, scything trees like corn stalks, and raising an immense cloud of snow dust.

Most avalanches end as cone-shaped masses, with the apex pointing uphill. The snow in the 'tip' may be 100 feet deep, and it is in this that any victims are likely to be buried. Electronic devices are used to locate victims in deep snow. Dogs and probing with long sounding rods are other, but slower, aids.

Dogs are, however, the best means of finding people buried in snow; they can sometimes locate a man even when he is buried 10 feet deep. There is a well-known Austrian story of how the postman of Zürs was one day overwhelmed by an avalanche. His dog came to the snow and remained standing at a particular spot; it refused to move. For three days it remained there and eventually the villagers dug into the snow beneath, to find the dog's master still alive. It must, however, be emphasised that this is most unusual; unless an avalanche victim is rescued in two hours or so, the odds are that he will never be rescued at all.

Another famous avalanche story, with a macabre ending, concerns the attempt to climb Mont Blanc in August 1820. An avalanche swept the nine-man team into a glacial crevasse, where they perished. From the known rate of travel of the glacier, it was forecast that the bodies would be carried slowly down, and should appear about 40 years later in the valley of Chamonix some 5 miles away. And, sure enough, 41 years later they duly appeared, according to some reports 'still looking in the bloom of youth'.

Many stories are told of remarkable escapes in avalanches. One recounted by J. Cecil Alter in the sober pages of the United States Weather Bureau's *Monthly Weather Review* concerns a man taking a shower at Bingham, Utah, on the morning of 17 February 1926. Suddenly a powerful avalanche swept down Sap Gulch and ran for 2 miles. It lifted the man from his shower, carried him 150 feet on the crest of the snow, and set him down comparatively unharmed.

No human escape from an avalanche can surpass that of the forestry worker of Glarus, Switzerland. In an airborne powder avalanche in 1900, he was seized by the wind and flung through the air at tremendous speed, 'head sometimes upward, head sometimes downward like a leaf driven by a storm'. He was blasted by snow from all sides, could not see and could scarcely breathe; he lost consciousness.

When he came to, he was lying in deep snow which had broken his fall and limited his injuries to a few fractures. The man thought that his flight had lasted a mere split second; in fact, he had been carried through a height difference of 2,200 feet and through a distance over the ground of more than half a mile. (Colin Fraser)

In powder-snow avalanches a potent cause of destruction lies in the mixture of snow particles and air (an aerosol) forming a dust cloud which behaves as a heavy gas, sweeping down the mountainside at near-tornadic speed ahead of the snow sliding on the ground. 'Avalanche blast can travel great distances. It can, and frequently does, precipitate avalanches on the opposite side of a wide valley. Its power is almost unbelievable.' (Gerald Seligman)

The most violent wind occurs when an avalanche is stopped abruptly. When the snow mass falls almost vertically on to a valley floor, air explodes in all directions like a bomb blast — and with all its vagaries. One house may be torn from its foundations, another only feet away left untouched. Again, the similarity to tornadic phenomena is obvious. Frequently the tops of trees in the path of an avalanche are snapped off, although the snow itself does not reach so high. Often, however, destruction is caused by the snow dust, which moves swiftly and envelops objects in its path. Sometimes the lateral components of the blast uproot trees 100 yards or so on either side of the avalanche. Fraser says that in the Grisons avalanche of 1806 a whole forest was destroyed. Trees were uprooted and flew over a nearby village; one landed upright on a roof, looking as if it had grown there.

In a restricted valley near the Grimsel Pass, Switzerland, avalanche blast destroyed a small bridge and hurled part of it about 150 feet up the mountainside; Sir Arnold Lunn told me that the snow itself never reached the bridge. This incident helps to render more credible the story of an Alpine stagecoach which was blown – coachman, horses and all – across a stream; the avalanche which caused this was said to have fallen so far away that the coachman neither saw nor heard it. Ordinary snow avalanches, unless they fall over steep gradients or carry heavy debris with them, make little or no noise. Ice avalanches fall with a noise like thunder.

According to Edwin Rohrer, however, the greatest destruction is caused inside the snowcloud, where the windblast is turbulent. Such blasts momentarily (one-tenth of a second) travel at speeds of up to 400 mph. Rohrer saw a $12\frac{1}{2}$-inch-thick reinforced concrete wall hit by a powder-snow avalanche: the concrete was blown out from the reinforcing wires, which were only slightly bent (quoted by Fraser).

Perhaps the greatest destruction caused by avalanche blast occurred in 1819; ice, not snow, was involved. Part of an Alpine glacier fell over a precipice. Although it landed on an uninhabited area, the houses in the nearby village of Randa were shattered by the terrific blast of air pushed ahead by the mass of glacial ice as it plunged and hit the valley floor. The steeple of a stone church was flung to the ground, and heavy millstones were tossed about like leaves in a gale. The village was almost totally destroyed.

Such are the vagaries of blast, however, that it is possible for a man to be within a few feet of an avalanche and feel nothing. F. F. Tuckett, an experienced mountaineer, says that he was on the Eiger in Switzerland when a great avalanche, estimated at half a million tons, fell so near him that he was covered with powdered snow, yet he felt no great wind blast.

In England avalanches are rare, but not unknown. Near Lewes, Sussex, there is an inn called 'The Snowdrop', a memorial to one of the greatest avalanches England has experienced. On 27 December 1836, after a heavy snowstorm, a huge mass of snow slid down from the South Downs and buried a row of cottages, causing the deaths of eight people. A contemporary account says:

Rescuers probing the snow with rods in attempts to locate victims of an avalanche. The snow in the 'tip' of an avalanche is sometimes 100 feet deep. (Ringier, Switzerland)

'A gentleman who witnessed the fall described it as a scene of the most awful grandeur. The masses appeared to him to strike the houses first at the base, heaving them upwards and then breaking over them like a gigantic wave to dash them bodily on to the road, and when the mist of snow, which then enveloped the site, cleared off, not a vestige of habitation could be seen – there was nothing but an enormous mound of pure white.' (Reprinted in the *Sussex County Magazine*, January 1927)

Avalanches are common in Scotland and account for a surprising number of deaths and casualties. In the winter of 1981/82, five people were killed.

The worst avalanche disaster in the United States is known as the 'Wellington Snowslide'. It occurred at the railroad station of Wellington, Washington, in the Cascade Range on 1 March 1910. A great mass of snow fell on the station, and three large locomotives, several carriages, a water tank and the entire station building were swept over a ledge into a canyon 150 feet below. Over 100 people were killed.

The avalanching snow of the European Alps, however, has claimed the greatest number of victims, especially in the years before the introduction of scientific preventive measures. The main reasons are the large number of tourists, and the fact that the Alpine slopes and valleys are dotted with farms and other dwellings. Another factor is the number of avalanches that occur: in Switzerland alone there are some 10,000 avalanche paths, although avalanches do not occur on every one in every year. In 1689 a tremendous avalanche wiped out Saas, together with its inhabitants. In 1719 Loèche was destroyed by an avalanche, and 60 people lost their lives. A year later, at Obergesteln, another of these 'thunderbolts of snow', as Lord Byron called them, demolished 120 houses and killed over 80 people.

During the first World War probably more soldiers were killed by avalanches in the Tyrolean mountains than by all the shells, bullets and other missiles of the combatants fighting in the area at the time. The winter of 1916 piled snow deeper than for half a century; mountaineers wise to the ways of snow knew that the eastern Alps were a deathtrap, yet the stern exigencies of war forbade retreat. On 13 December the snow began to thaw, and in 48 hours at least 100 avalanches plunged down the mountainside; how many soldiers died nobody knows. André Roch, a Swiss expert on avalanches, tells me that it was in the region of 10,000; he adds that the estimate for all the victims of avalanches in the war range between 40,000 and 80,000 (bodies were still being found in 1952).

By paying heed to avalanche warnings and advice from snow experts, the ordinary skier and tourist should be in very little danger. If skiers need to cross dangerous slopes they should do so one at a time and should also wear a transceiver (a device which emits a signal to guide searchers to the victim).

If you see an avalanche sweeping towards you, ski *across* the slope and try to reach a rock, tree, shrub or anything you can cling to. The longer you can avoid being swept away the better. Once in the swirling whiteness, keep your mouth shut and make strong swimming movements: this may help to keep you near the surface. As the avalanche slows down, bring an arm in front of your nose and mouth, thus creating a small breathing space if you are buried. Once all is still, make one determined effort to get to the surface. If you are not sure where this is: spit or dribble, see which way the saliva goes and try to move in the opposite direction! If you are unsuccessful, be still and try to be calm: this will greatly slow down the rate of oxygen consumption.

Compared with other natural hazards, the losses caused by avalanches are not great. The yearly average of deaths throughout the world is 150.[1] Property damage is comparatively trivial. These small losses are not due to any scarcity of avalanches; rather because the

vast majority occur in uninhabited regions, and the danger from those that occur where men live is lessened by forecasting and precautionary measures. For every avalanche that becomes news, tens of thousands remain unreported because they are harmless.

No country has suffered more from avalanches, or studied them more intensively, than Switzerland, but even here their scientific study did not begin until 1936. Much defence research and many snow studies are done at the Federal Snow and Avalanche Research Institute on the Weissfluhjoch, Davos. There are three main defences: forecasting, artificial release, and protective structures.

Avalanche protection barriers on a hillside above Hanningsvag, Norway. These anchor the snow thus preventing a slide from forming. (Frank W. Lane)

FORECASTING

It is generally possible for experts to know when and where avalanches are likely, and reports on their development can then be sent to threatened areas. In Switzerland avalanche bulletins are distributed to the press every Friday, and whenever the snow situation calls for one: a total of two or three a week on average.

ARTIFICIAL RELEASE

If snow masses can be brought down while they are comparatively small, dangerous avalanches will be avoided. Such harmless releases are induced by hand-thrown charges, by artillery or mortar fire, and by rockets. If conditions warrant it, officials on some of the Swiss mountain railways go out every morning before the traffic starts and direct fire at dangerous places on the higher snow slopes.

PROTECTIVE STRUCTURES

These prevent dangerous snow masses from forming. Trees growing close together, as in a thick wood, provide the best defence. Not only can no avalanche originate among them, they also arrest all except the most powerful ones. Trees are accordingly grown at various strategic points, such as the places above villages where avalanches might originate. Protective woods on Swiss Alpine slopes have been strictly preserved for centuries; at one time the penalty for cutting trees in them was death.

Artificial barriers are constructed on slopes where avalanches may start. These usually consist of rows of metal or concrete fences which hold the snow in place. The snow mass is thus contained at numerous points, and nowhere can a slide develop and peel off the whole surface. Long walls are also built at an acute angle to the snow slope, thus deflecting avalanching snow so that it descends at points where it can do the least harm. Some Swiss houses have their uphill-facing side built like a wedge, so that any avalanche which strikes it is split, the two halves harmlessly bypassing the house. Railways and transalpine highways, which are vulnerable targets, are often protected by tunnels or built-up galleries so that avalanches slide harmlessly over the protecting wall.

Despite the damage it causes, snow is, on balance, a decided asset. On natural beauty alone, what an irreparable loss it would be never again to see a snow-capped mountain or a landscape carpeted with glittering snow. Think of a snowless world where never again could children enjoy a snow fight or roll a giant snowball; where the thrill of the toboggan run, or the swish of a ski breaking the crust of a virgin snowfield, was a thing of the past, and you realise that the dangers and inconveniences are a small price to pay for such natural joys.

Snow is of considerable value to agriculture. The large amount of air trapped in its crystals makes it a very good insulator, better than sand. This insulation keeps the temperature of the soil almost constant, however much that of the air may change. Moreover, when a blanket of snow covers the ground, it greatly reduces heat loss. When snow which has lain for several weeks finally melts, the ground is often free of frost. Snow also holds water that is needed for irrigation later in the year, thereby forming a valuable reserve in some districts, especially in mountainous country.

Avalanches of snow are most common, but there are two other forms which, mass for mass, are more dangerous: ice and rock avalanches. Ice avalanches come from glaciers, parts of which sometimes break and hurl down millions of tons of ice. One of the most spectacular, and deadly, of this century occurred on 10 January 1962 in western Peru, where the ice-covered peak of Nevado de Huascarán, Peru's highest mountain, thrusts 4 miles into the sky. On the floor of the valley, 9 miles away, eight villages clustered around the township of Ranrahirca.

At 6.13 p.m. on the fatal day, a vast mass of ice broke from the north peak, carrying away more ice and blocks of granite and slate as it fell. As the colossal mass struck a funnel-like gorge, a terrifying roar echoed across the surrounding countryside. The avalanche, travelling at 1 mile per minute, then bounded down the twisting valley of the

White river of death. On 10 January 1962 over a million tons of ice plunged from a mountain in western Peru. This monstrous avalanche, gouging house-size blocks of granite from the mountainside as it fell, travelled ten

Ranrahirca River, rising high on the outside of the bends like a giant sled speeding down a bob-run. This monstrous journey was subsequently reconstructed by a survey on the spot.

As the avalanche descended it gouged blocks of granite, as large as houses, from the walls of the gorge. Soil and other debris added weight and volume. What had started as some 2 million cubic yards of ice became a mass of ice, rock and mud five times greater: a mass roughly equal to seven Empire State Buildings, weighing 7 million tons. It was this irresistible tide which swept over the valley floor around Ranrahirca. One moment this was a happy thriving township of a thousand or so buildings and over 2,000 people; a few moments later it was a vast graveyard covered with an impenetrable grey carpet of rock and mud. Only a score of buildings and 100 people on the outskirts of the town survived.

After burying Ranrahirca, the avalanche travelled a further mile to the Santa River and climbed 100 feet up the opposite bank before its momentum was finally spent. By then the leading edge of the vast mass was 1 mile wide and 45 feet deep. The avalanche had travelled about 10 miles in eight minutes. The final toll was nine villages, one town, 10,000 livestock and about 4,000 people (Bart McDowell, and Ronald H. Bailey).

Tremendous as this avalanche was, even greater ones have been known to fall in Peru. There is evidence from the distribution of ancient debris deposits that hundreds of years ago there was an avalanche far exceeding that of 1962, in both volume of ice and area covered.

More recently, on 31 May 1970, massed ice and rock again crashed from Nevado de Huascarán. This avalanche was even more massive, violent and destructive than that of 1962. With a front some 1,000 yards wide, it poured down the mountain with awesome speed and power. Kendrick Frazier says: 'The trajectories of thousands of boulders weighing up to three tons that were hurled more than 2,000 feet across the Llanganuco Valley indicate that its velocity reached 248 m.p.h.' The number of dead is unknown, but estimates range up to 25,000. It was by far the most destructive avalanche of which there is authentic record (George Plafker *et al.*).

Rock avalanches, or rockslides, are rare but potentially the most dangerous of all. Some of the worst have occurred in Switzerland. Sometimes in these tremendous rock falls a considerable part of a whole mountain plunges down. This happened at Plurs, Switzerland, when, on 4 September 1618, nearly half the side of a mountain fell and obliterated the town. Out of a population of some 1,500 only four were left: those who were away at the time.

Another Swiss rock avalanche occurred on 11 September 1881 near the village of Elm. Overshadowing the village was the Plattenbergkopf, the outermost buttress of a great mountain mass, the Glarner Alpen. Owing to careless slate-mining halfway up, the top of the Plattenbergkopf became undermined. There were sporadic falls of rocks and the villagers vaguely realised that the mountain would at some time fall. It fell sooner than they thought.

The 11 September was a rainy Sunday. Rocks fell more heavily than usual, and the mountain groaned and rumbled. Sightseers gathered and were 'rewarded' by the sight of part of the east side of the

miles in eight minutes. Four thousand people died. (George Plafker, US Geological Survey)

Plattenbergkopf breaking away. No-one was hurt, although rocks fell almost at the feet of some of the onlookers. Seventeen minutes later a larger mass fell from the west side of the mountain. By now even the hardened villagers felt some alarm and many flocked to the hillside opposite the groaning mountain. Little time was left.

Following the two large rockfalls, the top of the Plattenbergkopf was left balancing on a tiny neck of rock, like the top half of an hourglass. Millons of tons of rock teetered for four minutes, then hurtled down. The huge avalanche fell as far as the quarry, then the upper part shot forward horizontally across the valley, hit the Düniberg obliquely and was deflected down the valley, covering about 1 mile in less than half a minute. Elm was annihilated, and half of another village destroyed.

A few men raced the inexorable tide and won. The survivors, notably the village schoolmaster, have left a vivid description of what happened when the mountain fell. A great wind preceded the avalanche, whirling people into the air, uprooting trees and wrenching houses from their foundations. Some houses were carried whole through the air and set down safely beyond the reach of the avalanche. Other houses were seen to bend and shake, then 'break up like little toys' before the avalanche reached them. People caught by the flying rocks were killed instantly – 'as an insect is crushed into a red streak under a man's foot'. A house was cut in two by the sharply defined edge of the avalanche.

As abruptly as it had started, the avalanche ceased. For less than a minute the valley was filled with a continuous roar, then 'silence and stillness supervened. Survivors stood stunned where they were.

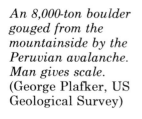

An 8,000-ton boulder gouged from the mountainside by the Peruvian avalanche. Man gives scale. (George Plafker, US Geological Survey)

Nothing moved. Then a great cry and wailing arose in the part of the village that was left. People began to run wildly about, some down the valley, some up. As the dust cloud grew thinner the wall-like side of the ruin appeared. It was quite dry. All the grass and trees in the neighbourhood were white with dust.'

About 10 million cubic yards of rock fell on Elm and its valley, burying some 150 men, women and children, and 1 million square yards of green fields, under a solid grey rock carpet (Martin Conway, and Ernst Buss and Albert Heim).

In North America, the most famous tragedy from a rock avalanche occurred in Canada when, on 29 April 1903, part of Turtle Mountain, Alberta, fell on the township of Frank, some 3,000 feet below. Turtle Mountain is composed of a thick layer of limestone overlying layers of softer rock and coal. The slope of the upper part of the mountain is steep, averaging some 50 degrees; the section which fell was even steeper. There was a coal mine at the foot of the mountain, and it is probable that the excavations caused the soft underlying rocks to collapse under the enormous weight of the limestone. Turtle Mountain was almost ready to go. H. E. Vokes says:

'The unseasonable weather determined the hour at which the calamity occurred. The unusual warmth of the past few days caused extensive melting of the winter snows, and this melted water had penetrated the open joint cracks. Then on the 28th there was a sharp change to cold weather, and the thermometer fell to zero in Frank on the morning of the slide. The water in the joint cracks froze. As it froze it expanded, tearing loose the last supports which held the mass in place, freeing it to hurtle down into the valley as one great avalanche of destruction.'

An estimated 80 million tons of rock hurtled down at a speed of 90 mph. The limestone was estimated to be half a mile square, and about 500 feet thick in the centre. As the locomotive-sized rocks crashed down, the roar was heard 25 miles away. The avalanche sealed the entrance to the mine, crushed the southwestern half of Frank, killed nearly 70 people, ploughed *beneath* the Oldman River, and carried water and river bottom 400 feet up the opposite side of the valley.

The first thing that the men in the mine, 300 feet down, knew was a blast of air that roared through the tunnel like a tornado, throwing men and horses to the ground. The entrance was sealed by a jumble of broken rocks. Two possibilities were open to the miners: to attempt to clear the entrance, or to try to hack a shaft to the surface from further back in the mine where the slope was steeper and the rocks less thick. They chose to dig the shaft and worked in desperate shifts from seven in the morning until five in the afternoon, when the first man came out and looked up at the mountain that had almost been his tomb. Its eastern face was entirely different, the valley a chaos of rock fragments. This largest known rockslide on the North American continent covered over 1 square mile and had an average depth of 65 feet.

NOTES

1. During the catastrophic winter of 1950/51, however, in the European Alps alone, 300 people were killed.

FLOODS

Water is one of the most abundant and important substances in life, the most precious of natural resources. Tasteless, odourless, colourless, it is yet vital to every living organism. In flood, however, it kills and destroys.

Water is composed of two atoms of hydrogen and one of oxygen: H_2O. For all practical purposes it is non-compressible, although at the bottom of deep oceans, with the weight of miles of sea above, it is slightly compressed.

It is because water is heavy that it is so destructive. One cubic foot of water weighs about 62 pounds, the actual weight varying slightly with temperature and the amount of dissolved salts. A large bathful (1 cubic

Protected by earthworks this house withstands the North Sea inundation of the Hamburg area of Germany in November 1981. (Hans Silvester/ Rapho)

yard) weighs three-quarters of a ton, and the water in a tank $30 \times 25 \times 20$ feet (15,000 cubic feet – about the size of a six-roomed house) weighs about 420 tons.

The destructive effect of water increases alarmingly with increase of speed. A wall of water striking at 20 mph is not four but 16 times more powerful than one travelling at 5 mph. Such facts explain why the destructive energy in even a moderate flood is the equivalent of millions of tons of TNT.

There are two main types of flood: inundation from the sea, and overflowing of inland waters. Occasionally, the two types combine. Inland floods are of two kinds: one seasonal, occurring at the same period each year (for example, the Nile); and the other sporadic. This chapter is concerned mainly with inundation and dangerous sporadic floods. The most violent flooding from the sea occurs with storm surges caused by exceptionally strong and persistent onshore winds combined with low atmospheric pressure, or from disturbance of the sea from earthquakes or volcanic eruptions (see later chapters).

England is no stranger to sea floods. There were great and disastrous ones on the east coast during the Middle Ages. In the 11th century extensive inundations occurred, the worst in 1099: the deaths, including those in Holland, were reputed to be in the region of 100,000.

In November 1236, an inundation of the sea in Norfolk destroyed flocks of sheep and herds of cattle, tore trees up by the roots and demolished houses; in one village alone, about 100 people died. Another terrible inundation occurred in this and other areas in December 1287. Again houses were destroyed, and in the village of Hickling the water was so deep that it overtopped the high altar in the priory by 1 foot or more. Some 500 people perished in East Anglia in this most fatal of all British floods (C. E. P. Brooks and John Glasspoole, and C. E. Britton).

The European country which has suffered most from sea floods is low-lying Holland. On 14 December 1287, the Zuiderzee area was inundated and 50,000 people drowned. On 18 November 1421, the southwestern part of Holland was inundated: 72 villages were destroyed and 10,000 people drowned. At intervals during the following centuries, the sea struck again and again. Stronger and better defences were built, and by 1953 the Dutch may well have thought that their ancient enemy was tamed. Then came the weekend of 31 January and 1 February. First, however, it was England's turn.

On the morning of 31 January, tremendous gales swept down the east coast of Scotland – among the worst northerly gales ever recorded in the British Isles: the wind at times reached over 100 mph. During the day the wind blew along the northern part of the North Sea, driving thousands of millions of tons of water to the south. The records of tidal stations show that the effect was to raise the level of the North Sea, in some areas by $1\frac{1}{2}$ feet above the highest previously recorded. The consequent surge against the coast reached its peak between southeast England and southwest Holland.

Wind alone, violent and persistent though it was, could not have caused these great floods. Several other factors combined to make the North Sea burst its containing walls, a combination of events that might not occur again for hundreds of years. The surge coincided with a high tide and an atmospheric depression: as the air pressure fell, the sea rose. The floods would have been even worse – several feet higher – had they coincided with the highest spring tides.

On the east coast of England, from Yorkshire to Kent, many square miles of low-lying land, most of it below normal high-tide level, were flooded. The sea either broke the coast defences or swept over them. The height of the sea as it struck the land varied, but at King's Lynn the River Ouse broke its banks and a 7-foot-high wall of water swept through the town. The power of such high seas, driven by hurricane-force winds, is enormous. At Wells-next-the-Sea some cliffs were cut back by 30 feet, and a neighbouring 7-foot cliff by 86 feet. Dunes and walls were washed away, beaches scoured to bare earth, and buildings shattered. The toll was 307 killed, over 32,000 evacuated, 24,000 houses damaged, and nearly 250 square miles of agricultural land spoiled for years (sea water is ruinous to such land).[1]

The floods hit hard at England, but even harder on the other side of the North Sea. The sea, Holland's ancient enemy, struck its cruellest blow for centuries. Violent onshore winds, which in gusts reached 90 mph, blew for some eight hours. Then, at high tide, the heaped-up waters battered against the Dutch dykes. These had withstood everything sea and wind could throw at them for many rough years, but on this terrible Sunday tide and tempest combined to breach them in scores of places along the coasts of Zeeland, Zuid-Holland and Noord-Brabant. (Some of the dykes had not been completely repaired following deliberate flooding during the Second World War.)

Dutch dykes are of three kinds: 'watchers', the biggest and strongest, bear the main assault; 'sleepers' act as a second line of defence; and the comparatively small 'dreamers' surround individual farms and fields. Once the watchers are breached, sleepers and dreamers are soon overwhelmed. Most of the dreamers are strongly reinforced on the seaward side, but when the sea has broken or overtopped them they are soon undermined from the rear.

On this fateful Sunday morning the sea rose until it was level with the 10-foot high dykes. Then came a sudden and unexpected surge which burst over 50 dykes almost simultaneously and sent a great sea raging over nearly half a million acres. This caught many people unawares, despite the warnings of the previous night. H. A. Quarles v. Ufford, of the Dutch Meteorological Institute, says: 'It is probable that no floods of such an intensity have occurred during the past 400 or 500 years.'

The cost of this invading sea was: 1,850 people killed and 72,000 evacuated; over 3,000 houses destroyed and 40,000 damaged; 625 square miles flooded; 9% of the agricultural and 3% of the dairy land covered by the sea. Over a quarter of a million livestock and poultry were lost.

Although by far the worst destruction from this flood occurred near the coasts of the countries affected, London itself was involved. The tidal surge swept up the Thames and, near the Houses of Parliament, reached the highest level on record: $17\frac{3}{4}$ feet. Another few inches and there would have been a major disaster. As it was, over 1,000 houses were flooded as the Thames poured into West Ham.

Thames floods have been recorded since 1099. Three occurred in the 19th century, the last in 1881. For nearly half a century afterwards the Thames was relatively peaceful until, on the night of 6/7 January 1928, it surged over the embankment and drowned 14 people in Fulham,

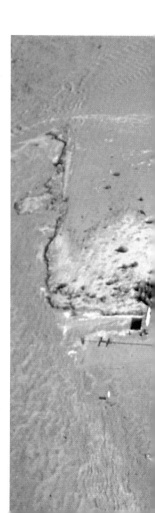

Westminster and Hammersmith.

Unless there were wholesale evacuation, a disaster of the greatest magnitude would engulf London if maximally adverse tide and weather conditions occurred simultaneously. The consequent disaster has been soberly assessed in Richard Doyle's novel *Deluge*: 60 square miles, involving $1\frac{1}{2}$ million people, inundated; 70 underground stations flooded, with appalling consequences; gas explosions, sewage pollution and electricity failures; 100,000 dead. Flood experts agree that this assessment is no exaggeration. A little-known but vital factor which increases London's vulnerability to flooding is that the centre of the city is slowly sinking. A fraction of an inch per year maybe but, since Roman times, those fractions add up to a considerable amount. Estimates vary, but they average about 12 feet. The Greater London Council is well aware of the danger, 'horrifying beyond measure'. River walls and embankments have been raised and strengthened, and enormous steel and rubber flood-gates constructed to protect the five major groups of docks.

The main work on London's defences began in 1974 and was operational in 1983. Seven large and two smaller concrete piers, with an abutment on each bank, have been built across the 570-yard-wide Thames at Woolwich, about 8 miles east of Westminster. There are ten steel gates between these structures: the four largest are each 200 feet long and weigh 3,300 tons. These gates are mounted on disc-like structures which rotate on trunnion shafts attached to the piers. They are normally recessed in concrete sills on the river bed, thus allowing

Like oases in a desert, buildings stand isolated in a muddy landscape after the main floodwaters have subsided. (US Government)

free passage of ships, but when flood conditions threaten the gates can be raised, thus providing a protective wall of steel between the flood and London.

Even the Thames barrier, however, will be dwarfed in a few years when the Dutch 'Delta Project' is completed. The Dutch meteorologist, C. J. van der Ham, tells me that 'this enormous enterprise, unprecedented in history aims (a) to raise the height of the dykes to a level to be surpassed by a North Sea flood only once in 10,000 years and (b) [to construct] a storm-surge barrier across the Eastern Scheldt with a length of 3,100 metres [nearly 2 miles], containing 63 steel flood gates'.

Although very destructive, sea floods are much less frequent than those resulting from the overflow of inland waters. With the development of more and more inland areas, these floods become ever more costly and dangerous.

The causes of inland floods are: rain, melted snow and ice; the accidental damming of rivers (landslides and earthquakes occasionally do this); rivers changing course; the build-up of river bottoms through accumulation of silt; and the bursting of riverbanks, dams and the containing walls of lakes and reservoirs. (Floods caused by volcanoes erupting beneath glaciers are dealt with on page 191.)

Rain is the primary cause of inland floods. It is formed when moist air rises and so becomes cooler, the moisture eventually falling to earth as rain, etc. To the meteorologist, rainfall is the total product of such precipitation (including snow, hail and sleet) and the amount in any particular place is measured by what is collected in a rain gauge.

For all places throughout the world, including the oceans, the average estimated annual rainfall is about 40 inches, but the extent varies greatly from area to area. It is least over large, flat, inland areas and greatest over areas where steep mountain ranges stand in the way of continuous warm moist winds. In large deserts, rainfall is practically non-existent,[2] perhaps 1 inch every two years; it has never been recorded at Calama in the Atacama Desert, Chile. At Cherrapunji in the Khasi hills, Assam, however, some 450 to 500 inches fall each year, and in some years twice that amount: from August 1860 to July 1861, 1,042 inches fell – nearly 90 feet of rain. Among the world's large cities, an average of 1.2 inches falls each year on Cairo, 95 inches on Singapore; London averages 24, Paris 24 and New York 43 inches.

The spiralling winds of hurricanes carry enormous quantities of water vapour from the oceans and pour them on the land as torrential rain (see page 21). Hurricanes are not, however, the only cause of great rainfalls. Whenever the meteorological conditions produce vast rising masses of moisture-laden air, heavy rainfall follows.

Occasionally, abnormal conditions cause exceptionally heavy falls over small areas, as in 'cloudbursts'. Such sudden downpours are generally triggered by a change in air currents. If these are rising at about 20 mph, or more, they prevent rain from falling and clouds become airborne reservoirs of vast amounts of moisture. If then the upward air currents rapidly cease, or drastically diminish, the heavens dump their liquid freight in a sudden cloudburst over a relatively small area.

A British authority on weather lore, E. L. Hawke, unearthed a little-known pamphlet written by Robert Harrison and published at Oxford in 1682: *Strange relation of the suddain and violent tempest which*

happened at Oxford, May 31 anno domini 1682. The 'suddain and violent tempest' occurred in the afternoon, accompanied by 'a huge blustering and boisterous wind'. The rain 'seemed one continued spout or stream; so that in less than half a quarter of an hour these pouring cataracts raised the water in a round and uniform vessel of about four feet diameter near two feet higher than before'. The consequent floods battered down bridges and demolished houses.

The valuable remark about the vessel, which in effect acted as a primitive rain gauge, enables a fair estimate to be made of the amount of rain which fell in a given time. Harrison's figures mean that about 1 foot 9 inches of rain fell in some seven minutes, a rate of 3 inches per minute. This rate exceeds all instrumental records for world rainfall. Some meteorologists, however, consider that this account should be treated with caution. The official world record for one minute's rainfall is $1\frac{1}{2}$ inches: at Barot, Guadeloupe, on 26 November 1970. The world record for 24 hours is 73.62 inches: at Cilaos, on the island of La Réunion in the Indian Ocean, on 15–16 March 1952. This means that 7,500 tons of rain fell on each acre.

Cloudburst and terrain can combine to cause 'flash floods'. The southwestern United States is especially prone to these sudden and sometimes catastrophic floods. Heavy rain suddenly falls over a comparatively small area which drains into steep valleys and gullies. These are quickly choked by a torrent, which may sweep for miles with bewildering speed: an area which has had no rain for weeks can suddenly be overwhelmed by a deluge. In the greatest flash floods, the walls of water are over 20 feet high.

Floodwaters engulf a small American town. (American Red Cross)

123

The raging waters scour the valleys of virtually everything movable: earth, vegetation, trees, rocks and miscellaneous debris. Sometimes a mass of earth as large as a house is washed out and carried away whole, occasionally with a tree embedded upright in it. During a flood in Davis and Box Elder Counties, Utah, on 13 August 1923, thousands of great boulders were carried along. At least a score weighed from 20 to 50 tons; the largest, a rectangular rock 14 feet long and weighing 80–90 tons, was carried 1 mile down a gentle slope of 6–8 degrees.

It is not the water alone which provides the great carrying power of flash floods. As the water courses down the valleys and gullies, earth, sand, clay and mud mix with it until a mudflow is formed: a thick mud porridge which flows with almost irresistible force and in which large boulders seem to float like corks. Inevitably, as the mudflow thickens and reaches lower ground, it slows down. It then spreads and moves like a huge sheet of wet mortar or concrete, sweeping all but the most solidly based objects before it: trees are carried away, either uprooted or snapped off at the ground, walls crushed in and small buildings pushed off their foundations.

One of the worst flash floods in American history swept down the 20-mile-long Big Thompson River and Canyon, Colorado, on the evening of 31 July 1976. The prelude to the disaster was a meteorological freak: a series of heavy thunderstorms, instead of moving across country, remained almost stationary over the headwaters of the canyon. Between 6.30 and 10.30 p.m. some 10 inches of rain fell. An estimated 50 million tons of water, with an energy equivalent of millions of tons of TNT, raged down the canyon. The Big Thompson River was over-

Mute evidence of the height reached by the waters of the great flood on the Cumberland River, Kentucky, in February 1937. (US Army Corps of Engineers)

whelmed. Its normal depth is 18 inches; it rose to over 20 *feet*. At the mouth of the canyon, normal flow is 165 cubic feet per second: this rose to 31,200, a *200-fold* increase.

The massed chocolate-coloured waters that thundered down the canyon swept away all but the most firmly anchored structures. Freighted with sand, mud, rock and debris, the water struck with the force of liquid concrete. Trees with trunks over 2 feet thick were gouged from the canyon's walls, and boulders 10 feet in diameter were rolled down the river bed.

Kendrick Frazier was in the canyon a few days before the flood. When he returned on the first weekend that it was re-opened to the public, he was shocked at the unimaginable change: 'The canyon walls were there, but much of everything else was gone.' Dotted about the canyon were many concrete slabs, all that remained of the buildings the flood had swept away. Spanning the mouth of the canyon, 15 feet above the highway, there had been a 9-foot-diameter water pipe. Full of water it weighed 600 tons. The debris-laden flood washed it away, carried it a quarter of a mile, and smashed it into a house.

Cynthia Russ Ramsay says:

'The violence of the water was indeed hard to believe. It smashed a two-storey municipal power plant at the foot of the canyon into a pile of brick rubble, and reduced a concrete bridge to gravel. It chewed U.S. Highway 34 into pieces of asphalt, bulldozed houses, and in a few hours turned Tom Hart's tomato patch into a ten-foot-deep ravine strewn with three-ton boulders.'

Not surprisingly, the last despairing cry over her CB radio of one victim as the waters engulfed her car was: 'My God! It's the end of the world!' The car was later found completely buried under mud and gravel, with the woman's body inside. Some cars were found buried 6 feet beneath the bed of the Big Thompson River.

The immense volume of water had one strange effect on some of the trees that resisted the frontal assault. The ground became so sodden that the roots could barely support the trunk and branches: 30-foot-tall pine trees could be felled by a vigorous push.

The flood finally spent itself on the plain around the small town of Loveland: the residents had been warned and there were no casualties, only damage to property. Total losses over the whole area were: 470 homes and buildings destroyed and a further 138 damaged; total economic loss estimated at 35½ million dollars; 145 people killed. It was the worst natural disaster in Colorado's history. (David McComb's *Big Thompson: Profile of a Natural Disaster* tells the story in great detail.)

It is not surprising to learn that the number one weather killer in the United States is flood. For many years lightning held that dubious honour, but in the 1970's water took the place of fire. The reason is not that there have been fewer thunderstorms and more floods, but because more people inhabit areas subject to flash floods. Mountain canyons and secluded valleys are ideal areas for those who want to 'get away from it all'; they are also the areas most subject to flash floods. Today, annual deaths from lightning average 110; those from floods, mainly flash floods, 130.

Great Britain has suffered many catastrophic floods from inland waters. One of the worst was on 18 March 1864, when Dale Dyke, about 8 miles from Sheffield, Yorkshire, burst and killed some 240 people.

Another disastrous inland flood occurred during the night of 15/16 August 1952 in North Devon, at and around the seaside town of Lynmouth. The rain gauge on Longstone Barrow, Exmoor, the tableland above Lynmouth, recorded 9.1 inches of rain in 24 hours. This has been exceeded only four times since official records began in Great Britain 100 years ago. Remember that ordinary steady rain for 24 hours means less than 1 inch in a rain gauge; 9 inches represents over half a million tons of rain per square mile. Throughout the whole area rainfall was about 3.7 inches, weighing about 90 million tons.

The state of the ground made conditions worse. It was already waterlogged, and just below the surface a layer of rock prevented any appreciable percolation of water. Moreover, the East and West Lyn Rivers, and their tributaries, fall 1,500 feet through funnel-like gorges into Lynmouth in under 4 miles. Down these gorges pounded millions of tons of floodwater. In dry summer weather the rivers have a depth of a few inches; now, at times, a solid wall of water up to 40 feet high raced down to the sea at 20 mph. At the peak of the flood, nearly 600 tons of water were estimated to plunge down the gorges *every second*.

Such a torrent is irresistible to everything except the heaviest and most solidly based objects. The water gouged out huge rocks and boulders, some weighing 15 tons, and carried them to the seashore. Trees felled by earlier gales, and others washed out by the roots, were swept into the sea. This heavy debris added to the lethal force of the flood. Structures that might have withstood the waters were knocked down by trees acting as outsized battering rams, and by rocks that had the impact of 100-pound solid artillery shells – weight making up for speed.

In the 4 miles between Exmoor and Lynmouth there were 17 bridges. The first soon gave before the battering of the debris-strewn waters, and added its weight to the force of the torrent; the next then collapsed, then the next, until every one of the 17 bridges was battered down. At times the mass of debris jammed to form a temporary dam. When the thousands of tons of piled-up water eventually broke through, the huge surge carried all before it. At a bridge in Lynmouth, however, the debris was so great that the floodwaters divided, temporarily forming another river.

Cottages, houses and other structures within range of the flood were soon destroyed. Overwhelmed by a house-high wall of water, battered by heavy trees and masonry from bridges, and struck by boulders weighing up to 10 tons, even the sturdiest dwellings collapsed and crashed into the raging tide. The floodwaters dug deep into the earth. Road surfaces were scoured away, and the soft earth of the verges was gouged as by a giant excavator, some gullies being 20 feet deep – right down to the bare rock. A vivid illustration of this gouging effect occurred at a Lynmouth garage: petrol tanks were scoured from their foundations and swept away without trace.

As in most disasters, there were many odd happenings. In one wrecked house a table, on which was a bowl of eggs, was left standing, and not one egg was even cracked. Elsewhere a cottage had been swept clean away, yet the wooden gate still swung from it hinges. In a car park all was darkness at one moment, a blaze of light the next: water

Top *The littered foreshore after the great Lynmouth, Devon, flood of August 1952. Millions of tons of water poured through funnel-like gorges. Soil, trees and boulders – some weighing 15 tons – were carried to the sea.* (Mirrorpic)

Above *The roof-top waters of the great Mississippi flood of May 1973. At Vicksburg, where this photograph was taken, the water eventually rose to 53 feet. Some 16 million acres in seven states were flooded, causing one thousand million dollars' worth of damage.* (US Army Corps of Engineers)

had shorted the electrical systems of some of the cars, thus switching on the headlights. A single car, lights blazing, was seen coming down a hill into Lynmouth. It slid under the flood and, lights still on, travelled like a weird submarine beneath the racing waters. Then suddenly its lights failed and, except for the lightning flashes, intense darkness prevailed again.

When dawn broke after this Walpurgian night, the scene on the foreshore was fantastic. It was littered with the debris of scores of wrecked homes and buildings; smashed cars; telegraph poles, tree trunks, branches and complete trees; the smashed and mangled remains of the undergrowth from the surrounding countryside; some 200,000 cubic yards of silt, mud, gravel, and stones, in some places massed 25 feet high; some 200,000 tons of rocks and boulders; iron girders and bridges; broken masonry and the bodies of birds, fish, animals – and people. Half a mile out to sea, hundreds of trees, presumably weighted down by rocks and soil entangled in their enormous roots, had their upper branches showing above the waves: a fantastic sea forest of stunted trees.

The flood altered the landscape. S. H. Burton, an authority on Exmoor, says: 'I knew Lynmouth well, but when I visited the town soon after the disaster, I could not find my way about. Combined bombardment from the sea and air could not have wrought more fearful devastation than these twin rivers in that dreadful night.'

The toll of this great flood was: 93 buildings destroyed or irretrievably damaged; 28 bridges destroyed or badly damaged; 132 vehicles destroyed; and 34 men, women and children killed or missing. On the credit side, the Lynmouth Relief Fund received, from subscriptions throughout the world, £1,336,425. Lynmouth was rebuilt and precautions taken which, it was hoped, would prevent Exmoor's wild waters from ever again destroying the little town. On 8 October 1960 these were put to the test. A 20-foot-high torrent of water, carrying trees and boulders, swept down on Lynmouth. The engineers had done their work well: the banks held (Eric R. Delderfield).

The suddenness, the violence, the damage and casualties made the Lynmouth flood one of the most dramatic weather disasters in British history. Yet in extent and duration it was far surpassed by the flood of March 1947, which affected almost the whole of the eastern three-quarters of England from a line drawn from Bournemouth to Harrogate, and part of southeast Wales as well. 'Never, in any history of which we have record, have nearly all the main rivers of the south, the midlands and the north-east of England swollen into such deep flood simultaneously, or persisted in flood for such a length of time.' (Dudley Barker)

This vast flood was caused by rain and snow: in March the average fall over the country as a whole was 6.78 inches, nearly three times the normal March precipitation. Then warm air moved across Britain and melted the masses of snow which had accumulated during the cold winter. Rivers were overwhelmed and burst their banks: water blanketed thousands of square miles. Viewed from space, much of England resembled one vast lake dotted with urban islands. In many areas the boat became the favourite means of transport. At Gloucester a bridal couple, having been carried through the flood to church, left by punt after their wedding ceremony.

The economic losses of this flood were, of course, disastrous. The exact figure is unknown, but it certainly exceeded £12 million. There were, however, no deaths: unlike Lynmouth, this flood gave ample warning and spread comparatively slowly.

North America has suffered greatly from floods and still does: property damage averages 1,000 million dollars a year. Severe flooding frequently results from hurricanes, owing to the immense rainfall in a short time, sometimes over 20 inches in 24 hours.[3] The ground is waterlogged and quickly flooded. Rivers, lakes and reservoirs are filled to overflowing. Soon the whole countryside is awash, and what were previously roads become canals where the only transport is rivercraft. Under pressure from the water, dams, bridges and buildings give way. Frequently, in great hurricane floods, the pounding waters wash wooden houses from their foundations and they sail away like huge mis-shapen boats.

John Hersey says that during the flood caused by hurricane Diane in August 1955 a wooden four-storey hotel at Winsted, Connecticut, floated away and was borne downstream in the Mad River. After travelling three-quarters of a mile, it settled on a playing field; it was upright but had only two storeys, the two lower ones having been broken off or worn away during the ride. A newspaper illustrator captioned a drawing of an incident in a flood caused by hurricane Agnes of 1972: 'House damaged by passing garage'.

In hurricane floods, the water at times rises dangerously fast. During the New England hurricane of September 1938, a man at Buzzards Bay, Massachusetts, crossed a street in ankle-deep water to rescue a child from a car; when he returned a minute or so later the water was up to his chest. F. Barrows Colton, who recounts this incident, tells of other strange happenings during these tremendous floods. Water shortcircuited the horns of cars and burglar alarms so that they added their cacophony to the shrieking of the hurricane; a flotilla of wooden cottages sailed up Narragansett Bay, Rhode Island; and a man's wooden legs, which the sea swept away from his house, were found a week later on a beach 20 miles away – both together!

The greatest floods in North America occur in the area of the Lower Mississippi. Waters from 50 tributaries (including the Ohio and Missouri Rivers), draining $1\frac{1}{4}$ million square miles, flow into North America's greatest river, the 2,348-mile-long Mississippi, 'Father of Waters'. In flood, the flow of water is about 30 times greater than at low level. (This is greatly exceeded in some other rivers; for example, on the Vistula, in Poland, the ratio is 1:120.) At no time in recorded history have all the great tributaries of the Mississippi been in dangerous spate simultaneously. Should this ever happen, it might well cause the greatest disaster in the history of the United States.

The Mississippi's lower reaches form a gigantic spout through which more than 60 cubic miles of water funnel during a flood period lasting from $1\frac{1}{2}$ to $2\frac{1}{2}$ months. The flood does not roar down the river like a vast wave; it is a slow inexorable tide, the flood crest sometimes travelling only 30 miles a day. Occasionally, the waters in the Mississippi rise higher than those in some of its tributaries: there is then a backflow, the local waters rise higher than their natural banks and artificial levees, and the land is flooded. This happened in the spring of 1927 when 26,000 square miles were inundated. Frederick

Simpich, of the National Geographic Society, who flew over part of the flooded area, says:

'A vast sheet of water as yellow as the China Sea at the mouth of the Yangtze, stretches practically from southeast Missouri down to the Atchafalaya Basin [Bay] of Louisiana. This sea is about 1,050 miles long and in places over 50 miles in width. Over 750,000 people normally live within its limits. Flying over it now in an airplane, you see the roofs of their houses, the smokestacks of their sawmills, their church steeples, the tops of their shade trees, and lines of telegraph poles sticking up from the water.'

During the relief work boats cruised among the treetops 15 feet above the ground. One experienced steamboat captain, with familiar landmarks obliterated, found himself and his 300-ton craft in a flooded forest. A girl is reported to have said: 'Noah oughta stuck around; he'd 'ave seen a real flood!' Some people actually built an ark for themselves and their animals. Unfortunately it leaked, and the would-be Noah fled to the nearest levee, his followers and animals coming after him 'two by two'. During another flood some people, hearing a voice broadcast warnings from an aeroplane, thought it was God announcing another deluge.

By the time the water had receded, and the overwhelming mess and confusion had been cleared, this flood had killed 313 people and rendered 637,000 homeless.

Although neither the most costly nor the greatest in extent, the most famous flood in the history of North America, and the most tragic in loss of human lives, was the Johnstown flood of 31 May 1889. The main cause was the bursting of a dam. The flood was the subject of a poem, *The Pennsylvania Disaster*, by William McGonagall – 'the best of all bad poets' – of which four lines will suffice:

The embankment of the dam was considered rather weak,
And by the swelled body of water the embankment did break,
And burst o'er the valley like a leaping river,
Which caused the spectators with fear to shiver.

Johnstown was an industrial borough of 8,000 people in the Conemaugh Valley in western Pennsylvania, at the junction of the Little Conemaugh River and Stony Creek. Some 12 miles to the northeast was the South Fork Dam, at that time the world's largest earth dam: 931 feet long, 72 feet high, over 500 feet thick at the base and approximately 40 feet wide at the top. This was 10 feet higher than the normal water level of the reservoir, which was 2 miles long, in places 1 mile wide, with a maximum depth of 70 feet. Capable of holding 5,000 million gallons of water (nearly 18 million tons), the reservoir was then the largest man-made lake in the United States.

Long before the fateful day there were warnings that the dam was unsafe. On 30 May came an added strain; a great storm, continuing for two days and nights, poured thousands of millions of tons of water on the surrounding countryside. By early morning on 31 May many of the streets of Johnstown were awash, and by afternoon the water was from 3 to 10 feet deep; the dam above was under enormous pressure.

As the day wore on, with no let-up in the downpour, some citizens thought of one of Johnstown's standard jokes: 'The dam has busted – run for the hills.' A few families did just that. They had not long to wait. At 3.10 p.m. there was a tremendous roar, and some 300 feet of the centre of the dam gave way. A treetop-high flood hurtled down the valley towards the already swollen river. The wall of water thrust before it a blast of air which flung down trees 6 and 8 inches in diameter.

Although the break in the dam was 300 feet wide, and eventually became 430 feet, there was so much water that it took about 50 minutes to drain away. Its initial mile-a-minute rush was not maintained. The immense mass of debris that the flood swept along as it bulldozed its way through the valley slowed it down. Sometimes, where the valley narrowed, this mass jammed against the walls and temporarily halted the flood. Then the overwhelming weight of water, still gathering volume from the draining dam, thrust forward again, sweeping all before it.

Above Johnstown there were several small communities. The flood practically washed them out of existence, like a steamroller crushing toy villages. A stone viaduct was snapped in two as if made of dry clay, then ground to pieces. An iron bridge high in the valley was torn from its foundations by a blow from the edge of the flood. Dozens of locomotives and passenger carriages, hundreds of freight cars and miles of track were swept forward as the monstrous river pounded down the valley. All these added immeasurably to the battering effect of the water.

Near Johnstown stood a factory – the Gautier rolling mills – with massive furnaces, boilers, heavy machinery and hundreds of large drums of steel cable and wire. The flood hit the steel mill and, according to an eye-witness, lifted and carried it bodily down the valley.

At 4.10 p.m. the flood swept into Johnstown, already awash from a day and a night of torrential rain. A lawyer named Horace Rose, who looked up the valley just before the flood struck, wrote:

> 'I saw stretching from hill to hill a great mass of timber, trees, roofs and debris of every sort, rapidly advancing toward me, wrecking and carrying everything before it. It was then in the midst of the Gautier works. A dense cloud hung over the line of the rolling debris, which I then supposed was the steam and soot which had arisen from the hundreds of fires in the Gautier works as the waves rolled over them. I stood and looked as the restless tide moved on and saw brick buildings crushed in and instantly dashed from sight, while frame tenements were quickly smashed to atoms.' (Quoted by Richard O'Connor)

Rose's own large brick-and-stone house was shattered and he suffered multiple injuries.

Certain houses, partly sheltered from the full weight of the flood, survived but many were crushed. Some wooden houses, wrenched whole from their foundations, floated on the vast muddy tide like ships; one was found afterwards tightly wrapped around with telegraph- and electric-light wires like some gigantic parcel.

Perhaps the most fantastic sight on this altogether fantastic day was the scene at Stone Bridge, 50 feet wide and based on seven 58-foot stone piers. It carried four tracks of the main line of the Pennsylvania Railroad to Pittsburgh and was built to last for centuries. The bridge withstood the flood then acted as a dam itself, reinforced by an amazing collection of debris.

Jam-packed against the bridge were the spoils of the flood's sweep down the valley; the wreckage towered over 50 feet and covered more than 60 acres. Behind it were mounds, 20–30 feet high. Steam engines and coaches; miles of track and steel cables; the wrecks of hundreds of wooden and brick buildings; parts of viaducts and bridges; telegraph poles, trees and timber; the carcases of horses, cattle and other farm animals; and men, women and children – alive and dead – spread for hundreds of yards in all directions in muddy meaningless confusion.

In the early evening, the wreckage caught fire: there were oil-soaked timbers, lime, crude petroleum – and live coals. Many escaped the water, only to die by fire.

As with every great natural disaster, the Johnstown flood abounded in freakish behaviour: of elements, humans and belongings. One lady insisted on finishing her hair-do before being rescued from her shattered house. Some women, with little clothing on, refused to be rescued until the men promised (a) to have coats or blankets immediately ready and (b) to turn their backs during the crucial seconds. Under two wrecked freight cars was a stable containing a cow, a dog and five hens – all dry and well. In one area, the only solid footing was a vast carpet of cigars, spilled from a nearby factory, while some of the best beds for several nights were coffins filled with straw. A

Below   A vivid illustration of the destructive power of water. After this South African flood the road was completely cut in two. (Rand Daily Mail)

Overleaf   Wrenched from its foundations, and lodged precariously atop a bridge near Cedar Cone, this house bears witness to the awesome power of the Big Thompson Canyon flash flood of 31 July 1976. It was the worst natural disaster in Colorado's history, causing 35 million dollars' worth of damage, killing 145 people. (David McComb)

partially wrecked house floated down the swollen river to Pittsburgh, over 60 miles away; it arrived nearly 24 hours later, and inside was a five-month-old baby alive and bawling. During the flood several babies were born prematurely: one was christened 'Moses' and two were named 'Flood'.

Nobody knows how many lives were lost. Estimates varied from 2,205 to 2,287. In addition, 967 were listed as 'not known to be found'. Among those who helped to clear up the appalling mess were 550 soldiers, 200 lumberjacks, 1,250 railwaymen, 6,000 labourers, nearly 250 sanitary workers – and 55 undertakers.

Those who have written on the Johnstown flood do not agree on the various statistics. In general I have used those approved by the Cambria County Historical Society. I have used Richard O'Connor's *Johnstown: the day the dam broke* as background material for this section.

Johnstown was not, however, finished with floods. There were several in the next 50 years, the worst on 17 March 1936, when 30 people died. In November 1943, after five years' work and the expenditure of nearly $8\frac{1}{2}$ million dollars, Johnstown was finally considered flood-proof. The channels of the twin rivers were widened and deepened, and their banks paved with concrete: nearly 3 million cubic yards of earth and rock were removed, and enough concrete was used to cover a two-lane highway 62 miles long.

Despite all these precautions Johnstown was not floodproof. During the night of 19/20 July 1977, water from the tributaries of the Conemaugh River and some small dams raged into the town, causing damage of 200 million dollars and killing about 80 people (the exact figure is unknown).

The great Boston molasses flood of 15 January 1919 had nothing to do with the elements, but its unique character makes it worthy of mention. A great storage tank of raw molasses (thick treacle) stood

134

near the inner harbour. It was 50 feet tall, 282 feet in circumference and held some 2 million gallons. At lunchtime the tank burst, and thousands of tons of molasses cascaded through the nearby streets, a monstrous thick brown wave about 15 feet high. Its initial speed was estimated to be 35 mph, and it struck with immense force.

Before the sticky brown flood was spent it had wrecked the elevated railway, caused over 1 million dollars' worth of property damage, killed 21 people, and given the municipal services the biggest clearing-up job in Boston's history. Years afterwards the smell of molasses could still be detected where the flood had pushed its sticky way. The cause of the burst was that the tank had been built of thinner plates than had been specified. It was also suggested that fermentation had built up explosive pressure (Ralph Frye; and *Boston Traveler*, 15 January 1954).

A weird and terrifying by-product arose in the Putnam, Connecticut, flood of 19 August 1955. In the midst of the deluge, startled onlookers saw flames shoot hundreds of feet into the air; their ears were deafened by thunderous explosions. Smoke from the fires could be seen 20 miles away. The floodwaters had poured into a warehouse containing 20 tons of magnesium, a chemical which ignites on contact with water. 'The warehouse erupted in flame, and hundreds of barrels of burning magnesium were carried downstream in the churning river. Firemen could only watch helplessly throughout the night as the barrels exploded, each blast lighting up Putnam like a giant flash bulb.' (Champ Clark)

The greatest floods of all occur in Asia, the scene of Noah's deluge, when 'the water prevailed exceedingly upon the earth; and all the high hills, that were under the whole heaven, were covered'. The Hebrew idiom uses universal expressions – 'the whole heaven' – for restricted areas; here it is Mesopotamia. There are references in other ancient writings to a great flood in this area.

Archaeology has shown that a gigantic flood did occur in ancient times in lower Mesopotamia. While excavating at Ur of the Chaldees, Sir Leonard Woolley found a heaped-up deposit of water-laid clay with a maximum depth of 11 feet. Such a mass of clay indicates a flood of at least 25 feet in that particular spot. It also proves that the area was overwhelmed by a flood unparalleled in its later history. Sir Frederic Kenyon says that the deposit was not due to a long period of submersion but to a sudden flood.

According to Genesis: 'Fifteen cubits upward did the waters prevail.' This is roughly the maximum height estimated by Woolley, who considers that in the flat low-lying land of Mesopotamia the flood probably covered an area of 300 × 100 miles.

'It was not a universal deluge; it was a vast flood in the valley of the Tigris and the Euphrates which drowned the whole of the habitable land between the mountains and desert; for the people who lived there that was all the world. The great bulk of those people must have perished, and it was but a scanty and dispirited remnant that from the city walls watched the waters recede at last. No wonder that they saw in this disaster the gods' punishment of a sinful generation and described it as such in a religious poem; and if some household had managed to escape by boat from the drowned lowlands the head of it would naturally be chosen as the hero of the saga.'

There has, of course, been speculation on the cause of this most famous of all floods. The most likely explanation seems to be that the Tigris and Euphrates overflowed their banks, that there was torrential and long-continued rain and that there was a tidal bore or invasion from the sea: '. . . all the fountains of the great deep [were] broken up' (Genesis 7: 11).

More books have been written about Noah's flood than on any other natural disaster, and possibly on any other single incident in the world's history. Werner Keller says that, up to 1980, 80,000 works in 72 languages had been published on it.

Since Noah's day, the greatest and most disastrous floods have occurred in the Indian subcontinent and in China. The worst ones in India are associated with typhoons, and are dealt with under 'hurricanes'. In the Bay of Bengal area, 300,000 people have been killed in one such flood.

Terrible as these floods were, they are surpassed by some Chinese floods, particularly from the overflowing of the Hwang-Ho or Yellow River – 'China's Sorrow'. As this meanders over its surrounding plains, it is an ever-present threat to the 50 million farmers and peasants living on the 50,000 square miles of rich farmland (by one of Nature's ironies, the vast slimy sea of liquid mud left after a flood is an excellent fertiliser). The river rises in the Tibetan highlands and, after a circuitous course of nearly 3,000 miles across China from west to east, empties into the Yellow Sea at the Gulf of Po Hai. In places it is 1 mile wide.

The river's English name comes from the yellow windblown loess (a mixture of clay and sand) which the swift current whirls down from Inner Mongolia in millions of tons. Its turbid waters have twice the amount of silt carried by the Mississippi. It is estimated that each year the river washes away over 1,200 million cubic yards of soil. (When the Panama Canal was made, about 200 million cubic yards of earth and rock were excavated.) As the Hwang-Ho slows down on reaching the Great Plain of North China, an appreciable part of the loess falls to the river bed, so that for some 500 miles the channel grows shallower each year. The bed rises an average of about 3 feet a century. The result is that at low water the river, contained by high levees, runs about 15 feet above the general level of the plain; at high water it runs 25 to 30 feet above, and in flood way over that.

These conditions make the Hwang-Ho the most flood-prone river in the world. In addition, floods sometimes alternate with droughts on the Great Plain. Controlling the Hwang-Ho thus becomes a water engineer's nightmare. It is also his supreme challenge for, as Oliver J. Todd, an engineer who worked on the Hwang-Ho for over 20 years, says: 'On the Great Plain . . . lies the greatest outdoor laboratory in the world for flood control.'

How long the Chinese have tried to tame the Hwang-Ho is not known but the Emperor Yü, who was an engineer, worked on flood control over 40 centuries ago. He is said to have succeeded by dividing the flow and dredging the river bed continually. It is believed, however, that the river carried less silt in those days that it does now.

Above right One of the avid sightseers who came to Johnstown after the devastating flood of 1889 surveys the ruins from a perilous perch. This most famous of America's floods claimed some 3,000 lives. (Carnegie Library of Pittsburgh)

Below right London's defence against the Thames' floodwaters. The barrier is sited at Woolwich, eight miles east of Westminster. There are ten steel gates, the four largest being 200 feet long and weighing 3,300 tons. (Greater London Council)

The Hwang-Ho holds the unenviable record of causing the world's most lethal floods. In September and October 1887 the river rose until it overtopped 70-foot-high levees: 50,000 square miles were inundated, 300 villages swept away, some 2 million people made homeless; at least 900,000 died. An even higher toll has been claimed for a later flood, but the reference books do not agree on either the date or the number of victims. The Chinese Society of Hydraulic Engineering tells me that the 1933 flood covered an area of some 4,500 square miles and affected over $3\frac{1}{2}$ million people, '18,000 of whom died'.

On 30 October 1952, Mao Tse-tung climbed to the top of a levee and proclaimed: 'Work on the Yellow River must be done well!' Since then an enormous amount has been done to prevent the flood tragedies of the past. There have been setbacks, but no devastating floods have occurred since Mao's invocation.

As avalanches have played their part in war (see page 112), so has the Hwang-Ho. In April 1938, in an attempt to halt the Japanese army, troops of Chiang Kaishek dynamited a hole in the southern levee, releasing a raging flood that drowned the surrounding countryside. Whatever effect this had on the Japanese, it was disastrous for the Chinese: 4,000 villages flooded, 6 million people made homeless, half a million drowned.

One of the most famous floods of the 20th century occurred in northern Italy in 1966. The main cause was exceptional rainfall. On 3 and 4 November, 19 inches of rain fell on the Arno River watershed: a third of its average annual rainfall in 48 hours. The consequent flood swept into 750 villages, covered 3,000 miles of highway, and killed 127 people and 50,000 cattle.

It was, however, the damage to Florence and its art treasures that caught the imagination of the western world. The city had $7\frac{1}{2}$ inches of rain in 24 hours: nearly a quarter of the average annual rainfall in one day. The floodwaters were augmented by water from the Lévane dam, 35 miles upriver. Even the dam's near-$6\frac{1}{2}$ million cubic-yard capacity was overstrained by the torrential rainfall, and part of its reservoir overtopped the dam to swell the flood that bore down on Florence with the speed of a galloping horse. At times the Arno's waters, channelled by the narrow streets, raged through Florence at 80 mph.

Whenever the Arno is in full spate, Florence is in danger. The river runs through hills and its bed forms a gutter; when that overflows, the water pours into Florence and beyond. Disastrous floods have swept through the city's streets and squares on seven occasions during the past six centuries. The flood of 1966 rose higher than ever before; at the Via dei Neri the highest water mark was 16 feet 2 inches; in one square, surrounded by buildings, the waters rose to 20 feet. The force of the rushing waters tore out concrete walls, swept motorcars from roads and flushed fuel oil from basements. Mud, trees and vegetation, dead animals, and the contents of the sewers swelled the flood, and this noisome torrent poured into the Nazionale Library (Italy's largest). It dowsed priceless paintings and statues, wrecked treasured exhibits in museums. Estimates of the damage vary, but £50 million is probably not too high.

As soon as news of the flood reached the rest of the world, help in various ways poured into Florence. A small army of young people from a dozen countries in Europe and some 500 from the United States, who were in Florence to study, exchanged pens and notebooks for shovels and brushes, and helped to clear up the mess and rescue the treasures (*National Geographic*, July 1967).

World losses from floods, both in lives and money, are immense. In the United States alone, they have cost around 1,000 million dollars in a year. Much time, thought, energy and money is therefore devoted to flood control, although this, important as it is, is only one category of public measures against floods. Others are insurance; land-use regulation; structural adjustment; forecasting and warning services[4]; and emergency action.

Flood control necessarily varies with the situation, such as terrain, stretch of river, surroundings and previous history. Controls suitable for one stretch of river in one country may be unsuitable for a similar stretch in another, or even in the same country. Controlling flooding near a large city, for example, is a very different matter from that in unpopulated country.

Nowhere in the world has greater effort been given to flood control than on the lower Mississippi. A glance at a map and a rapid reading of its history show why: over 50 major floods in 250 years of settlement. The first controls were begun soon after the founding of New Orleans in 1717. Ten years later the city was guarded by a levee 3 feet high, 18 feet wide and 5,400 feet long. Today, there are about 1,700 miles of levees on the main Mississippi River, with an average height of 25 feet (maximum 40 feet). The base width is about ten times the height. Many have a 25-foot-wide road at the crown. There are also some 2,000 miles of levees on the tributaries. Many levees are sited a long distance from the river – up to 5 miles in places – to give an additional area for excess water.

The Mississippi levee system is one of the greatest feats of American engineering; it is longer than the Great Wall of China. It is also profitable: for every dollar spent on the levees, there is an estimated return of almost nine dollars in increased agricultural land and improved waterways.

Over 250 years' experience of the river, however, has shown that more than levees are necessary. Engineers have therefore provided controls which can be used when the river rises dangerously. The first is a series of reservoirs; should these be filled to overflowing, floodwaters can be released into channels and flood plains, where minimum damage and disruption will be caused.

The main flood controls are, of course, federal projects involving vast labour and expense, but it is not generally realised that smaller local measures can do much to reduce floods. Contour-ploughing, that is ploughing lengthwise across hillsides rather than up and down the slopes, produces a 'terracing' effect, which tends to hold water or delay its travel downhill. Trees are one of the best natural defences: forests can absorb more rainfall than moorlands. The planting of deep-rooted grasses, ploughing, and the building of small earthen dams at strategic spots also help to prevent heavy rainfall from causing floods.

As so often with natural violence, even floods have their benefits. Some of the most fertile land in the world lies beside great rivers, and every time they overflow a fertilising deposit of sediment covers the area. Nile floods are the basis of Egyptian agriculture; the valley is fertile solely because the world's longest river floods its banks regularly each year.

NOTES

1. Appealing for help, the Lord Mayor of London said: 'I doubt if in the past century so much devastation and misery has ever fallen on our country in 48 hours in peace-time.' The flood is commemorated in an excellent 900-page monograph, *The Great Tide* by Hilda Grieve. It deals mainly with the inundation of Essex, where 119 died.

2. But certainly not in the Sahara. When a six-year drought in the Spanish Sahara ended in torrential rain in August 1975, a man was drowned! (*The Daily Telegraph*, 6 August 1975).

3. Hurricane Claudette deposited a United States record 43 inches of rain on Alvin, Texas, in 24 hours during 25–26 July 1979 (*Weatherwise*, August 1980).

4. Many people have been needlessly drowned because, not knowing how a flood was going to develop, they have panicked and been swept away as soon as the front door was opened. Had they stayed upstairs until the flood abated, they would have been safe.

METEOROIDS

'I could more easily believe that two Yankee professors would lie than that stones would fall from heaven.' So said Thomas Jefferson, then President of the United States, when told that two Yale University professors had reported the fall of over 300 pounds of meteorites at Weston, Connecticut, in December 1807. The remark was typical of the attitude which prevailed in scientific circles at the time.

Yet the true origin of meteorites had been recognised by the ancients. In a list of treasures compiled by a Hittite king in the 16th century BC, there is a reference to 'black iron of heaven from the sky'. Livy mentions the fall of a shower of stones in Rome about 654 BC, and there is a Chinese record of a meteorite in 616 BC which is alleged to have broken several chariots and killed ten men. References in the writings of other ancient civilisations indicate that meteorites were regarded as having a celestial origin.

During the Middle Ages, and in later centuries, there were various records of meteorites. Subsequently, the notion that the earth was sometimes under bombardment from outer space was regarded as a vulgar superstition. In the 18th century learned men were unable to believe stories of fiery bodies falling from the sky with loud explosions. Some European museums even discarded genuine meteorites in their collections as relics of a superstitious past.

There were various theories to explain the optical phenomena which were alleged to accompany the falls, such as lightning or a 'phlogistous gas catching fire in the upper regions of the atmosphere'. That rocks did fall from the sky was, however, beyond admission.

Nevertheless, accounts of falls were accumulating, despite the scepticism of scientists. In the afternoon of 13 September 1768, a meteorite fell at Lucé, France. The French Academy of Science, then the foremost scientific body in the world, sent a commission which received the unanimous testimony of numerous eye-witnesses, and were given the 'rock' itself. The commission concluded that it did not fall. The statement of one of the witnesses was actually altered to make it fit the explanation that the rock was merely a terrestrial body which had been struck by lightning.

A further example of obscurantism was to come. On 24 July 1790, a shower of meteorites fell in southwest France, burying themselves in the earth. Some 300 written statements by witnesses were sent to scientific bodies and journals, and pieces of the stones were produced. Still official science would not reverse its *ipse dixit* that 'stones do not fall from the sky'. Well might Charles P. Olivier say:

> 'In the face of all this evidence, we have an example of stupidity and bigotry, exhibited by the foremost body of scientists of the day – men who doubtless considered themselves, and were so considered by others, the most advanced and "modern" of their time – which for all ages should stand as a warning to any man who feels that he can give a final verdict upon a matter outside his immediate experience.'

These are words which any scientist would do well to ponder when confronted with evidence running counter to long-cherished opinions.

Several events finally made the French Academy and the scientific world recognise the true origin of meteorites. The Vienna Museum had preserved an iron meteorite. This was studied by Ernst Florens Friedrich Chladni, a German who was both a scientist and a lawyer. It was his legal training that was to prove invaluable. Chladni carefully studied the eye-witness reports of alleged falls and realised that here were no garbled fairy stories of impossible events, but the statements of ordinary men honestly striving to describe what they had seen.

In 1794 Chladni published his report. He defended the trustworthiness of witnesses to alleged falls, stated that meteorites enter the atmosphere from outer space, and made some shrewd observations concerning their nature. Chladni's report certainly provoked discussion, but scientists were not immediately converted to his revolutionary view of the origin and nature of the 'stones from the sky'.

In the year the report was published there was a fall of meteorites in Italy; another in England during the next year; and in 1798 another in India. In 1803 Edward Howard, an English chemist, published his own and a fellow scientist's analyses of some meteorites. The conclusions supported Chladni's views.

On 26 April 1803, Nature provided the final evidence. In clear daylight, a large shower of stony meteorites fell near the village of L'Aigle in northwest France. Many witnesses said that just before the fall they saw brilliant lights in the sky and heard loud explosions. Some of the stones were still hot when discovered. They weighed from a

A Perseid meteor of 14 August 1983 blazes across the night sky. Large meteor showers occur regularly each year in mid-August. (Chuck Fields)

141

quarter of an ounce to nearly 19 pounds, and fell along a path some 8 miles long. The French Academy sent one of their members, Jean Baptiste Biot, to investigate on the spot. His report finally convinced his sceptical colleagues that, after all, stones do fall from the sky.

Even today, however, there is much discussion concerning the precise origin of meteorites. Some of the discarded theories are that: they were parts of the earth which had been thrown up in violent volcanic eruptions; they were formed in the upper atmosphere by condensation of dust and gases; they have grown in interstellar space by the accumulation of small bits of solid material. It is now generally agreed that meteoroids are fragments of asteroids (small planets) or comets.

An enormous number of meteoroids stream into the earth's atmosphere every 24 hours. On a clear moonless night, a single observer will see an average of about ten meteors an hour, but his field of view is so restricted that he can see only those which appear in a tiny part of the sky. Moreover, many meteors are too faint to be observed by the naked eye and can be seen only through a telescope, or detected by radar. An estimate by Harvard Observatory is that over 100,000 million meteoroids encounter our atmosphere every 24 hours. Although only a small proportion reach the earth, thousands of tons of meteoritic dust fall every year. That is why the earth puts on weight.

The average meteor that can be seen with the naked eye is first visible approximately 60 miles above the earth and is seen for about half a second, hence the popular name 'shooting star'. It follows that every visible meteor must have sufficient mass to render incandescent a cylinder of air several miles long which can be seen at least 60 miles away. Few meteors come nearer to the earth than 35 miles, although brilliant fireballs descend as low as 10 miles.

It might be thought that meteoroids, to cause such a great band of light, must have considerable mass. Most astronomers, however, believe that few are larger than a pea.

Very few meteoroids reach the earth: about 1,000 or so per year over the whole land surface. Our almost complete immunity from bombardment is due to two factors: the earth's protective layer of air, and the high speed of the missiles. Although the atmosphere extends several hundred miles above the earth, only below 70 miles is it dense enough to cause meteoroids to glow. The total effect of this layer of air is to provide the earth with a 'cushion' of tremendous stopping power.

Although the protective armour of air prevents the vast majority of meteoroids from reaching the ground, the rare blockbuster[2] (with an initial weight of not fewer than 20 pounds or so) sometimes gets through. Probably only a few ounces of a 20-pound meteoroid reach the earth. Friction first melts then ablates, or rasps off, layer after layer of the outer parts so that only the central core or fragments land on earth.

There are several kinds of meteor light trails. The brief pencil of light – shooting star – that momentarily streaks the night sky is an ordinary meteor. If the meteoroid is coming directly towards the observer, it appears as a brief stationary point of bright light. The brilliant torch that illuminates hundreds of cubic miles is known as a fireball; it has a luminosity equalling or exceeding that of the brightest planet. A spectacular fireball may be caused by a meteoroid weighing no more than 1 pound.

The earth orbits at 18.5 miles per second (mps). Meteoroids enter the atmosphere at any angle and at varying speeds. One travelling in exactly the same direction as the earth has a speed relative to the earth of 6.8 mps; one entering head-on has a relative speed of 45.4 mps. All speeds between these two extremes are possible. To realise what the speed of 45.4 mps means, imagine a race between a meteoroid and a train from London to Glasgow (a 400-mile journey). The meteoroid would reach Glasgow before the last of the train's carriages had left London's Euston Station!

All but the very largest meteoroids are so retarded by their passage through the atmosphere that they land with no more force than if dropped from a high building. On 1 January 1869, some meteoroids fell on a frozen lake at Hessle, Sweden; although some of them weighed several pounds, they did not break through the ice. Other meteorites, however, have buried themselves several feet in hard earth.

When a meteoroid, travelling many times faster than a high-powered rifle bullet, collides with the atmosphere, the air in its path is violently compressed. If the meteoroid is large enough, the boom from the sonic shock wave is heard several minutes after the fireball has passed.

The speed of the meteoroid causes the air to press against it with such force that the friction generates tremendous heat: sometimes 3,000°C, half the surface temperature of the sun. The heat melts the meteoroid's surface, which the air rasps back over the sides to form the fiery tail. This process continues until friction slows the meteoroid down; when the speed is insufficient to ablate it, it strikes the earth. The vast majority of meteoroids disintegrate in the air; probably fewer than one in a million reaches the earth as a solid body.

Large showers of meteors occur regularly each year, such as the Perseids in mid-August. When a dense swarm comes into the earth's path, a 'meteor storm' blazes over some part of the world. This is one of the most beautiful and awe-inspiring sights in Nature. One[3] of the greatest storms in historic times occurred on 12 November 1833, when the night sky was turned into a superb firework display. Spreading out like the spokes of an umbrella from a point (the radiant) in the constellation of Leo, a rain of celestial rockets poured into the earth's atmosphere. Olivier, referring to the United States, says:

'Meteoric astronomy really began with this shower. [It] was so remarkable that the impress upon the popular mind has never been obliterated and the interest then aroused in meteors has never died out. . . The writer has often had the old Negro cook of his family give him a vivid account of how she saw " the stars fall" when a girl of ten. Though the shower occurred 60 or 70 years before, the impression never left her which had been made on her mind when a child, and she vividly described the terror of the Negroes as "the stars fell, and fell, thick as snow coming down in a snowstorm," and of how all thought "the Day of Jedgment had sho' come".'

It was claimed that 35,000 meteors could be seen each hour in this spectacular display.

Thirty-three years later the swarm was again carried into the earth's path. Sir Robert Ball, the distinguished Victorian astronomer, thus describes this shower:

Overleaf above
The artist's brush complements the camera's lens. The picture shows in detail a meteor trail and fireball as the meteoroid explodes. (Amédée Guillemin, The Heavens, London 1867. Ann Rowan Picture Library)

Overleaf below
The Wasserburg fireball of 31 October 1977 plunges earthwards. It was taken with a fish-eye lens at the Churanov Station. The white streaks are due to the movement of stars during the time-exposure. The breaks in the meteor's trajectory, caused by a rotating blade, are 8/100ths of a second apart. The irregular light trail to the right of the meteor was caused by a flashlight at the station. (Dr Zdeněk Ceplecha, Ondřejov Observatory, Czechoslovakia)

'For the next three or four hours we witnessed a spectacle which can never fade from my memory. The shooting stars gradually increased in number until sometimes several were seen at once. Sometimes they swept over our heads, sometimes to the right, sometimes to the left, but they all diverged from the east.

'Sometimes a meteor appeared to come almost directly towards us, and then its path was so foreshortened that it had hardly any appreciable length, and looked like an ordinary fixed star swelling into brilliancy and then as rapidly vanishing. Occasionally luminous trains would linger on for many minutes after the meteor had flashed across, but the great majority of the trains in this shower were evanescent. It would be impossible to say how many thousands of meteors were seen, each one of which was bright enough to have elicited a note of admiration on any ordinary night.'

In the early morning of 24 March 1933, one of the most brilliant fireballs ever seen in the United States blazed erratically across nine Southern states, being seen for distances over 100 miles from its line of flight. It was described as 'the largest ever seen' and 'terrifying' by people who were many miles away. Seasoned cattlemen, accustomed to facing the vicissitudes of life and who ordinarily knew no such thing as fear, despaired of their lives during these 'terrible moments'. Yet they were 75 miles from the fireball's nearest approach. (See note 5.)

Nininger, who investigated the passage of this meteoroid – named Pasamonte – and the material it dropped, says of the photograph (page 151) taken near Clayton, New Mexico, by a farmer who hastily snatched a camera and snapped as the fireball blazed past : 'The great luminous sphere which forms the centre of the picture was six miles in diameter, while the column stretching behind it was over a mile in width.' Most of this, of course, was incandescent gas.

This meteoroid left a cloud of dust which filled 1,000 cubic miles. People in the vicinity of its lower passage through the air said that they noticed a peculiar sulphurous odour for some hours, and suffered a throat irritation for several days. The passage of such a body sometimes affects radio and television reception, blacking them out completely for several minutes.

The vast majority of meteorites fall in the sea or on uninhabited or sparsely populated areas. Since towns and cities cover a relatively small area of the earth's surface, this is not surprising. Some have been picked up on mountain tops, and one was drawn up in a fish net from the bottom of a shallow lake. Many of the meteorites which fall in populated areas are so small, and so like ordinary debris in appearance, that the chances of their being correctly identified are extremely slight.

Known meteorites range in weight from a dust particle to many tons. The heaviest is the Hoba meteorite, a roughly rectangular 9×8-foot block, which lies near Grootfontein, Southwest Africa; it is estimated to weigh some 60 tons.[4] As it is believed to have fallen over a million years ago, weathering has greatly reduced its original weight, probably by about half (J. D. Fernie). Unless they fall on very soft ground, meteorites of more than 100 tons or so are unlikely to survive intact; the tremendous shock of the impact usually shatters them.

The heaviest meteorite known to have fallen in Great Britain is the

Wold Cottage stone, weighing 56 pounds, which fell within 10 yards of a man working in a field near Scarborough on the afternoon of 13 December 1795. It is now preserved in the Natural History Museum in London. Twenty-two known meteorites have fallen in Great Britain since 1623.

The largest meteorite found in the United States, and the fourth largest in the world, was discovered in 1902 near Willamette, Oregon. It is a conical mass of iron weighing about 14 tons, but erosion has eaten much of it away. Originally, it probably weighed between 20 and 25 tons.

It may be imagined that the possibility of seeing a meteorite fall is remote indeed. Nininger (1933) says: 'To witness the actual impact of one of these extramundane visitors may be considered the rarest of human experiences.' There are, however, about 500 eye-witness accounts, although many more (unrecorded) falls must have been seen. There is no known photograph of a meteorite hitting the earth. In Czechoslovakia, however, Zdeněk Ceplecha observed a fireball, photographed it on his two-station cameras, and estimated the fall so accurately that four meteorites were recovered.

One story concerns a farmer who was ploughing when a shower of meteoroids began falling around him. He rushed into town and called on the sheriff to protect him from his enemies, whom he believed were pelting him from ambush! Such a tale is reminiscent of another man who, during the First World War, observed a meteor storm and concluded that the Germans had opened long-range artillery fire on the United States . . .

In medieval annals there are several accounts of people being killed by what may have been direct hits from meteorites, but I know of no modern record of such a fatality. It has been estimated (how I do not know) that the chances of a meteorite strike on a human being in the United States are once every 9,000 years.

It has been suggested that some unsolved mysteries of death by violence may be referable to meteorites. In Michael Innes's *The Weight of the Evidence* (1944), a fictional meteorite plays a prominent part in the plot, although there is no suggestion that it fell directly on the victim from outside the atmosphere. The American humorist Robert Benchley, asked why he did not sunbathe in a deckchair, replied: 'What, and risk being hit by a meteor!'

There are several records of airmen seeing meteoroids plunging earthward. The best account I have read is by a civil airlines pilot, Bill Coyle. Cruising during the night of 23/24 March 1933, 2 miles above Adrian, Texas, he was surprised by what he took to be a giant floodlight turned on in the sky. He soon realised that it was a brilliant meteor (the Pasamonte), 'big as the Wichita hangar', flashing across the sky:

'In a second or two it became too bright for me. We were at about the same altitude. In a moment I caught sight of its tail and could tell it was going north of me. Its line of flight was probably 40 or 50 miles distant; at any rate it was so close I could see fragments of the [meteoroid] whirling away from it and dropping back into the tail. It left a deep red trail with a bluish tint which hung in the sky until daylight.' (Quoted by Hubert J. Bernhard)

It disappeared with a thunderous rumble that was heard in several states.

Nininger told me that he made a careful survey of this meteoroid and proved that the fireball ended 17 miles above the earth, although some material reached the ground. He points out that very few meteoroids approach nearer to the earth than 4 miles; they are very much farther away than most pilots who see them believe. One pilot dipped a wing to 'avoid' one that was about 100 miles away!

There are various kinds of meteorites, each with its own name. *Aerolites* are composed almost entirely of stone and constitute about 90% of all known falls; the stone is quite different in texture and composition from most of the rocks of the earth's crust. *Siderites* are composed chiefly of iron, with about 10% nickel. *Siderolites* are a mixture of metal and stone and are very rare. All the largest meteorites are siderites, as the other kinds are more easily crushed. These three main groups are subdivided into numerous classes; the Rose-Tschermak-Brezina system lists no fewer than 76 (A. Brezina).

Probably no meteoritic object has caused so much controversy as the smooth, curiously shaped, glassy lumps known as *tektites*. The largest known weighs about 7 pounds. Some scientists are doubtful whether they are meteorites at all. They differ from all other known meteorites in composition, shape and distribution. The most likely theory on their origin is that they are parts of the rocky crust of the earth, melted and thrown out when the earth was hit by a comet or large meteorite. The great majority of all known tektites are found in Australia, the East Indies and the Philippines (John O'Keefe). Robert Hutchinson deals in detail with various aspects of tektites in *The Earth's Beginning* (1983).

Scientists believe that some meteorites and comets contain ice. There is evidence that there is ice in the solar system (the satellites of Jupiter appear to consist largely of ice), and it is possible – allowing for part of the mass to be ablated – that pieces of ice may land on the earth (Mary F. Romig). (See also pages 78–9.)

Meteorites are of great value to scientists. They are samples of some of the material of the solar system beyond our planet. Until material was brought back from the moon, meteorites were the only such samples.

Meteorites are of commercial value, both direct and indirect. They can be sold for money, the actual price depending on several factors, chiefly rarity. Pieces from a very rare meteorite were bought for more than the price of platinum, although such a price is exceptional. Platinum, diamonds and gold have been found in meteorites, but only in minute quantities.

Meteoritic iron is extremely tough: a lump about 2 feet high wore out 82 bandsaw blades before it was cut in half. Not surprisingly, therefore, early man used iron meteorites as weapons. Fragments of a dagger unearthed at Ur of the Chaldees dating from before 3,000 BC are of meteoritic nickel-iron. Attila possessed a 'sword from heaven', and even in the 19th century Alexander, Emperor of Russia, had a sword made from meteoritic iron.

From prehistory to the Space Age, meteoroids have been Nature's own space probes. Their behaviour, especially when entering the atmosphere, has provided valuable information to scientists concerned with the intricate problems of space travel. When John Glenn's capsule started its return to earth, its speed approached that of a 'slow' meteoroid. At this speed (about 5 miles per second), the protective heat shield glowed white-hot at a temperature of 1,500°C (Robert B. Voas).

And so to 'pwdre ser', an appropriately bizarre name for one of the weirdest stories in the whole realm of natural science – or mythology. The words are Welsh and mean 'star rot'. Other names for the alleged phenomenon are star jelly, rot of the stars and gelatinous meteor. The French name is *crachet de lune*, 'moonspit'.

Occasionally, after a meteorite has landed, people have claimed to have found an offensive-smelling jelly-like mass at the site of the fall. Whatever the truth may be, this relationship between meteors and jelly is deeply embedded in folklore. Jeremy Taylor refers to 'staring upon a meteor or an inflamed jelly'; John Dryden has the line: 'When I had taken up what I supposed a fallen star I found I had been cozened with a jelly'; and Walter Scott puts these words into the mouth of a character in *The Talisman*: 'Seek a fallen star and thou shalt only light on some foul jelly.'

One's immediate reaction is to say that anything remotely as soft as jelly would be burnt up in the atmosphere (but what of ice meteorites?). Perhaps a credulous observer has found a terrestrial object, such as a half-digested meal regurgitated by an animal, and concluded that it came down with the meteor he has just seen blaze to earth. It is, however, questionable if such a pat explanation is adequate for all accounts and, moreover, the misplaced bigotry over the origin of meteorites engenders caution in dismissing out of hand anything connected with the subject. 'Stones from the sky' no doubt seemed as outrageous a concept to our scientific forebears as 'gelatinous meteors' do to us.

In a communication to *Nature*, Professor Frank Schlesinger relates that, after a public lecture, he received a letter from the daughter of a man who was walking along a street in Lowell, Massachusetts, when he saw a meteor flash to earth very near him.[5] On examination of the site, he found a jelly-like mass 'almost intolerably offensive in smell. I have often heard my father allude to this event, which greatly interested him, he being a close observer and an extensive reader.' While Schlesinger did not accept that there was any connection between meteor and jelly, he said: 'It may be well to put this piece of evidence on record.'

The man Schlesinger referred to did not see the jelly fall to earth, but Monica Ephgrave did. During a heavy rainstorm at Cambridge, England, on 23 June 1978 she saw a jelly-like mass, about the size of a football, glide down and settle on her lawn; smaller pieces of the same substance were seen nearby. She did not notice any smell and saw no meteor. The mass had completely disappeared by the morning (*The Journal of Meteorology*, England, December 1978).

Professor McKenny Hughes, of Cambridge University, wrote in *Nature* for 23 June 1910:

'We have a well-known substance which may be of different origin in different cases, respecting the general appearance of which, however, almost all accounts agree. The variety of names under which it is known point to its common and widespread occurrence. We have in every name, and in every notice in literature, a

Overleaf   A close encounter of the real kind. On the afternoon of 10 August 1972 a brilliant meteor blazed 1,000 miles across North America from Utah to Alberta. The journey took about 100 seconds. The photograph shows it passing over the Grand Tetons, Wyoming. The nearest the meteor came to earth was 36 miles. It eventually escaped the earth's atmosphere and re-entered outer space. Had the meteoroid plunged to earth in an inhabited area it would have caused great devastation. Obviously its weight can only be guessed at but 500 tons is a reasonable estimate. (Z. Ceplecha, 1979) (James and Linda Baker, Lillian, Alabama)

recognition of the universal belief that it has something to do with meteors. What is it, and what is the cause of its having a meteoric origin assigned to it?'

William R. Corliss (1977) says:

'The testimony of legends and folk lore is overwhelmingly in favor of the reality of gelatinous meteors. Obviously, this does not mean that all gelatinous masses found in meadow and field fell from the sky, but neither can we deny the possibility of gelatinous meteors just because terrestrial nature does produce lumps of gelatin.

'Scientists who have tried to explain pwdre ser always opt for the terrestrial interpretation; that is, some form of plant or animal life or possibly some half-digested matter disgorged by an animal. It seems that a common characteristic of pwdre ser is its smell and general rottenness. But if rotten fish can fall from the sky, why not offensive gelatin? Pwdre ser often has one other interesting feature: it seems to evaporate away rapidly, removing all evidence of the unusual phenomenon. Genuine animal matter is not so fleeting and ephemeral.'

In an article in *Notes and Queries* for 1 January 1938, 'Hibernicus', after quoting many references to star jelly, suggests that it is *Nostoc*, a gelatinous alga. (See *The Journal of Meteorology*, England, April 1980, for other references)

Although pwdre ser is of only peripheral interest to meteoriticists, a phenomenon so deeply embedded in literature, whatever its explanation, calls for discussion in a book primarily designed for laymen.

Before satellites and space capsules actually began to orbit the earth, it was thought that collisions between them and meteoroids would be a major hazard. Experience has proved that this fear was greatly exaggerated, although it is possible that a capsule could be destroyed by such a collision. Owing to its high speed, a meteoroid is, weight for weight, vastly more destructive than TNT. A pinhead-sized iron meteoroid could blast a hole in a capsule; one the size of a grape could destroy it. Astronauts clambering about the outside of the capsules, clad only in their space suits, are even more vulnerable. Nevertheless Millman, in *The Meteoritic Hazard of Interplanetary Travel*, writes: 'Although the hazard of penetration by meteoroid impact is never of zero probability, a suitable design of the spacecraft and the space suits can minimize the probability of serious damage to such an extent that this hazard becomes relatively small compared to the other problems of interplanetary travel.' Up to now experience has proved Millman right, but a tiny meteorite chipped a window of the Russian *Salyut-7* orbital space station, and other stations have shown evidence of similar impacts.

The most spectacular effects of meteoritic falls are the 'meteor craters', found in various places on the earth's surface, which mark the fall of very large meteorites. Meteoriticists are not agreed on the number of such craters, but it is almost certainly between 100 and 200. How they are formed has been described by Fletcher G. Watson:

'As the [meteoroid] plunges into the ground its forward motion is

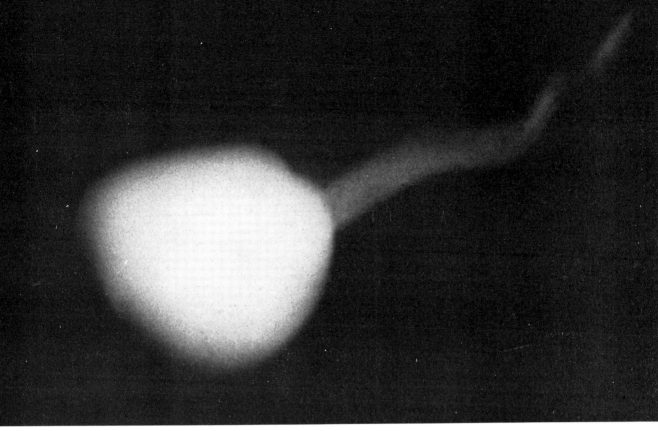

checked in a minute fraction of a second. Through this braking action the outer parts of the meteorite and the contacting ground are tremendously compressed, heated and partly turned to vapor. This gas, with steam from the omnipresent ground water, expands in a terrific explosion, blowing much of the meteorite back out of the ground, tearing a gaping crater. The meteorite is shattered and widely scattered over the surrounding area: at best a fraction of the original body remains in the crater. An intensely hot air blast spreads out burning and destroying the nearby vegetation and life. Simultaneously strong earth-waves spread from the crater, warping and shattering the surrounding rock strata.'

The best-known meteor crater lies near Winslow, Arizona. It is certainly the biggest hole that I have ever seen – the Grand Canyon excepted. Meteor Crater is square with rounded corners, four-fifths of a mile across. Around the edge is a parapet which was forced up by the enormous pressure of the explosion when the meteorite struck (the same phenomenon can be seen on a small scale around a bomb crater). This parapet varies from 130 to 155 feet in height. The depth from the parapet to the floor of the crater is now about 575 feet; originally it was deeper, weather action having partially filled it in. If two St Paul's Cathedrals were placed on the bottom, one on top of the other, only part of the dome and cross of the upper cathedral would protrude above the crater's rim.

Various estimates have been made of the size of the meteoroid that blasted out Meteor Crater. A large body with a slow impact speed would cause the same devastation as a smaller body with a faster speed.

The explosion of the great meteoroid that blazed across the southern United States on 24 March 1933. As the photograph was taken the fireball was 25 miles above the earth. The head was six miles across, the trail over a mile wide. (Charles M. Brown from H.H. Nininger)

A reasonable estimate is a nickel-iron mass about 80 feet across, weighing about 70,000 tons and travelling at 10 miles per second.

Imagine a body of this size hurtling through the air and approaching Winslow from the northwest. Friction with the air makes the surface incandescent as the oxygen in the atmosphere blow-torches the iron. From this great flying mass sputtering chunks fly off as the meteoroid, travelling at a low angle, nears the ground. A huge cylinder of superheated air is forced along by the meteoroid and, as it strikes, this air is forced across the surrounding countryside in a fiery blast. At the moment of impact, the whole earth is jolted. The meteorite tears its way through a quarter of a mile of solid rock. A wall of flame shoots miles high and the thunder of the colossal impact is heard thousands of miles away.

As this is a book about extreme violence in Nature it is appropriate, in the only chapter on astronomy, to mention the greatest known violence in the universe. This was once thought to be a supernova, a star which blows itself up in a paroxysm of celestial energy radiated at a rate hundreds of millions times greater than the energy output of the sun. There is now evidence that there are bodies vastly more powerful: the so-called quasars (quasi-stellar objects). They have been described as perhaps the most remarkable objects yet discovered by man.

Quasars are about 10,000 times smaller but 100 times brighter than the brightest known galaxy. Some are thousands of millions[6] of light years away, and are receding into the abyss of space at about 90,000 miles per second – half the speed of light. It is estimated that some quasars consume energy at the rate of 100 of our suns each year, one sun for fuel every $3\frac{1}{2}$ days. Nuclear processes are probably too weak for such energies; it is possible that they come from a source of which earth has neither measure nor faintest parallel.

Located near Grootfontein, SW Africa, the Hoba meteorite is the heaviest yet found. It is roughly rectangular, measures nine feet by eight and is estimated to weigh 60 tons. It is believed to have fallen over a million years ago, since when weathering has reduced its original weight by about half. (J. Donald Fernie)

Man learned about quasars from the electro-magnetic radiation they emit. It is a fascinating commentary on modern science, and the power of the human mind, that we have learned about the universe's vastest energies from its tiniest. The total amount of quasars' radiated energy so far collected by telescopes on earth is not sufficient to raise the temperature of a gram of water by one-millionth of a degree Centigrade.

In comparison with that violence for which man has no conceivable measure, the largest meteorite ever to blast this earth is less than the pop of a Christmas firecracker. Nevertheless, in view of the tremendous effects of large meteoritic impacts and their occurrence in past millennia, the question arises: what are the possibilities of an asteroid or giant meteoroid striking the earth today? These possibilities are very real: this century has witnessed the passing fairly near to us, astronomically speaking, of a dangerously large mass; and a direct hit from a mass weighing thousands of tons (see pages 154–7).

Great devastation could also be caused by a large body that did not actually hit the earth. If such a body passed near enough it would raise immense tides and deflect the spin axis of the earth, which would in turn produce drastic climatic changes. Some writers believe that there is evidence from prehistory scars that the earth has suffered from such near-misses (Peter Warlow).

On 30 October 1937, the asteroid Hermes – $1\frac{1}{2}$ miles wide, 1,000 million tons in weight – came to within half a million miles of the earth. Judged by standards of terrestrial measurement, that may seem a comfortable enough distance; in terms of the astronomical yardstick it is not. The astronomical measure is the light year: the distance which light, travelling at some 11 million miles a minute, will cover in one year. It takes eight minutes for the light from the sun to reach us, but four years for the light from the nearest star to travel across the vast distances of interstellar space and reach this planet. By that standard (i.e. the light year and not, of course, its actual speed), Hermes missed this earth by only three seconds! Put another way, a mass capable of blasting London or New York City into oblivion missed us by only 1–2 degrees in the inclination of its orbit and a slight difference in its speed relative to the earth. Hence the description of the near-miss in *The New York Times*: 'The two bodies just scraped past each other during the night, in an astronomical sense.'

Hermes is only one of hundreds of asteroids, with diameters between half a mile and more than 400 miles, travelling around the sun. These flying mountains normally have stable elliptical orbits, but the attraction of other planets affects their course, sometimes bringing them near to the earth. In their book, *The Great Extinction* (1983), Michael Allaby and James Lovelock put forward the theory that the much-debated disappearance of the dinosaurs was due to a huge asteroid hitting the earth. This theory has, however, been severely criticised, not least because there is evidence that some dinosaurs were still roaming the earth after the date of the supposed catastrophic impact. (Among the plethora of theories to account for the dinosaurs' disappearance are that they suffered from slipped discs, gigantism, a reptilian Black Death and constipation – not all at once of course!)

In view of the possibilities of an asteroid strike, which could cause the greatest calamity in recorded history, NASA has proposed a

'Spacewatch' project. Movements of the 800 or so known asteroids could be checked. If one were getting dangerously close, efforts would be made to prevent it striking the earth.

In 1967 engineering students at the Massachusetts Institute of Technology produced a plan to save the world from being hit by the mile-wide asteroid Icarus. Although at its nearest point of passage in 1968 it came within an estimated 4 million miles of the earth, the students assumed that it would be deflected to a collision course.

If Icarus had hit the earth the most likely area for the impact was estimated to be mid-Atlantic, 2,000 miles east of Florida. The thousand cubic miles of water displaced would cause tidal waves 100 feet high to break on Atlantic shorelines. Seaports, including New York and Boston, would be engulfed and the whole of Florida drowned. A crater, 10–15 miles wide, would be blasted in the ocean floor. As the shock of the titanic impact pulsed around the globe, it would trigger earthquakes 100 times more violent than any in recorded history.[7]

The students' plan to prevent such worldwide mayhem involved launching a series of Saturn rockets equipped with 100-megaton hydrogen bombs. It was estimated that computers would enable the rockets to be manoeuvred to within 100 feet of Icarus and would then detonate the bombs, either breaking up the asteroid or deflecting it from its earthbound trajectory. The idea for the film Meteor, which was released in October 1979, was credited to the MIT's 'Project Icarus'.

At a meeting of the British Association in 1908, Sir Napier Shaw drew attention to some unexplained oscillations in the microbarograph record. These showed that powerful air waves had passed across England from north to south on 30 June 1908. The scientists at the meeting could find no satisfactory explanation of these mysterious 'kicks'. On the same day, some seismographs in Germany and Russia had registered mild earthquake shocks. Calculations located the focus of the earth tremor in Siberia, a region where earthquakes were virtually unknown.

Another series of unusual phenomena was noticed at the same time. On 30 June, near Gothenburg, Sweden, 'an extraordinarily strong light' appeared in the sky about an hour after sunset and lasted until after 2 o'clock in the morning; a book could easily be read by it. At 10 o'clock on the same night, at Aberdeen, Scotland, the light, instead of continuing to fade from the sky, suddenly grew brighter – 'almost as bright as daylight'. A similar lengthening of the hours of daylight was noticed in other parts of Europe. There were also spectacular sunsets: for several days the evening skies were a blaze of bright green, golden-red and pure yellow.

These four events – the strange kicks in the microbarograph record; the disturbance of the seismograph record, apparently from a non-earthquake region; the lengthening of daylight; and the brilliantly coloured sunsets – were duly noted and filed. Natural science was not yet sufficiently integrated to notice any relationship between disturbed air pressure, ground shocks, a lengthening of the hours of daylight and brilliant sunsets.

The years passed, and then came the First World War. Men had other things to think about than unexplained records buried in scientific archives. Early in the 1920s, however, reports began to filter out from a remote part of Russia, to which access was very difficult, that a

Opposite above
Meteor Crater, the imprint of a colossal meteorite that slammed into the Arizona desert near Winslow, Arizona, thousands of years ago. The depth from floor to parapet is nearly 600 feet. It has been estimated that the meteorite weighed 70,000 tons as it struck the earth at ten miles per second. (Spence Air Photos)

Left *A few of the millions of trees felled when part of a comet crashed into the Tunguska forest in Central Siberia on 30 June 1908. Trees over an area of 2,000 square miles were affected in the tremendous explosion, calculated to have equalled that of a 50-megaton bomb.* (Fotokhronika, Tass)

tremendous explosion had occurred some years before the outbreak of the war. Later, these reports became more definite: the explosion had occurred in Siberia some time during the summer of 1908. The forgotten records were then remembered . . .

Russian scientists, headed by L. A. Kulik, mounted several expeditions to Siberia, photographing, interviewing people, examining the area both on the ground and from the air. From the information collected, it is now possible to construct a fairly accurate picture of what had happened to cause the four unexplained phenomena recorded so many years before. (E. L. Krinov)

At about 7 a.m. on 30 June 1908, over the Tunguska forest in Central Siberia, a great incandescent mass flew through the air. There was a terrific explosion and the earth shook. A man who was at Vanavara, 40 miles south of the point of the cataclysm, said:

> 'There was a fiery flame in the northwest, which gave off such heat that my shirt nearly caught fire. I felt as if I were enveloped in flame. I noticed that this miracle covered a space of not less than two kilometres [a little over 1 mile] . . . I only had time to note the extent and the flame disappeared. After the flame disappeared there was an explosion which threw me off my feet a distance of 7 feet or more . . . The glass and frames of the house broke and clods of earth were spit up from the square in front of my hut.'

Additional facts about this great cataclysm were gathered by the various investigators. At the time the body struck, observers at three widely separated places, 300–400 miles distant from the actual site, saw in the bright sunlight a huge column of fire rise to an estimated height of 12 miles. From Vanavara, this fiery column appeared to be 1 mile across. A great pillar of smoke rose into the air at least as high as the flames.

The sound effects were as impressive as the spectacle. On a river over 100 miles away there was such a cannonade that the crew on a ship rushed to the cabin for safety. The blasts grew in intensity and lasted for over three minutes. Six hundred miles away, near Turokhansk, an observer said: 'Away to the east I heard three or four dull thuds in succession, like distant artillery fire.'

Some of the mechanical effects of the explosion have already been described in the accounts of witnesses. There were others. Reports told of whole families being wiped out; certainly, if they had been within 20 miles of the searing heat and tremendous concussion, they would have been killed instantly. Three hundred miles away men and horses were flung off their feet.

It was not until many years later, when Kulik and his companions explored the immediate area of the fall (61°N, 102°E), that the most spectacular evidence of destruction was seen: the wreckage of 80 million trees over an area of nearly 2,000 square miles! Over more than 400 square miles not a tree was left standing. Towards the perimeter of this area trees were found uprooted, broken and stripped of branches. There must have been an instant obliteration of life throughout the whole of this region.

A puzzling feature was the absence of any crater at all compatible with the vast destruction caused. At the centre of the area of obliteration the ground was shattered and the rocks were 'folded into small wrinkles', but there was nothing resembling a meteor crater.

The answers to the questions which puzzled the scientists at the 1908 British Association meeting will now be fairly obvious. The kicks in the microbarograph records were caused by the great atmospheric wave set up by the explosion. It took five hours for this wave to reach Britain, 3,500 miles away. The disturbances of the seismograph records were due to the ground wave and explosion of the fragments crashing into the earth. The lengthening of the hours of daylight and the brilliant sunsets were caused by the vast cloud of dust and smoke that was flung miles into the air. A vast dust cloud high in the atmosphere catches the sun's rays and reflects them downward, for a time even after the sun has sunk below the horizon.

It has been estimated that the total energy involved in this tremendous explosion was roughly equal to that of a 50-megaton bomb. For many years the explosion was believed to have been caused by a gigantic meteorite. Today this theory is discarded. Almost certainly it was the result of collision with a fragment of a comet, probably Encke's. John Baxter and Thomas Atkins, in their book *The Fire Came By* (1976), suggest that the cause was a nuclear-powered craft from outer space which ran out of control and blew up a mile or so above Siberia. This melodramatic explanation is not shared by any professional meteoriticist known to me.

When *The Elements Rage*, in which I dealt with these events in Siberia, was published in April 1945 (four months before the atomic bomb was dropped on Hiroshima), someone drew it to the attention of the director of intelligence of the British Air Staff, remarking that one of the photographs indicated that an atomic bomb had been exploded before. That was not the explanation of the photograph, of course, but the remark has disturbing implications. If a similar explosion were reported today, there is the possibility that it would be mistaken for a nuclear explosion. Fortunately, the danger has been foreseen: it was the subject of a letter from W. E. Le Gros Clark and Kenneth P. Oakley in *The Times* for 25 September 1961. I hope that the warning has been heeded.

NOTES

1. Meteoriticists – students of meteorites etc. – use the following terminology for the various aspects of the subject:
Meteoroid: any solid natural body smaller than an asteroid (minor planet) moving in space, including the earth's atmosphere.
Meteor: the light phenomenon caused by the entry of a meteoroid into the earth's atmosphere. It is also used as a general adjective, e.g. meteor crater.
Meteorite: a meteoroid that has landed on the earth.
2. Peter M. Millman comments: 'Even very heavy meteoroids may not reach the ground if they are of the friable type and enter the atmosphere at the higher velocities (greater than 20 to 30 miles per second), for example the Tunguska event.' (See page 156)
3. The greatest storm of historic times occurred on 17 November 1966 over the western part of the United States. An estimated 60,000 meteors were seen during a 30-minute period.
4. The weight of large meteorites is usually given in metric tons: 1 metric ton = 1,000 kilogrammes or 2,204.6 pounds. The meteorites are named after nearby towns or landmarks.
5. Millman comments: 'There are a great many cases where an observer believed a meteor fell close to him when actually it was 50 to 150 miles distant. Unless a meteoroid is very large it falls as a dark object.'
6. One discovered in 1982 is 18,000 million light years away, and is calculated to be emitting the energy of 100,000 million suns.
7. In the *New Scientist* for 24 November 1983, Digby McLaren points out that evidence is amassing that the havoc caused by outsize meteorites has altered the evolution of the planet.

EARTHQUAKES

Although not so spectacular as a volcano, a great earthquake makes an ineffaceable impression. We are so accustomed to living on solid earth that when *that* begins to shake the mind is overwhelmed.

'The concrete floor just exploded. Tables and dishes flew into our faces and we were all hurled into a mad dance, bouncing about like popping corn. When at last I got near the doorway, I hurled myself at it. But the floor shifted, and I smashed into the crumbling wall a yard farther along.' (Carl Mydans, decribing the onslaught of the Fukui, Japan, earthquake of 28 June 1948. Quoted by Bryce Walker)

Throughout the world many thousands of earthquakes occur every year. The vast majority are slight; about 20 are serious but do not occur in built-up areas; and about half a dozen kill and destroy. The British Isles have an average of three newsworthy earth tremors each year; the United States averages 700.

The ancients had various theories to account for earthquakes. The Algonquin Indians believed that the earth was supported by a great tortoise, and that when the earth shook he was shuffling his feet. In Mongolia the earthshaker was a pig, and in India a mole. The early Japanese believed that the quakings of the earth were caused by the movements of an underground spider. Later Japanese theorists thought that the troublesome creature was a catfish; a rock rested on its head to keep it quiet, but presumably the fish occasionally wriggled free to set the world a-shaking.

Volcanic eruptions sometimes cause local earthquakes, but the origin of the most severe quakes is nearly always deeper in the earth. The earth's crust is not rigid and immovable but consists of great rafts or plates, like ice floes on a polar sea. In continental areas these plates extend to depths of about 60 miles; they are 'thinnest' in the oceans, in some areas probably about 5 miles. They are in slow movement, 1 inch or so a year. There are ten major plates, and they carry the continents and ocean basins with them. Most earthquakes occur at plate boundaries as the plates grind and crush together, but both earthquakes and volcanoes sometimes occur nearer the centre of plates. The Hawaiian volcanoes, for example, are in the centre of the Pacific plate.

Miles below the surface, a strain develops inside vast masses of rock. Something gives way, generally along a fault or weak line, and the sudden adjustment of these huge masses of the earth causes a shiver to pulse through the entire globe. The shock in the immediate area rarely lasts for more than a minute, and generally only for seconds, but milder aftershocks may continue intermittently for a long time after a large quake, often for years.

About 95% of all earthquakes occur in one or the other of two great belts which together encircle the earth. The first belt runs around the margins of the Pacific (with branches into the West Indies and the Southern Antilles); the other passes through the East Indies, the Himalayas, the Caucasus and the Mediterranean. This is roughly the same course as that followed by the earth's major volcanic belts.

Dragon's ball + frog's mouth = earthquake. A BBC model of an ancient Chinese seismoscope. When an earthquake jarred the dragon, the ball dropped.

In the United States the most active earthquake regions are in
Alaska and California. The San Andreas fault system runs some 700
miles from northern California to Mexico, its west side grinding
northwards at an average rate of about 2 inches a year. It has been
called 'California's Mighty Crack of Doom', and with good reason. In
1857, a shock rocked a sparsely populated area near Los Angeles; in
1906, San Francisco was wrecked by a major earthquake when the
fault 'jumped' 15–20 feet; during 1979–80, there were four moderate
earthquakes between San Francisco and San Diego; and seismologists

Above left and right *The Saada Hotel, Agadir, Morocco before and after the earthquake of 29 February 1960.* (American Iron and Steel Institute)

believe that another devastating quake could strike California any day – or night.

There is an elaborate chain of instruments throughout the world for recording earthquakes. Known as seismographs, they have a long history. The first earthquake recorder appears to have been made about 130 AD, by the Chinese astronomer Chang Heng. It consisted of a bronze dome fixed to the ground, inside which was a delicately balanced inverted pendulum. Set equidistantly around the rim were eight dragons' heads, each with a bronze ball balanced on the tongue of its open mouth. Below each dragon was a bronze toad with its mouth agape (the Chinese symbols for heaven and earth are, respectively, the dragon and the toad).

The slightest jarring of this contraption shot the balls nearest in line with the path of the earthquake wave out of the mouth of the dragon and into that of the toad waiting below. The occurrence and approximate direction of earthquakes were thus recorded long before news arrived by messengers from the stricken areas.

Most modern seismographs work on the basis of the inertia principle. When the earth moves, heavy bodies which are not rigidly fastened to it have sufficient inertia to prevent an immediate response.

In older seismographs, a heavy weight, sometimes 20 tons, is suspended on a pendulum from a framework connected directly to the earth. When an earthquake occurs it agitates the framework, but the pendulum, because of its inertia and suspension mechanism, does not move. In most modern instruments, the weight is much smaller and is linked to an electro-magnetic system which conveys the movements to the recording device.

The movement of the earth is recorded in various ways as a series of agitated lines. In early models, a needle, attached to the pendulum, recorded on to a continuously running band of smoked paper. In modern seismographs, the recording is mostly photographic (a beam of light – the 'pen' – on sensitised paper) or electronic (magnetised tape). Smoked-paper seismographs, however, still give the sharpest line, and are becoming popular again in modern field instruments. Seismographs are generally grouped in threes: two for recording horizontal movements, one for vertical.

The actual movement of the earth at places many miles distant from the earthquake is naturally extremely slight, sometimes as little as one forty-millionth of an inch. When big quakes are near, the total movement is inches, or even feet.

By electrical and mechanical means the movement is magnified over 1 million times in the most delicate instruments. If a seismograph's weight is touched by a feather, the needle agitates violently. Spiders crawling about a seismograph vault have produced oscillations on the record, and children dancing have shaken the earth sufficiently to leave their mark.

When an earthquake occurs, it sends out waves which travel faster than the swiftest bullet. The first wave, called P (for primary), travels through the earth at speeds of a few miles per second. Then follows the S (for secondary) wave, which rocks from side to side, moving at little more than half the speed of the P wave. Some writers call P and S waves 'Push' and 'Shake' respectively, as these terms describe their behaviour more graphically. Other waves follow, and by studying the seismograph record seismologists are able to tell with tolerable accuracy where and when an earthquake occurred and its probable magnitude.

It is a tribute to the ingenuity of seismologists that such information can be obtained at all. It requires considerable scientific detective work to deduce from a series of squiggles on a moving band of paper what is happening below the earth's surface in places hundreds – or thousands – of miles away. To quote Bryce Walker:

> 'With its layered panoply of materials, the earth responds to the impact of an earthquake by vibrating in a maelstrom of wave forms of all frequencies, sizes and velocities. If the frequencies were audible it would be as though a full-sized symphony orchestra were blaring out all the notes of all its music at once, every instrument playing fortissimo in every possible key, producing utter cacophony. When depicted visually on a seismogram, the earthquake's tumult of conflicting and overlapping seismic waves presents an apparently bewildering hodgepodge of zigzag lines.'

In seismically active areas of the world, especially sensitive seismographs are activated about once an hour, occasionally much more frequently. Widely recorded earthquakes occur at the rate of just under two a day, major quakes once a week. These figures are not as alarming as they sound, because about two-thirds of all earthquakes occur under the sea, and of the remainder many occur in uninhabited or sparsely inhabited areas.

Seismologists have compiled scales to measure (a) the intensity of shocks and (b) the magnitude of the earthquake causing them. The two types of scale are often confused in popular accounts of earthquakes, but they are quite distinct.

Like the Beaufort Wind Scale, earthquake-intensity scales are based on the effects produced, which vary with the distance from the epicentre (the site of the earthquake). Practice varies from country to country. One of the most widely used is the Modified Mercalli Intensity Scale, based on the one originally propounded in 1902 by the Italian seismologist, Giuseppe Mercalli, and modified by the American seismologists, Harry O. Wood and Frank Neumann. Versions of this scale, some abbreviated, others with additional comments, have appeared in several books on earthquakes (see pages 182–3).

The energy involved in a severe earthquake is enormous: there is no such thing as an immovable object, even mountains are moved. The only comparable release of energy is in the most powerful volcanic eruption or an exceptionally heavy meteoritic impact.

The best-known magnitude scale is Charles Richter's (1935). It is based on the maximum reading or deviation on a standard seismograph. Each increase of a whole number on the scale represents an increase in the release of seismic energy of some 30 times. Thus an earthquake of 8.0 magnitude is not twice, but 800,000 times greater than one of 4.0.

It must be emphasised that the figures given for the magnitude of any earthquake are only approximate. Different seismologists often give different figures for the same earthquake. This is understandable when it is realised that seismograph readings vary according to the location of the station relative to the earthquake, and the travel path of the earthquake waves.

In 1966 the Japanese seismologist, Keiiti Aki, suggested a more accurate way of measuring earthquake magnitude based on the 'seismic moment'. This quantity is a measure of the amount of slip integrated over the entire area of fault surface. Seismologists adopted Aki's suggestion, and since 1977 have used the Seismic Moment Scale as well as Richter's (Hiroo Kanamori). Here, I have given all magnitudes on the Richter Scale.

The highest figure so far recorded is 8.9. This magnitude has been reached only twice: on 31 January 1906, near Quito, Ecuador; and on 2 March 1933, at Honshu, Japan, at the boundary of the Pacific and Eurasian plates.

The actual place in the earth where the quake originates is called the focus, and the point on the surface immediately above is the epicentre. The length of the fracture which causes a big earthquake varies greatly. The longest measured on land appears to be that of the 18 April 1906 California quake, in which faulting occurred along a line of some 270 miles of the San Andreas fault. The breadth of any individual fracture is often only a few inches, but it is sometimes measured in feet.

In a large earthquake the vibrations are felt over hundreds of thousands of square miles. This was well illustrated in the great Lisbon earthquake of 1 November 1755. The shock was felt over an area of some 1,300,000 square miles, more than one-third of Europe. Inland waters, including Loch Lomond, Scotland, over 1,000 miles from Lisbon, were oscillated as the earthquake waves raced through the earth.

One of the best-known stories of that cruel day tells that a newly built quay at the mouth of the Tagus, on which a number of people were standing, sank out of sight and all the people were drowned. Sir Charles Lyell says 'perhaps a narrow chasm opened and closed again in the bed of the Tagus, after swallowing up some incumbent buildings and vessels'. Yet the story was disproved as soon as Portuguese engineers examined the site shortly after the quake.

It was stories like this which made people believe that in severe quakes the earth opened and swallowed people. It is easy to understand such a belief, for many earthquake photographs show what appear to be yawning chasms. Fissures do appear in the upper surface, but there is no evidence that these are more than a few feet deep; they are quite different from the deep-seated earthquake faults. It must be added, however, that in the great Fukui, Japan, earthquake of 1948 a woman was certainly trapped and killed in a fissure. She was working in a paddyfield when the quake struck and 'fell into a fissure which, it was said, opened to about four feet in width. It closed upon her to the chin, instantly crushing her to death.' Richter (1958), who quotes this from an official report of the earthquake, says: 'This is the only properly documented case of the kind in recorded history, even in Japan, except for that of the cow in the California earthquake of 1906.' A correspondent who read *The Elements Rage*, however, alleged that in a South American earthquake a man returning home saw his house tumble into a huge rent in the ground, which then closed over it; his wife and three children were inside. Unfortunately, my correspondent gave no further details.

In addition to surface fissuring, several other movements of the ground occur during an earthquake. Frequently, the ground moves horizontally: one part of a road may move several feet in relation to another part, and fences are likewise displaced. Vertical displacement also occurs; part of the ground sinks or is pushed up. In the Alaskan earthquake of 10 September 1899, a beach became a cliff overnight.

Among the most spectacular movements are the visible waves which accompany the greatest earthquakes. They have been described as the earth's clumsy efforts to imitate the ocean. Some seismologists consider them to be an optical illusion: the combination of the shaking earth, clouds of dust and general terror causing eye-witnesses to imagine that the surface of the earth itself is rippling. There are, however, a number of detailed descriptions which make it hard to dismiss the waves as an illusion. Kendrick Frazier quotes several eye-witness accounts of the waves accompanying the great San Francisco earthquake of 18 April 1906. Police Sergeant Jesse Cook said: 'The whole street was undulating. It was as if the waves of the ocean were coming toward me and billowing as they came.' Another witness said: 'The street seemed to move like waves of water.'

The effect of all the various movements and accompaniments of an earthquake is to induce a feeling akin to sea-sickness, and sometimes hallucinations. During the Lisbon earthquake, priests in the great church of São Vicente de Fora said they saw the building suddenly rock and sway like a wave-tossed ship. John Harpum, however, tells me that such reports of rocking are probably the result of disturbance of the balancing mechanism of the ear caused by shock waves: 'I have experienced the same from near bomb misses.' On the other hand,

Devastation following an earthquake in Nepal. Throughout the world earthquakes, with their accompanying fires and floods, are the greatest of all natural destroyers of human life and property. Earthquakes, on average, kill some 15,000 people every year. (League of Red Cross Societies)

George Plafker, who made a study of the great Alaskan earthquake of 27 March 1964, informs me: 'It took two minutes of hard shaking for one six-storey building in Anchorage to collapse. Many others were not even seriously damaged.'

The Assam earthquake of 15 August 1950 was one of the greatest ever recorded, registering 8.6 on the Richter Scale. Rivers were dammed; major floods drowned the countryside; mountains and hills split open, and square miles of their surface covering were stripped off; rain came down as mud owing to the dust-choked air; and the geography of the region was permanently changed. This earthquake was experienced by the British botanist, Frank Kingdon-Ward, and his wife Jean. They were in a valley at Rima, Tibet, about 25 miles from the epicentre. Seismology is the richer for their vivid accounts of their terrifying experiences. The first shock came early in the night. They went out of their tent, Frank Kingdon-Ward carrying a lantern:

'Two paces more and we were thrown violently to the ground, which was now shuddering like a mad thing beneath our feet. The lamp also fell with a crash and went out instantly, leaving us in darkness. Bewildered and annoyed, we tried to pick ourselves up and behave with a little dignity, only to find that it was impossible to stand, or indeed even to sit, while the world broke up all around us. With the first big shock there came a deep rumbling noise from the earth itself, full of menace, which quickly swelled in volume to a deafening roar that filled the valley. Mixed with it was a terrrifying clatter, as though a hundred rods were being rapidly drawn over sheets of corrugated iron. The noise was unbelievable, agonizing. Never before had our ears been subjected to such an onslaught of sound.'

Their two servants managed to fight their way to them across the heaving earth. All four lay face downwards, gripping hands:

'We waited in indescribable terror for the enraged earth to open beneath us and swallow us whole. It seemed impossible that any of us could escape that fate, for the convulsions beneath us never ceased for minutes on end; and how long, I wondered, could the tortured sand bear our weight upon it? Helpless as we were in the grip of the earthquake, every one of us, I think, experienced that night the uttermost depths of human fear.

'Incredibly, after an interval that can only be measured in terms of eternity, we found ourselves back in the more familiar dimensions of space and time. The deep rumbling gradually died away, and only then was it possible to distinguish which elements of the confusion and uproar had been earthquake noises and which the thunder of the landslides. We got up and looked around us in the darkness.'

Throughout the night the ground shook every few seconds, and an endless barrage of rocks and earth cascaded down the mountains. The stars were blotted out by an immense pall of dust. It began to rain.

At dawn they looked out. The earth was still trembling, but the shocks were neither so strong nor so frequent. Dust was everywhere, blotting out the rising sun. A stream had dried up, there were fissures in the ground, and a rope bridge across a river had snapped like cotton.

But the birds still sang; 'no eggs though, for with one accord every hen in the valley ceased to lay'.

The Kingdon-Wards and their servants joined with others to escape to India, about 100 perilous miles away. They arrived after a terrifying journey lasting more than two weeks. One of the hazards was rock avalanches, which continued for months after the earthquake. Jean Kingdon-Ward, describing one avalanche, says:

> 'A wedge of granite broke away with a savage roar from the cliffs above the river, toppled over very, very slowly, then crashed hundreds of feet in one bound till it hit a projecting spur. There it exploded into smaller blocks, which fell hundreds of feet again down the sheer mountain wall, breaking into still smaller fragments as they bounced off the cliff once more and plunged headlong into the muddy waters of the Lohit. After the barrage ceased, the whole cliff smoked with clouds of pulverized rock, white and brown and yellow. No sooner was it clear again than the awful performance was repeated. The noise alone was terrifying.'

Earthquakes sometimes cause rivers to flow backward. In the New Madrid, Missouri, quakes of 1811 and 1812, the uplift of the bed and caving in of the banks caused a temporary rise in the water level of about 6 feet and a reversal of the current. According to Victor Hugo Boesen, some panic-stricken men, who took to their boat to escape the violence of the quake, found themselves 'carried upstream with the speed of a galloping horse'!

It was in this great series of earthquakes that parts of a forest were seen to fall. The shaking is sometimes so violent that the soil around the roots loosens and trees topple over. Trees over fissures are sometimes split in half: in New Madrid, large oak trees were split for 40 feet up the centre of the trunk, the halves standing on either side of the fissure. James Penick has written a detailed study of these great quakes in which many true 'stranger than fiction' stories are recounted.

It is not generally realised that a large earthquake has an effect on the atmosphere. As the earth's surface vibrates, like the skin of a drum, it produces atmospheric pressure waves which, although small, spread vast distances and reach the ionosphere some 40 miles above the earth.

In a violent earthquake this vertical motion shoots objects into the air. Large stones bounce up and down like peas on a drum and potatoes jump out of the ground. During the Calabria, Italy, earthquake of 5 March 1783, a stone well shot 8 feet above the ground. In the Japanese earthquake of 1 September 1923, wells jumped out of the ground, some rising 10 feet before breaking into fragments. Even more remarkable was the appearance, 3 feet above the surface, of some 2-foot-wide wooden pillars: they had been submerged well below the surface, and proved to be supports for a bridge built in 1182 whose existence had been completely forgotten.

It was the jolting action of an earthquake which was responsible for one of the most macabre incidents of which I have ever read. During the earthquake at Arica, Chile, on 8 August 1868, a cemetery on a mountainside was disturbed. The dead had been buried upright in concentric ranks, as in an amphitheatre, all facing the same way. The

Earthquake and earthquake-triggered landslide shattered this bridge in Guatemala on 4 February 1976. The earthquake caused one of the worst disasters in the Western hemisphere. Some 23,000 people were killed, over a million left homeless – about one in five of the population.
(World Food Programme/United Nations)

nitre-impregnated soil had so preserved the bodies that awe-struck watchers suddenly saw uncovered on the mountainside a close-packed army of the dead – rank upon rank of mummified corpses. Coupled with the appalling effects of the earthquake, this was the last touch of horror to convince them that it was the end of the world (Haroun Tazieff).

A variety of sounds accompanies an earthquake, 'the cracking and twisting of all creation'. In some, the 'awful rumblings' of the straining earth have been so deafening that the individual crashings of buildings and trees have not been heard as separate noises.

Strange noises, strange lights. The following lights have been reported before, during, or after the earthquakes themselves: lightning-like flashes; luminous spots and narrow bands; diffuse lights in the air; globes, streamers, and columns of fire; and numerous sparks and luminous vapours. The colour of these lights varies, but the most common are red, blue and white.

The lights are not confined to the land. During the Sanriku, Japan, earthquake on 15 June 1896, the sea partly receded and the bed of the ocean was seen tō glow with a bluish-white luminescence. When another quake occurred in the same area on 3 March 1933, similar lights were seen; in addition the crests of the waves emitted a dim continuous light, and the whole surface of the sea glittered. When the waves broke over the shore, the coastline was faintly illuminated by bluish light.

The sea lights are almost certainly caused by tiny luminescent organisms which are disturbed by the violent agitation of the sea. The lights over the land are not susceptible of such a simple explanation. Some may be caused by factors unconnected with earthquakes, such as lightning and meteors. Others may be the result of secondary earthquake action: disturbance of electricity-supply lines and earthquake-induced fires. Earthquakes generate considerable heat, and trees overhanging a fault are sometimes scorched.

During earthquakes in Szechuan Province, China, during August 1976, many earthquake lights were seen. They were described as being in the form of columns, fans, balls and sheets. Several seismologists witnessed a 'fireball' from a distance of about 100 yards. It was originally about 1 yard in diameter, but later shrank to the size of a table-tennis ball. The fireball shot up to a height of about 40 feet, then curved over and fell to earth. Its brightness waxed and waned, and wisps of white smoke swirled around it. There was a slight crackling sound and a sulphur-like odour. Almost certainly the cause was the release of natural gas by the earthquakes (Robert E. Wallace and Ta-Liang Teng).

Some of the lights may result from electrical discharges quite distinct from lightning. There is an increase of ionisation in the atmosphere above an earthquake. Another suggestion is that earthquake stress on piezoelectric quartz produces luminescence. Finding the explanation for earthquake lights is no mere academic exercise. If geophysicists knew what caused pre-quake glows it would help in earthquake prediction, but at present, to quote one scientist: 'Earthquake lights constitute the darkest chapter in the history of seismology.' A review of the subject was published by John S. Derr in 1973.

The most severe American earthquake since the magnitude scale was invented occurred in Alaska on Good Friday, 27 March 1964. The length and complexity of the rupture made it difficult to assess the evidence, but the magnitude was estimated to be between 8.3 and 8.6. Moreover, calculations based on the 'seismic moment' (see page 163) indicate that the energy release was much greater – perhaps 10 to 20 times greater – than that indicated by the Richter figures.

There is no doubt that this was among the two or three mightiest quakes of the century. It has been extensively described, and I shall give here only a few stark details. The epicentre was the head of Prince William Sound, about 80 miles east of Anchorage. One hundred thousand square miles of the earth's surface had been either uplifted or dropped,[1] the largest area to be affected by an earthquake since records began. A swath of destruction was cut for 500 miles, from Cordova to Kodiak Island; and buildings in Seattle, over 1,000 miles away, swayed as waves from the monstrous quake shuddered beneath them. Tsunami (quake-induced waves: see page 179) from the earthquake spread havoc far beyond Alaska. Speeding at 400 to 500 mph across the Pacific, tsunami hit Vancouver Island, California, Hawaii, and even Japan, 4,000 miles from Alaska.

As a result of this major quake, 75% of Alaska's commerce and industry were ruined, an estimated loss of 750 million dollars. The death-toll was 115: fortunately, the state is sparsely populated.

To seismologists, the Alaska earthquake provided a rich field of study, of which they took full advantage. So much material had to be assessed that it was not until 1973 that the report of the National Academy of Sciences was published: eight volumes, 4,705 pages. The United States Government appointed two committees to study earthquakes and their prediction. Clusters of instruments, some in holes nearly 2 miles deep, measure earth tremors, and computers process the information.

Earthquakes are by no means unknown in Great Britain: there are records of at least 1,500, dating from the 7th century. I experienced one in Altrincham, Cheshire, on the night of 29 December 1944: it was extremely mild where I was located, but elsewhere people were bounced out of bed, crockery was smashed, and ceilings were cracked. In all British earthquakes, however, only a few deaths have been reported. In that of 6 April 1580, which shook the whole of England and was particularly severe in London, stones fell from the top of a church and killed two apprentices. London earthquakes average about three per century.

The worst earthquake in Great Britain occurred on 22 April 1884 in East Anglia, and was felt over an area of some 50,000 square miles. It has been estimated that its magnitude was 5.5. Twelve hundred buildings were damaged and, although the records of casualties vary, at most only five people were killed.

In 1983 Robert Muir Wood reported to the British Association for the Advancement of Science, that it is statistically inevitable that a damaging earthquake will strike the British Isles. He did not hazard a time-scale, but pointed out that an earthquake occurred under the southern North Sea on 7 June 1931. Had its epicentre been 100 miles or so to the west it would have devastated Hull, probably killing hundreds of people. And what if an earthquake hit Canvey Island in Essex with its array of liquid-gas tanks? Or a nuclear power station?

Earthquakes have occurred in both Washington DC and New York City. The most severe in Washington was on 31 August 1886, when an intensity of V was recorded but little, if any, damage was done. The worst New York quake was on 10 August 1884 with an intensity of VII, causing damage to houses in the Jamaica and Amityville districts.

The greatest earthquake disaster of modern times occurred in the Peking area on 28 July 1976. The magnitude was registered as 8.3 by the United States Geological Survey Station at Golden, California. The mining and industrial centre of Tangshan, with a population of over 1 million, was devastated; nearly 300,000 perished. The Chinese, in accordance with policy, refused all the proffered aid from foreign countries.

Throughout the world, earthquakes and their accompanying fires and floods, are the greatest of all natural destroyers of human life and property. Their only rivals are hurricanes, with their attendant floods, and volcanoes; but neither of these has taken the same toll throughout the centuries as earthquakes which, on average, kill 15,000 people

Ground fissure caused by the Beni Rashid, Algeria earthquake of 10 October 1980. Very occasionally such fissures open and close on people. (Chris Dammers/ Oxfam)

every year. The most lethal of recorded earthquakes occurred on 23 January 1556 in the Shenshi Province, China: it killed approximately 830,000 people. Since records began (in China, about 1,000 BC), earthquake deaths throughout the world total nearly 14 million.

Some interesting observations on the psychological effects of an earthquake were made by William James, the American pioneer psychologist. In 1906, when he was 64 years of age, he was the visiting professor at Stanford University, California. Before James left Harvard, a friend said to him: 'I hope they'll give you a touch of earthquake while you're there.' At 5.30 a.m. on 18 April 1906 the wish was granted: the most famous earthquake in American history struck San Francisco, 35 miles from where James was staying.

'[When] I felt the bed begin to waggle, my first consciousness was one of gleeful recognition of the nature of the movement. "By Jove," I said to myself, "here's B's old earthquake, after all!" And then, as it went *crescendo*, "And a jolly good one it is, too!" I said.

'Sitting up involuntarily, and taking a kneeling position, I was thrown down on my face as it went *fortior* shaking the room exactly as a terrier shakes a rat. Then everything that was on anything else slid off to the floor, over went bureau and chiffonier with a crash, as the *fortissimo* was reached, plaster cracked, an awful roaring noise seemed to fill the outer air, and in an instant all was still again, save the soft babble of human voices from far and near that soon began to make itself heard, as the inhabitants in costumes *negligés* in various degrees sought the greater safety of the street and yielded to the passionate desire for sympathetic communication.

'The thing was over, as I understand the Lick Observatory to have declared, in 48 seconds. To me it felt as if about that length of time, although I have heard others say that it seemed to them longer. In my case, sensation and emotion were so strong that little thought, and no reflection or volition, were possible in the short time consumed by the phenomenon.

'The emotion consisted wholly of glee and admiration; glee at the vividness which such an abstract idea or verbal term as "earthquake" could put on when translated into sensible reality and verified concretely; and admiration at the way in which the frail little wooden house could hold itself together in spite of such a shaking. I felt no trace whatever of fear; it was pure delight and welcome.

'"Go it," I almost cried aloud, "and go it stronger!"'

Keiiti Aki, who read this chapter for technical accuracy, commented: 'I especially enjoyed the story of joyous Professor William James. To tell the truth, I feel the same thrilling joy every time I feel an earthquake.'

James went to San Francisco to observe how the catastrophe affected the victims. Two things impressed him most: the rapid way that people improvised to bring order out of the tremendous and unprecedented chaos; and 'the universal equanimity . . . Not a single whine or plaintive word did I hear from the hundred losers whom I spoke to. Instead of that there was a temper of helpfulness beyond the counting.'

At Stanford University, the prevailing emotion seems to have been one of gaiety:

> 'Everybody was excited, but the excitement at first, at any rate, seemed to be almost joyous. Here at last was a *real* earthquake after so many years of harmless waggle! Above all, there was an irresistible desire to talk about it, and exchange experiences.
>
> 'Most people slept outdoors for several subsequent nights, partly to be safer in case of a recurrence, but also to work off their emotion, and get the full unusualness out of the experience. The vocal babble of early-waking girls and boys from the gardens of the campus, mingling with the birds' songs and the exquisite weather, was for three or four days a delightful sunrise phenomenon.'

It may seem difficult to find a single practical blessing for which most of us are indebted to earthquakes. Yet, strange as it sounds, an earthquake may be regarded as a safety measure, saving us from even worse disasters. Earthquakes release the stresses and strains of the rocks before they build up even more titanic forces and wreak even more devastation.

Earthquakes provide knowledge of the deep interior of the earth (the conduits of volcanoes reach only a comparatively short way). The quiverings of the thin-skinned earth alone reveal something of those vast depths which no man can reach. Earthquake waves vary in behaviour according to the substance they pass through: they are faster through granite than through sand; and S waves will not pass through molten rock – only P waves do that. By studying such wave behaviour, seismologists can picture roughly the composition of the earth's interior.

The nearest to an immediate human benefit comes from this kind of investigation, which enables scientists to locate valuable minerals and other deposits beneath the earth's surface. In this geophysical prospecting, small seismic sources, such as artificial explosions and hydraulic vibrators, trigger waves which are monitored with the help of portable seismographs. By studying records, and using knowledge of the terrain and existing data, it is possible to learn something of what lies below the surface. Today, seismic prospecting is used throughout the world for a number of purposes, from tracing accumulations of oil and coal to investigating dam sites and polar icecaps.

In this Nuclear Age, every seismologist has a politician breathing down his neck. This is because the detection of underground nuclear tests is bedevilled by their similarity to earthquakes: both send similar waves pulsing through the earth. Improvements in detecting apparatus, and greater experience in interpreting the seismograph records, will make distinction easier. In particular, arrays of seismographs facilitate detection and interpretation of earth movements. An array in Montana has 525 instruments deployed over a circle 120 miles in diameter.

Seismologists have given much attention to lessening the danger from earthquakes. One way is to trigger small quakes before the pressure builds up for a big one. The 'trigger' is water pumped between unstable rock layers. Much work has also been done on earthquake forecasting, a harmless enough pursuit but one which occasionally meets unexpected obstacles. British seismologists working in the Himalayas in 1980 had their instruments damaged by villagers: it was against the will of Allah to attempt to predict earthquakes.

The leaders in forecasting are the Chinese, which is understandable in view of the appalling losses they have suffered from earthquakes. As knowledge and experience increase, and instruments become more refined, the signs of a forthcoming earthquake can be more clearly interpreted. Such signs include: local changes in the earth's crust; tiny shifts in the deformation of the landscape; glows from the earth; and changes in well water, both in the level and in the radon content (radon is a gas given off by the decay of radium in rocks; when they crack under increased stress extra radon sometimes escapes).

Some people who have experienced earthquakes say that the atmosphere seems unnaturally still shortly beforehand. On the evening before the Quetta earthquake of 30 May 1935, Betty Montgomery drew the attention of her husband, later Field Marshall Lord Montgomery, to a skein of silk in her hand. Every strand stood out separately, as stiff as wire. Was this coincidence? (Robert Jackson)

Warning is often given by animals. In the introduction to the papers presented at the United States Government-sponsored conference on *Abnormal Animal Behaviour Prior to Earthquakes* (1976) it is stated:

'From a geophysicist's point of view, an animal can be considered as a complex, highly sensitive sensor capable of detecting and responding to variations in any or all fields routinely measureable by geophysical means. It must be our working hypothesis that, if an animal can sense a premonitory signal or complex of signals adequate to perturb his behaviour prior to an earthquake, we can potentially design and deploy equipment adequate to measure such signals.'

Pheasants have frequently been heard to call before an earthquake was felt by humans. (In the Second World War pheasants called at the fall of distant bombs of which the birds' human neighbours were unaware.) About half an hour before the earthquake at Sofiadhas, Greece, on 30 April 1954, storks took to the air in an agitated manner; many villagers, noticing this, feared that a catastrophe was coming and took to the open, thereby saving their lives.

Such reactions are not confined to birds. Before the Chinese earthquake of 4 February 1975, snakes were observed coming out of their lairs in frozen ground. Pandas in Chinese zoos have been seen acting strangely before earthquakes, and there have been similar reports from other countries of unusual mammalian activity prior to major earthquakes.

Wallace and Teng say:

'Abnormal [animal] behaviour prior to earthquakes has been a part of the Chinese folk wisdom for so long that the scientific community seems to accept it as fact. Although no explanation is offered at this time, laboratory work on the neurophysiological responses of animals to various physical-chemical stimuli is being carried out in the Shanghai Biophysical Institute to place the evidence on a sounder scientific footing.'

The authors reproduce photographs of unusual behaviour by animals before earthquakes: rats scrambling onto telephone and power lines; a rabbit on a roof (safer than on the ground?); and pigs trying to escape from their pen.

Experiments with catfish have shown that they become restless some hours before an earthquake. In one seven-month experiment, ten catfish acted abnormally in advance of 85% of earthquakes (*Wildlife*, July 1979). One theory is that animals detect the electrostatic charges caused by strains in the earth before the quake. Although it appears contradictory to the above, some people claim that before a quake a marked hush descends on the animal kingdom, birds and insects in particular ceasing their normal activities.

Although seismologists have so far failed to devise any accurate means of forecasting earthquakes,[2] they do at least point out areas where earthquakes are likely. But what if it is impossible to avoid living in an earthquake area? Japan, for example, is exceptionally earthquake-prone, and nothing less than a mass evacuation could ensure complete immunity from disaster. In such regions, the architect, in collaboration with the seismologist, can do much to reduce the danger. The best foundation on which to build in order to resist earthquakes is hard rock; the worst is soft ground or 'made' land – filled-in shallow land alongside rivers, lakes, or sea.

Some types of buildings are particularly vulnerable, others very resistant to damage. Model buildings are tested on 'shaking platforms' where, as far as possible, earthquake conditions are simulated. As a result of such tests and direct quake experiences, the most earthquake-resistant structures have been evolved. The findings are: if you live in an earthquake zone, choose either a tent or a skyscraper! Wood-frame structures are also recommended; they have a good record in earthquakes.

The best-known successful attempt to build an earthquake-proof building is Frank Lloyd Wright's Imperial Hotel in Tokyo. By contrast, the Olive View Hospital in San Fernando, which had been built to meet the local earthquake regulations, was damaged beyond repair in the Californian quake of 9 February 1971.

It has been suggested that a steel box-like structure would withstand any earthquake. Probably the only building that approximates to such a structure is a six-storey bank in Los Angeles: virtually all steel and 'guaranteed' to withstand an earthquake of a magnitude of 8.4. Even this building, however, would be severely tested if it were over the epicentre and the earth fissured widely beneath. In such circumstances other well-built structures have been torn apart.

Buildings with thick and heavy walls are disadvantaged: it is difficult to give them the necessary strength to resist the lateral stresses induced by an earthquake. In violent quakes, such buildings are shaken down and bury those within. Brick buildings, especially if not very well built, often collapse. Heavily tiled roofs are a menace; the shaking sends the tiles crashing down often on to the heads of people below.

Well-built simple structures often come through earthquakes unscathed. During the Charleston, South Carolina, earthquake of 31 August 1886, a Negro family in a log cabin slept unharmed right through the quake. Wooden buildings in thickly populated areas, however, can be very dangerous because of the fires which break out after nearly all severe earthquakes.

Modern American skyscrapers are good examples of earthquake-resistant buildings; they are safe unless close to the epicentre of one of great magnitude. What happens then may be judged from an eye-witness description of the Japanese earthquake of 1 September 1923[3] by Henry W. Kinney, an experienced American journalist and editor. He was in a train approaching Yokohama.

'I glanced out just as the stone face of an embankment shot down over the tracks. It did not slide or tumble down: it literally shot down, as if compelled by a sudden, gigantic pressure from the top, the stones spreading in a twinkling over the wide right-of-way. A four-storey concrete building vanished, disintegrated in the flash of an eye. Tiles cascaded with precipitate speed from the roofs. The one predominating idea that struck the mind was the almost incredible rapidity of the destruction.'

Eighty million tons of rock dam the Madison river and state highway after the earthquake of 17 August 1959 in the Gallatin National Forest. Ringed vehicle gives scale. (US Forest Service)

6

It was this earthquake that tested the famous Imperial Hotel in Tokyo. The hotel came through this terrible ordeal with comparatively little damage, as did the majority of modern buildings. It was the subsequent fires which caused the havoc (Noel F. Busch). But not to the Imperial. Its designer, Wright, had insisted that the hotel should have a large ornamental pool; when the earthquake destroyed the city's water services, this pool provided the water which saved the hotel.

It is important to know what to do in an earthquake. First, get under something that will protect you from falling debris and count to 40 seconds (although occasionally earthquakes last much longer than this). Then turn off the gas and electricity, and get into open ground – fast. Jean Kingdon-Ward says: 'There is a powerful instinct that urges one to get out of doors in an earthquake.'

Landslides are often started by earthquakes. During the Calabria, Italy, earthquake in 1783, acres of land moved half a mile across a ravine. Yet flowers and corn and large oak and olive trees were unharmed; they continued to flourish as well at the bottom of the ravine as their companions, from which the landslide had separated them, did 500 feet above and half a mile away. The answer to Macbeth's question – 'Who can impress the forest, bid the tree unfix his earth-bound root?' – is: 'A landslide'.

The greatest landslide in North America within historic times occurred on 23 June 1925 in Wyoming's Gros Ventre Mountains, near the southern boundary of the Yellowstone National Park. It was not caused by an earthquake. Heavy spring rains moistened the clay in an underlying section on the side of a valley. Eventually, the section slipped and an enormous mass of sandstone rock covered with forest – an estimated 50 million cubic yards – slid across the valley and rammed against the opposite side to a height of 350 feet. This, in turn, dammed the Gros Ventre River, which then formed a huge lake 3 miles long. Nearly two years later part of the dam burst and a great flood, 15 feet high, swept down the valley, drowning the little village of Kelly. There is still a lake at Gros Ventre, a permanent memorial to America's greatest landslide (William C. Alden).

The greatest landslides in recorded history were those of 16 December 1920 in Kansu, central China. They followed severe earthquakes, and occurred on a monumental scale over an area of 30,000 square miles comprising ten cities and numerous villages. In one area there were 17 immense landslides within a 20-mile semicircle. The nature of the soil and the terrain explains what happened. Loose earth carpeted hills which, shaken by the great earthquake, sent untold millions of cubic yards of soil cascading into valleys and plains. The scars left by some of the slides were so clean that they appeared to have been scooped out by a gigantic trowel.

The Chinese coined the phrase *Shan tso-liao* – 'The mountains walked' – to describe the fantastic results of this greatest of all known landslides. Upton Close and Elsie McCormick, in their report in *The National Geographic Magazine* for May 1922, say: 'One astonished peasant looked out of his window in the morning to find that a high hill had moved on to the homestead, stopping its line of march within a few feet of his hut.' Elsewhere, a mountain slid into a valley, complete with the temple which had been erected on its top. The death-toll was

180,000, the worst known from landslides.

Slides or flows of various kinds occur in special conditions, some of which have no relation to earthquakes. Sudden heavy rain falling on mud on a steep gradient sometimes causes a mudflow, a huge mud river with tremendous carrying power. Heavy rain may burst bogs, unleashing a flow of half-liquid peat. Such bog bursts occur in Ireland, as may be expected, but one of the worst was in Stanley, Falkland Islands. Following heavy rains in June 1886, a peat river, 4–5 feet deep, flowed through the town; streets were blocked, houses wrecked and people killed (C. F. Stewart Sharpe).

One of the most curious – and dangerous – slides occurs with quick-clay, which can rapidly change from a solid to a liquid. It is composed of very fine mineral particles and water. If a small cube of quick-clay is held in the open hand and shaken, it becomes moist and loses its shape; if a lump that has been supporting 20 or so pounds is put in a perfectly

Cars are dwarfed by this large landslide in Hong Kong on 18 June 1972, which was caused by intense rainfall. Such slides are often triggered by earthquakes. (Hong Kong Government Information Services)

dry beaker and stirred, it will turn to liquid and can be poured out. (This property of thixotropy is used in non-drip paints.)

Normally, quick-clay is as firm and solid as earth, supporting houses, offices, factories, a whole township. On rare occasions, however, an earthquake shock or other disturbance will turn sloping ground that has been solid for thousands of years into a soupy lake which slides away, carrying everything with it.

On 12 November 1955, part of the centre of Nicolet, Quebec, slid into the Nicolet River. Another quick-clay disaster occurred at Vaerdalen near Trondheim, Norway, during the night of 19 May 1893, when about 1 square mile, involving about 60 million cubic yards, slid into a valley. The earth was turned into a heavy liquid that washed down the valley towards the fjord below. A score of farms were destroyed and 111 people killed. Some farmers were rescued after sailing $3\frac{1}{2}$ miles down the clay river perched on the roof of their house (Per Holmsen).

During the Second World War, in Norway, several quick-clay slides were triggered by bombing. In the south of the country British bombers, trying to hit a nitrogen factory, started a slide over an area of some 50,000 square yards which carried away ten houses. In the north, near Petsamo, Russian bombers set off a huge slide which swept down a valley, destroying a bridge, military depots and artillery positions. Professor I. Th. Rosenqvist, who told me this, adds: 'These two incidents are all I know about bomb-triggered slides, and in many cases heavy blasting of bedrock has taken place in the neighbourhood of quick-clays without any slides being caused.'

Finally, there are the quakes beneath the sea. These seaquakes do little direct damage beyond breaking submarine cables and disturbing bottom-feeding fish. Sometimes the fish migrate to more equable surroundings, thus affecting fisheries.

Seaquakes have two indirect, or secondary effects, both owing to the fact that they displace unconsolidated material on steep slopes (as also do some earthquakes that occur near the sea). One result of such displacement is avalanches of mud, sand and sludge which occasionally cascade down the slopes of the continental shelves. In some of these submarine slides the initial speed is 50 mph. Such a speed, although held for only a fraction of the total path, is maintained against the tremendous braking power of water. Seaslides have been proved to travel as much as 300 miles along the ocean floor.

The second, and much more dangerous, effect of a displacement of the ocean bed is that it may generate large sea waves that race across the oceans at great speed. They are often called tidal waves, but they have nothing to do with tides. To avoid confusion, oceanographers call them by the Japanese word *tsunami*, whether the waves are caused by quakes or volcanoes.

Strangely enough, tsunami (the word is both singular and plural) are virtually undetectable at sea. Although from crest to crest they sometimes measure 600 miles, their height from trough to crest is only 1–2 feet. It is the tsunami's speed which is remarkable, and the greater the depth of water the greater the speed. A wave driven by the strongest wind rarely travels more than 60 mph; tsunami sometimes travel at 500 mph, or even faster. As the tsunami reaches shallow water near land – it may be 3,000 miles away – the speed is greatly reduced.

Often, strange as it sounds, the first sign of an approaching tsunami is the sea going out. This is because there is an abrupt collapse of part of the ocean bed which, in turn, causes the sea above it to drop, leaving a depression on the surface. The surrounding seas rush to fill the depression, there is a wild turmoil of waters, and then the seas flow back again – but higher and faster than they went out. This process is often repeated several times following a seaquake. The first return wave generally appears within 15 minutes, although two hours have sometimes elapsed. Many people have died because the return wave came before they expected it: when a 75-foot high tsunami hit Honshu, Japan, on 15 June 1896, some 26,000 people were drowned.

A tsunami's effect on reaching shore varies according to its violence (speed) and the nature of the coast. A medium tsunami crashing against high cliffs will probably damage nothing but objects, and people, on the beach. The same tsunami crashing against a shallow shore will sweep inland and, in built-up areas, cause great destruction.

Opposite Houses collapse when shaken by the Good Friday 1964 Alaskan earthquake, the severest in America since the invention of the magnitude scale. The quake affected 100,000 square miles; buildings over 1,000 miles from the epicentre were shaken. Damage was estimated at 750 million dollars. Deaths were 115. Fortunately Alaska is sparsely populated. (Steve McCutcheon)

The greatest violence occurs when a tsunami sweeps into a funnel-shaped bay and the sea piles up to crash inland as a vast wall of water. If the tsunami is already of exceptional violence, the resulting disaster is unimaginable.

The sea defence does not exist which can repel a great tsunami: a vast wall of water 50 feet, 100, even 200 feet high, weighing untold millions of tons, crashing inland at 100 or even 150 mph. A tsunami of 210 feet was recorded at Cape Lopatka on the southern tip of Kamchatka, Siberia, in 1737. The height of the vast majority of tsunami, however, is much less than this.

By far the highest waves occur in bays and enclosed bodies of water, when a vast mass of earth or rock suddenly plunges down. These waves are not strictly tsunami, although earthquakes often cause the fall of material. On 13 September 1936, at Loen Lake, Norway, about $1\frac{1}{4}$ million cubic yards of rock fell into the water, sending a wave to a maximum height of 230 feet crashing on to the opposite shore.

This and all other known records for giant waves are, however, surpassed by those which sometimes race across Lituya Bay, a T-shaped, ice-scoured, nearly landlocked bay on the northeast shore of the Alaskan Panhandle. Deep water, precipitous topography at the head of the bay, plus ice and rock slides appear to be the reasons. At least four times in 100 years these great waves have swept high into the forests lining the bay, felling thousands of large trees, sweeping the fjord-like sides clear to the bare rock.

The greatest wave of all, and by far the highest in the recorded history of man, occurred here on 9 July 1958. An earthquake shook 40 million cubic yards of rock, weighing 80 million tons and falling from a maximum height of about 3,000 feet, into Gilbert Inlet at the head of the bay. This is roughly equivalent to the simultaneous launching of 2,000 battleships from a slipway half a mile high.

The tremendous rockfall sent a vast wave racing across the bay at a speed of about 100 mph, and caused water to surge over the opposite wall of the inlet to a maximum height of 1,740 feet – a third of a mile, nearly twice the height of the Eiffel Tower, over four times the height of St Paul's Cathedral! Four square miles of forest, extending inland for two-thirds of a mile, were destroyed. Large trees 50 feet high with diameters of 4 feet were either washed out or snapped off near the ground. (Don J. Miller)

A vivid description of what it is like to be caught on a ship in a tsunami has been given by Rear Admiral L. G. Billings. At the time, he was a lieutenant aboard the flat-bottomed United States Navy steamship *Wateree* when she was off Arica, Chile, on 8 August 1868.

'We were startled by a terrific noise on shore, as of a tremendous roar of musketry, lasting several minutes. Again the trembling earth waved to and fro, and this time the sea receded until the shipping was left stranded, while as far to seaward as our vision could reach we saw the rocky bottom of the sea, never before exposed to human gaze, with struggling fish and monsters of the deep left high and dry.

'The round-bottomed ships keeled over on their beam ends, while the *Wateree* rested easily on her floor-like bottom; and when the returning sea, not like a wave, but rather like an enormous tide,

Opposite San Francisco's modern pyramid, 853-feet high, is an example of earthquake-resistant architecture. The opposite of such sophisticated buildings – wood-frame structures – are also relatively safe in earthquakes. (Transamerica Corporation)

came sweeping back, rolling our unfortunate companion ships over and over, leaving some bottom up and others masses of wreckage, the *Wateree* rose easily over the tossing waters, unharmed.'

When the main return wave struck, the *Wateree* was overwhelmed, but struggled through to the surface. She was carried by the immense waters like a matchbox on a fast-flowing stream. The wave carried her 3 miles up the coast and nearly 2 miles inland. She was lifted over sand dunes, a valley and a railway track, and finally deposited high in a little cove. Billings says that they found near them the wreck of another ship with her anchor chains wound around her as many times as they would go, indicating that she had been rolled over and over by the force of the water. Had the *Wateree* not been a flat-bottomed ship, she would almost certainly have perished.

MODIFIED MERCALLI EARTHQUAKE INTENSITY SCALE

Because the performance of masonry is such an important criterion for evaluating intensity, this version specified four qualities of masonry, brick or otherwise, as follows:

Masonry A Good workmanship, mortar, and design; reinforced, especially laterally, and bound together using steel, concrete, etc; designed to resist lateral forces.

Masonry B Good workmanship and mortar; reinforced, but not designed in detail to resist lateral forces.

Masonry C Ordinary workmanship and mortar; no extreme weaknesses like failing to tie in at corners, but neither reinforced nor designed against horizontal forces.

Masonry D Weak materials, such as adobe; poor mortar; low standards of workmanship; weak horizontally.

INTENSITY

I Not felt. Marginal and long-period effects of large earthquakes.

II Felt by persons at rest, on upper floors, or favourable places.

III Felt indoors. Hanging objects swing. Vibration like passing of light trucks. Duration estimated. May not be recognised as an earthquake.

IV Hanging objects swing. Vibration like passing of heavy trucks, or sensation of a jolt like a heavy ball striking the walls. Standing motor cars rock. Windows, dishes, doors rattle. Glasses clink. Crockery clashes. In the upper range of IV, wooden walls and frame creak.

V Felt outdoors; direction estimated. Sleepers wakened. Liquids disturbed, some spilled. Small unstable objects displaced or upset. Doors swing, close, open. Shutters, pictures move. Pendulum clocks stop, start, change rate.

VI Felt by all. Many frightened and run outdoors. People walk unsteadily. Windows, dishes, glassware broken. Knickknacks, books, etc., off shelves. Pictures off walls. Furniture moved or overturned. Weak plaster and masonry D cracked. Small bells ring (church, school). Trees, bushes shaken visibly, or heard to rustle.

VII Difficult to stand. Noticed by drivers of motor cars. Hanging objects quiver. Furniture broken. Damage to masonry D, including cracks. Weak chimneys broken at roof line. Fall of plaster, loose bricks, stones, tiles, cornices, unbraced parapets and architectural ornaments. Some cracks in masonry C. Waves on ponds; water turbid with mud. Small slides and caving-in along sand or gravel banks. Large bells ring. Concrete irrigation ditches damaged.

VIII Steering of motor cars affected. Damage to masonry C; partial collapse. Some damage to masonry B, none to masonry A. Fall of stucco and some masonry walls. Twisting, fall of chimneys, factory stacks, monuments, towers, elevated tanks. Frame houses moved on foundations if not bolted down; loose panel walls thrown out. Decayed piling broken off. Branches broken from trees. Changes in flow or temperature of springs and wells. Cracks in wet ground and on steep slopes.

IX General panic. Masonry D destroyed; masonry C heavily damaged, sometimes with complete collapse; masonry B seriously damaged. General damage to foundations. Frame structures, if not bolted, shifted off foundations. Frame cracked. Serious damage to reservoirs. Underground pipes broken. Conspicuous cracks in ground. In alluvial areas sand and mud ejected, earthquake fountains, sand craters.

X Most masonry and frame structures destroyed with their foundations. Some well-built wooden structures and bridges destroyed. Serious damage to dams, dikes, embankments. Large landslides. Water thrown on banks of canals, rivers, lakes, etc. Sand and mud shifted horizontally on beaches and flat land. Rails bent slightly.

XI Rails bent greatly: Underground pipelines completely out of service.

XII Damage nearly total. Large rock masses displaced. Lines of sight and level distorted. Objects thrown into the air.

In the foregoing, each effect is named at the level of intensity at which it first appears frequently and characteristically. Each effect may be found less strongly, or in fewer instances, at the next lower grade of intensity; more strongly or more often at the next higher grade. A few effects are named at two successive levels to indicate a more gradual increase.

MANUAL OF SEISMOLOGICAL OBSERVATORY PRACTICE

Editor
P. L. Willmore
Institute of Geological Sciences, Edinburgh, Scotland
September 1979

Published by World Data Center A for Solid Earth Geophysics
U.S. DEPARTMENT OF COMMERCE

Seismologists point out that the scale is based on eye-witness accounts but is of limited value since factors other than the intensity of the earthquake are involved. A poorly constructed building near the epicentre would suffer more damage – and thus indicate a more intense earthquake – than a modern skyscraper miles away.

NOTES

1. In Anchorage's Fourth Avenue, the main business thoroughfare, one side dropped 11 feet, leaving a twisted tangle of destruction. The other side of the street was left intact.

2. One frustrated seismic forecaster summed up his studies with the wry prophecy: 'The longer it's been since the last one, the closer we are to the next.'

3. In addition to the earthquake, the hapless victims were assailed by typhoon, tornado, fire, tsunami, landslides and floods.

VOLCANOES

An erupting volcano is Nature's greatest spectacle. The vast display of energies; the violent uprush of liquid rock and gases from deep below the surface to miles above it; the shake and tremble of the earth; the flash of lightning and the roar of thunder; the brilliant firework display of the glowing and exploding lava; and the multitudinous sounds of the belching crater – these make an ineffaceable impression upon the mind of the beholder.

Frank A. Perret, after witnessing an eruption of one of the most famous volcanoes in the world, Vesuvius in 1906, wrote: 'Strongest of impressions was that of an infinite dignity in every manifestation of this stupendous releasing of energy. No words can describe the majesty of its unfolding.' Perret was present before, during and after the eruption, and was thus able to study it in detail. His monograph (1924) is one of the classics of geological literature.

Vesuvius was almost ready to go in May 1905, but then part of the side of the main cone fissured, releasing some of the pent-up lava. Eleven months later, however, in April 1906, she literally blew her top. Molten lava issued from the crater on 4 April, and thereafter there were continuous eruptions for days. After midnight on 7 April, there were violent earthquake shocks, and terrific explosions in the crater. It was impossible for observers to stand still. The whole of Vesuvius was humming and vibrating like a gigantic boiler under a colossal head of steam.

Millions of tons of lava, ash and dust-charged gas were exploding from the crater, accompanied by various electrical discharges: St Elmo's fire, 'flashing arcs' and other forms of lightning. The lightning flashes forking through the dark volcanic clouds added greatly to the impressiveness of the scene.

After two days of violent eruption the throat of Vesuvius appeared to be clear. Then, from unknown depths, there rushed up a tremendous blast of volcanic gas which shot 7 miles into the sky, where it formed a gigantic cauliflower-shaped cloud. The compression of the gas while imprisoned in the earth, and its acceleration within the shaft of the volcano, must have been colossal. This enormous blow-off lasted throughout the daylight hours of 8 April, accompanied by a Niagara-like roar.

At times the ash clouds were lit by incandescent jets of molten lava and vivid lightning flashes, so that they formed a gigantic torch, miles high, which illuminated the Gulf of Naples from Capri to Cape Miseno.

The next stage in this grand display was the emission of jet-black clouds. Near the volcano it was pitch dark; Perret says that it was impossible to see a compass held in the hand. Fine ash penetrated everywhere.

A gigantic pall hung over Naples and the surrounding country for a fortnight, and men might well have thought that 'the last eternal night of story had settled on the world' – the words used by Pliny the Younger to describe the Vesuvius eruption of 79 AD. Lightning forked through the darkness, ash rained down upon the landscape and hot ash avalanches plunged down the mountainsides.

Water vapour condensed in the cloud over the crater and formed soft mud balls, some as large as hens' eggs. Finally, rain fell in torrents and streams of mud flowed across the surrounding country, causing great damage and some loss of life. Then, on 30 April, after $3\frac{1}{2}$ weeks of almost ceaseless activity, Vesuvius was quiet.

Before dealing with the mechanism of volcanic eruptions, it is necessary to have a general picture of the nature of the earth's interior. How such information is obtained is dealt with on page 172.

Broadly the composition of the continental part of the earth's surface is: at the top there is a thin covering of earth, sand and clay. Below this there is a layer of various kinds of rock, which have an average density and composition similar to that of granite. This granitic layer grades into another, which has the density and composition of basalt.

The average depth of the combined granitic and basaltic layers of the continents is about 20 miles, but is deeper under mountain ranges. Beneath these layers is the mantle, a great section of heavy rocks extending some 1,800 miles. Then there may be an outer core of molten nickel-iron 1,300 miles thick, surrounding an inner core of solid nickel-iron with a diameter of 850 miles. As yet this is very speculative, because the properties of materials at enormous pressures and high temperatures are by no means certain.

Beneath the oceans there is no granitic layer, only sediment up to half a mile thick which rests directly on the basaltic layer, which is 3–6 miles thick. The deepest hole ever drilled, a gas well in Oklahoma, is 5.95 miles. In terms of distance to the centre of the earth, this hole is the equivalent of a mosquito stinging an elephant!

Temperature increases steadily with depth, but there are wide variations in different places. Generally, a temperature of 100°C, the boiling point of water, is reached at about 10,000 feet. Despite the extremely high temperatures of the earth's interior, there is no liquid mass of fire at the heart of the earth as was once believed. With increase in depth there is also increase in pressure, and this is so great in the centre that it must keep the potentially molten rocks in a solid state.

Although in general the earth is believed to be solid rock for nearly 2,000 miles, there are pockets of partially liquid material (magma) which fuel volcanoes. By processes which are still not fully understood, the magma forces its way to the surface through conduits, resulting in a volcanic eruption. As far back in geological time as it is possible to go, volcanoes have lived and died, leaving their lava-strewn monuments across the face of the earth.

With few exceptions, the deep fractures in the crust which give rise to volcanoes (and many earthquakes) are today located in great chains along the margins of major plates (see page 158). Most land volcanoes are found in the Pacific Girdle of Fire (the margins of the Pacific), and in a chain running from the East Indies to the Mediterranean. Most oceanic volcanoes occur in a chain running north to south through the centre of the Atlantic Ocean, eastward across the southern Indian and Pacific Oceans, and along the eastern Pacific into the Gulf of California, with a major branch running through the Indian Ocean

Overleaf Curtain of fire formed by molten lava erupting from Hawaii's Kilauea's volcano in May 1969. The eruptions continued for five years, burying 10,000 acres and creating the new volcano Mauna Ulu. (US National Park Service)

Above *The cauliflower-shaped ash-cloud that formed over Vesuvius during the eruption of March 1944.* (US Navy)

Right *The graceful billowing cloud that towered miles above Vesuvius in the eruption of 1873.* (Goursat/Rapho)

into the Red Sea. Land volcanoes are most likely to occur where there are great variations in altitude: high mountains alongside deep oceans.

The above, together with pages 158–97, give a very simplified account of the earth's interior and the origins of earthquakes and volcanoes. Readers wanting more detailed information of the lithosphere (the earth's outer shell) and plate tectonics should refer to the technical books mentioned in the Bibliography, for example *The Cambridge Encyclopedia of Earth Sciences* edited by David G. Smith (1981).

Estimates vary, but probably not fewer than 500 volcanoes have been active in historic times. They may be dormant for many hundreds of years, then erupt. The volcanic island of Tristan da Cunha was dormant from its discovery in 1506, yet erupted in 1961 – after a known interval of 455 years.

As about three-quarters of the earth's surface is beneath the sea, it is virtually certain that there are many more volcanoes on the ocean floor than on land. Of these sea volcanoes, about 60 are known to have erupted within the last 200 years or so. Authorities differ in their views on the exact number of both land and sea volcanoes.

Today, active land volcanoes range from cones the size of a haystack to some of the loftiest mountains in the world. The matter ejected from a volcano consists of gas and either tiny rock particles (ash), liquid (lava) or solid rock, or a combination of these, varying with the volcano and type of eruption. Gas is always present, and some 20 different kinds have been detected; steam is the most abundant.

The forceful agent in a volcanic eruption is gas, especially steam. When water turns to vapour, its volume increases about 1,000 times. It is as if vast stores of dynamite were suddenly exploded inside the volcano. Sometimes the lava breaks through fissures at the sides of the volcano, rather than by flowing over the top.

Volcanic eruptions are complex phenomena and are therefore difficult to classify. They vary from a comparatively mild outflow of lava to tremendous violence. During the course of a single eruption, which sometimes lasts for weeks, or even months, there are frequently several types of activity. The classification most widely accepted appears to be that of Gordon A. Macdonald (1972). He lists ten types, the main ones of which are as follows.

Hawaiian: The discharge of streams of lava, with mildly explosive liberation of gas. The action is sometimes rapid, lava cascading down the sides of the crater at 25 mph.

The name for this phase derives from Hawaii, with its two active volcanoes, Mauna Loa and Kilauea. Mauna Loa is the greatest volcano in the world. Rising from a base over 70 miles wide on the ocean floor, it towers nearly 30,000 feet, 13,675 feet being above sea level. Its crater is not funnel-shaped like most volcanoes, but is a vast flat-floored cauldron (caldera) with vertical sides. When Mauna Loa erupts, great fountains of lava shoot upward, sometimes reaching a height of 1,000 feet. When the crater overflows, a torrent of lava pours down the volcano's sides in the typical Hawaiian phase of volcanic activity.

J.D. Dana wrote of an eruption of Mauna Loa: 'Its deep unearthly roar waxed louder and louder as we drew nearer the action, until it resembled the roar of the ocean's billows when driven by the force of a hurricane against a rock-bound coast, or like the deafening roar of Niagara.' He says that the intense heat (over 1,000°C) created

Overleaf above
Protected by a heat-resistant suit a scientist measures the temperature of lava. Once exposed to air the temperature drops rapidly. (Stephen Sparks)

Overleaf below
Old Faithful, America's most famous geyser, spouts steam and hot water 130-feet high in Yellowstone National Park, Wyoming. After each spout, which lasts for between two and five minutes, the geyser is quiet for about 70 minutes. (Susan W. Kieffer, US Geological Survey)

189

miniature tornadoes (whirlwinds?) which 'stalked about like so many sentinels, bidding defiance to the daring visitor'.

The immense temperatures of molten rock and other volcanic materials cannot, of course, be measured by ordinary thermometers. An approximate temperature can, however, be obtained by an optical pyrometer, an instrument used in steel furnaces to determine the heat of molten metal. By matching the colour of the object – steel or lava – against a scale on the pyrometer, a temperature reading is obtained. Thermocouples are widely used today: these measure temperatures below the surface. The greatest known temperature for lava is about 1,400°C, recorded at Vesuvius.

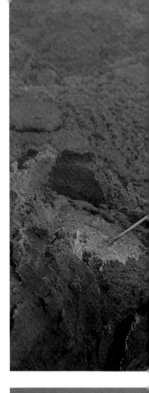

Strombolian: An intermittent but comparatively mild volcanic discharge. The name derives from Stromboli, in the Lipari Islands north of Sicily – 'The Lighthouse of the Mediterranean'. Stromboli has been continuously in action since before the dawn of human history. Mild explosions occur at the rate of one to 30 per hour, lava and gas being thrown into the air. John Harpum tells me: 'Volcanic bombs [lumps of lava] are very common on Stromboli. I have counted ten bombs in the space of two minutes, rolling down the side of the cone and hissing into the sea.'

Vulcanian: A much more explosive type of volcanic action. Magma gradually accumulates in the heart of the volcano over a period of years, the exposed lava at the top of the conduit acting as a plug which prevents it from erupting. When sufficient magma has accumulated at the base, the explosive gases and boiling lava burst the rocky plug and the volcano erupts. Masses of solid and liquid rock burst out, and great cauliflower-shaped clouds of vapour and ash form over the crater.

Plinian or *Vesuvian*: A violent outburst of magma highly charged with gas. (This chapter opened with a description of a typical Plinian eruption.) Violent Plinian eruptions sometimes culminate in a stupendous blast of gas which shoots miles into the stratosphere (see page 184). The name Plinian comes from Pliny the Younger, who first recorded such an outburst during an eruption of Vesuvius. The material from such eruptions reaches the jet streams, and is often carried great distances. Robin T. Holcomb of the United States Geological Survey tells me:

'One striking phenomenon is the shock wave that is occasionally seen propagating outward from the sources of various volcanic blasts of the Vulcanian, Vesuvian and Peléean types. These shock waves can be seen because of the changes they induce in the refractive index of air. The wave expanding outward at supersonic speeds can appear as a transparent sphere centered on the apex of the volcano. One I saw at Sakurajima Volcano in Japan expanded out and then appeared to reverse itself and contract back within a fraction of a second, followed by the oral and tactile sensations of the shock and the sudden rise of the eruption column. An unforgettable experience that few people have ever heard of.'

Icelandic or *Basaltic flood*: The discharge from fissures of great

volumes of fluid basaltic lava, which spread over the adjacent countryside, in some eruptions for thousands of square miles. The only examples of such flows in historic times have been in Iceland, which consists entirely of volcanic material, mostly basaltic lava.

One of the greatest Icelandic eruptions began on 8 June 1783. Tremendous explosions came from the area near Mount Laki, followed by vast ash clouds. The initial explosive phase was followed by an enormous outpouring of lava from many vents along a fissure 10 miles long: the total flow was estimated to be about 3 cubic miles, the greatest outpouring of lava in historic times.

The effects were disastrous. Most serious was a noxious haze which lay over the country during the summer, spoiling the grass and causing famine. The final cost to Iceland of this eruption was one-half of its cattle, three-fourths of its sheep and horses, and one-fifth (about 9,500) of its population.

During the colder stages of the Pleistocene Ice Age, Iceland was almost completely covered with an ice sheet over half a mile thick – and sometimes volcanoes erupted underneath. A faint idea of the shattering paroxysms which then occurred can be gathered from what happens today when there is an eruption beneath a glacier – a rare example of the meeting of fire and ice. The hot lava melts the ice for hundreds of feet deep, causing tremendous floods. During the violent eruption of Iceland's Mount Katla in 1918, water from melted glaciers reached a maximum flow of some 100,000 cubic yards per second. The maximum discharge of the Amazon, the greatest waterway in the world with a mouth 50 miles across and 150 feet deep, is not much greater than this.

Peléean: A highly dangerous form of eruption in which enormous clouds of superheated steam, charged with pulverised rock (*nuée ardente*), are ejected at high speed, often from the side of the volcano.

St Pierre was a prosperous town on the northwest coast of Martinique in the Caribbean. About 5 miles away was Mont Pelée, a volcano which had been quiet for 50 years but whose previous eruptions had clothed the countryside in rich volcanic ash, making the soil fertile for valuable sugar-cane plantations.

In April 1902 Pelée awakened. There were earthquake shocks and mild eruptions which dusted the streets. The activity increased, and by the end of the month Pelée had cleared its throat and was raining noxious ash on the town. On 5 May, a cataract of boiling mud coursed down the mountain at express-train speed and overwhelmed a sugar mill, killing 30 workmen.

Panic spread in St Pierre: some people left, and more made preparations to go. Then, during the night of 7 May, Pelée gave its final warning as the darkness was cleft by a magnificent display of natural fireworks. People stared in wonder. Some were frightened, and again prepared to leave; but others were thrilled by the brilliant spectacle, and stayed.

The next morning dawned bright and sunny; the only sign of activity on Mont Pelée was a huge vapour volume rising high into the heavens. At 7.50 a.m. an eruption burst from the main crater, and at the same instant the volcano's side opened with a roaring explosion. A vast black cloud shot out horizontally at tremendous speed. The other three rocky sides of Pelée formed the mouth of a gigantic cannon from which shot a bolt of superheated vapour, gas and white-hot fragments of molten rock. St Pierre was set ablaze from end to end almost instantaneously.[1]

At this moment, the ship *Pouyer-Quertier* was lying some 6 miles out to sea west of St Pierre. The crew saw two giant flashes from Pelée; then 'light appeared in the direction of St Pierre, and 30 seconds later the binoculars showed the town to be in flames. The whole flank of the mountain on the side towards St Pierre was glowing red.'

Most of St Pierre's 30,000 inhabitants were wiped out before they knew what hit them. One breath of that fiery cloud and a man's lungs shrivelled away. Some bodies, however, were found in positions indicating that an attempt had been made to flee.

After devastating St Pierre, the blast swept across the harbour. With the exception of two steamships, every craft in the harbour capsized and was totally wrecked. The steel masts of the steamer *Roraima* broke across their bases 2 feet above the deck, snapping off perfectly clean like clay-pipe stems struck with a stick. Her funnel, bridge and boats were swept away and tons of ash were deposited on her devastated decks; she was set ablaze fore and aft. Most of her crew, and all but two of her passengers, were killed. The other ship to survive, the *Roddam*, staggered out of the harbour with over 100 tons of volcanic ash on her decks. Ash fell on ships hundreds of miles out at sea, and on Barbados, 150 miles south of Pelée, an estimated *2 million* tons of ash rained down.

This vivid eye-witness account has been left by Assistant Purser Thompson of the *Roraima*:

'I saw St. Pierre destroyed. It was blotted out by one great flash of fire. Of 18 vessels lying in the Roads, only one, the British steamship *Roddam*, escaped, and she, I hear, lost more than half on board. It was a dying crew that took her out. Our boat arrived at St. Pierre early Thursday morning. For hours before we entered the roadstead, we could see flames and smoke rising from Mt. Pelée. No one on board had any idea of danger. Captain G. T. Muggah was on the bridge, and all hands got on deck to see the show. The spectacle was magnificent. As we approached St. Pierre, we could distinguish the rolling and leaping of the red flames that belched from the mountain in huge volumes and gushed high in the sky.

'Enormous clouds of black smoke hung over the volcano. The flames were then spurting straight up in the air, now and then waving to one side or the other a moment, and again leaping suddenly higher up. There was a constant muffled roar. It was like the biggest oil refinery in the world burning up on the mountain top.

'There was a tremendous explosion about 7.45, soon after we got in. The mountain was blown to pieces. There was no warning. The side of the volcano was ripped out, and there hurled straight toward us a solid wall of flame. It sounded like thousands of cannons. The wave of fire was on us and over us like a lightning flash. It was like a hurricane of fire, which rolled straight down upon St. Pierre and the shipping.

'The town vanished before our eyes, and then the air grew stifling hot and we were in the thick of it. Wherever the mass of fire struck the sea, the water boiled and sent up vast clouds of steam. I saved my

life by running to my stateroom and burying myself in the bedding. The blast of fire from the volcano lasted only a few minutes. It shrivelled and set fire to everything it touched. Burning rum ran in streams down every street and out into the sea. Before the volcano burst, the landings of St. Pierre were crowded with people. After the explosion not one living being was seen on land. Only 25 of those on the *Roraima*, out of 68, were left after the first flash. The fire wave swept off the ship's masts and smokestack as if they were cut with a knife.' (Quoted by L. Don Leet)

In the whole of the afflicted area some 30,000 people had been living. As far as could be ascertained, only 30 of these escaped death, and of these only four were uninjured. With one blast Pelée killed 30,000 people, sank 14 ships and incinerated 10 square miles of country.

Yet another horror was to come. Torrential rain swept tens of thousands of tons of volcanic ash down Pelée's slopes. A deluge of soft pasty mud cascaded into St Pierre, burying many houses to the rooftops. Rushing into the sea, it produced a small tidal wave which was felt at Fort de France, 12 miles away. Chief Officer Ellery S. Scott of the *Roraima* writes:

'After the stones came a rain of hot mud, lava apparently mixed with water, of the consistency of very thin cement. Wherever it fell it formed a coating, clinging like glue, so that those who wore no caps it coated, making a complete cement mask right over their heads.'

When the first rescue party eventually entered the town, a scene of unparalleled devastation met their eyes: just one vast heap of dirty blackened rubble. There were some remarkable examples of the effect of the volcanic whirlwind: 3-foot-thick walls of stone and cement blown down and torn to pieces, as though they had been children's bricks; century-old trees plucked from the ground, roots and all; heavy siege guns, 10 feet long, blown from their mountings; and a statue of the Virgin Mary, weighing 3 tons, flung some 50 feet from its pedestal. It has been estimated that a wind speed of some 300 mph would have been required to accomplish this last feat.

When the blast first shot from the volcano it was probably travelling at this speed. Peléean blasts are propelled by continuously expanding and exploding gas previously dissolved under pressure in the magma they carry with them.

The condition of some of the corpses gave a vivid impression of how death had come. Here was a clerk bending over a ledger, pen still in hand, frozen in the immobility of death. There was a man bent over a washbasin from which the water had evaporated. Some, who had evidently staggered a few steps, lay with contorted bodies, hands clutching at scalded mouths and throats.

Numerous bodies were found without a vestige of clothing. Many others had burst abdomens and split skulls, but with no other signs of injury; such wounds indicate that a sudden reduction in the surrounding air pressure had caused their bodies literally to explode. Two of the survivors on the *Roraima* said: 'While the blast lasted it was too hot to breathe much, and immediately afterward there seemed to be nothing

The 'Tower of Pelée': the 1,000-foot high rock spire that rose in the crater of Mont Pelée after the volcanic blast of 8 May 1902. It gradually disintegrated and finally disappeared in November 1904. (Lacombe)

we *could* breathe. We gasped as if in a vacuum, without being able to get anything that satisfied the lungs.'

A short while after the disaster, a young traveller, A. L. Koster, visited St Pierre to take the first photographs of the dead city. No date is given, but it was probably shortly after the second blast, on 20 May. He was particularly impressed by the complete silence, and the carpet of fine talcum-like powder that was almost everywhere. The ground was still so hot that it was uncomfortable to walk about.

'Evidence of terrific heat was everywhere. The bodies of victims strewn among the ruins were greatly reduced in size. It was as if most of the moisture had suddenly been extracted from them. But as they were not burned, and as trees and other pieces of wood were barely charred, I concluded that either the duration of the heat had been extremely brief or that the heat had failed to ignite anything because of an absence of oxygen . . . A tidal wave attending the blast drove sailing vessels ashore. Their masts had shrunk to a mere fraction of their original diameter inside the protective iron collars at deck level.'

One of St Pierre's few survivors (accounts vary from one to four) was a prisoner, a 25-year-old Negro named Auguste Ciparis who was trapped in the dungeon of the jail. The tiny window of his cell faced away from the volcano, and the massive stone walls of the prison resisted the heat and blast so effectively that he learned of the catastrophe only when he was rescued. For four days he waited, starving and terrified in his tiny underground cell. At last his cries for help were heard; he was rescued and lived to recount the story of his amazing escape. History contains none more marvellous. This fact did not escape the famous American showman, P. T. Barnum: he exhibited Ciparis as one of his circus curiosities.

The tragedy of St Pierre had one good result. It shocked the world into awareness of the importance of volcanology, and the importance of having trained watchers at dangerous volcanoes.

Hot clouds like those from Mont Pelée sometimes produce vast deposits of ash, as happened when the Novarupta volcano near Mount Katmai, Alaska, erupted during several days in June 1912. It was the greatest volcanic explosion of the 20th century, and left a permanent memorial – The Valley of Ten Thousand Smokes.

First, a column of ash and pumice was hurled 25 miles into the stratosphere. Then, from an area near the western foot of Mount Katmai, millions of tons of red-hot lava particles suspended in hot gases poured down the 15-mile-long valley. Pulverised rock covered an area of 42 square miles. Fortunately – unlike St Pierre – the surrounding country was barren and unpopulated. It is estimated that Mount Katmai ejected ten times more material than Pelée.

The tremendous hot blanket vaporised ground water, so that shortly after the eruption the whole floor of the valley was smoking with thousands of steam jets (fumaroles) – hence its name. The superheated steam from some fumaroles reached nearly 500°C, hot enough to melt zinc. Today the valley is part of Katmai National Monument, one of the largest national parks in the United States, comprising 4,215 square miles.

North America was the scene of one of the most widely publicised eruptions of all time: Mount St Helens, Washington, during May 1980. It was the 'Fujiyama of western America', a symmetrical mountain whose snow-clad dome thrust nearly 10,000 feet into the skies above the Cascade Range.

St Helens was known to be volcanic; it had last erupted in 1857. Then, for over a century, it was quiet, but on 20 March 1980 there was an earth tremor near the mountain: the first sign that St Helens was active again. Subterranean activity increased, accompanied by outbursts of dust and steam. By the middle of May, an ominous 300-foot-high bulge had built up on St Helens' northern flank, a sure sign of tremendous pressures inside the volcano. Then, between 8 a.m. and 9 a.m. on Sunday 18 May 1980, the top of St. Helens exploded in an eruption with the energy equivalent of 10 million tons of TNT – 500 Hiroshimas.

The final trigger was an earthquake. The bulging flank broke and slid northward as a giant landslide. With the confining pressure thus removed, gas and pulverised rock blasted from the side of the mountain. As from the mouth of some gigantic cannon, St Helens hurled millions of tons of ash and burning rock, some travelling at 230 mph at northwest Washington State. A geologist, monitoring the volcano from an observation post on a ridge 5 miles away, shouted into his microphone: 'This is it!' Then the fiery avalanche swept him and his observation post into oblivion. The farthest destructive reach of this fan-shaped blast was 17 miles.[2]

There were two blasts: one from the base of the landslide, another near its head. These were followed by a Plinian column, from the base of which pyroclastic flows (rapidly moving masses of rocky fragments) swept across the devastated landscape. Nearly every living thing in an area of some 230 square miles was annihilated. The total amount lost from the mountain, in blast and landslide, was in the region of 1 cubic mile.

The destructive phenomena of St Helens were not confined to volcanic debris; there were also floods and mudflows formed by melting snow and ice from the mountain.[3] Racing across the ravaged land at speeds of up to 50 mph, the muddy tide, coarsened by volcanic and other debris which it swept up in its passage, smothered or swept away trucks, bulldozers, cabins, railcars and bridges. It choked rivers so that they overtopped their banks, and spread a carpet of destructive mud for hundreds of yards on either side.

Bare facts indicate the enormous destruction that the eruption caused: 153 miles of trout and salmon streams obliterated, along with 26 lakes; 1–2 million birds, mammals and fish killed; economic loss estimated at 1,000 million dollars; the landscape permanently altered.

The most spectacular effect was on the thick forest of trees which stretched for many miles to the north. St Helens' superheated windstorm felled trees, some of them 17 feet in diameter, as easily as a child blows down matchsticks; they were either snapped off just above the ground, or wrenched clean out. In the area of the blast 130,000 acres of trees were felled, representing about 3,700 million board feet (1 board foot = the cubic content of a piece of wood 1 foot square and 1 inch thick), enough to build a quarter of a million houses.

Estimates of what these figures mean in terms of individual trees necessarily vary, but it is virtually certain that not fewer than 6 million mature trees were felled or seriously damaged. It is not possible to estimate the number of smaller trees affected because they vary greatly in numbers per acre. Many of the larger ones have been salvaged; St Helens performed the biggest logging operation of all time!

The human death-toll was 35, with a further 25 missing. Fortunately the eruption occurred on a Sunday, otherwise 330 loggers would have perished when the hurricane of incandescent ash levelled the forests where they worked.

Very few people lived in the area covered by the eruption; if it had been densely populated, there could have been the greatest catastrophe in American history.

Such were the effects in the immediate vicinity of the volcano, but one result of the eruption affected areas many hundreds of miles away – and lasted for days. St Helens shot a 12-mile-high plume of volcanic ash into the atmosphere – millions of tons of finely pulverised rock. This vast cloud created its own weather as lightning flickered through its darkness, followed by roll after roll of thunder. The sun was blotted out, turning midday into midnight. The ash was carried by winds across the continent to the Atlantic Ocean; then, in ever-attenuated form, it circled the globe in 17 days, carried by 8-mile-high winds and jet streams.

Aeroplanes and trains were affected because of poor visibility, and some operations were cancelled; pilots reported damage to engines, wings and windshields. In places hundreds of miles from the volcano people had to wear face masks and goggles in attempts – not always successful – to keep at bay the abrasive grey ash. Many cars stalled, their air filters clogged by the all-invading particles.

Viewed from an aeroplane, the whole landscape north of St Helens was a realm of almost total grey, a lunar landscape. When President Carter flew over the area, four days after the initial eruption, he said: 'The moon looks like a golf course compared to what's up there.' In places near the volcano the ash was 4 feet deep. On Yakima, some 100 miles east of St Helens, there was an ashfall estimated at 600,000 tons. Five hundred miles away, in eastern Montana, it was half an inch deep in places, quite enough to make life decidedly uncomfortable.

Some idea of what it was like to live with the ash may be gauged from the following quotation from a publication produced by the newspaper of the region, *The Columbian*:

> 'Even when the mountain wasn't erupting, the ash was everywhere, kicked up by traffic and continually blown about by the wind.
>
> When it rained during an ashfall, the powder and moisture combined to make a muddy substance that defied windshield wipers and window cleaners. Homeowners swept or washed the stuff from sidewalks and houses, only to find them coated again with more windblown material.
>
> Homeowners were urged to remove heavy amounts of ash off flat or low-pitched roofs; otherwise they might buckle under the weight. People were advised to stay indoors during heavy ashfalls. If they had to venture outdoors they should wear surgical masks, or at least hold a wet cloth over mouth and nose. If ash came in contact with skin it should be rinsed off with plenty of water, not just wiped off.'

It was reports of the human toll from the dust that revived the use of the longest non-nonce word in the English language: pneumonoultramicroscopicsilicovolcanoconiosis. These 45 letters mean the disease caused by inhaling contaminated air. Disastrous as it was, the ashfall was not however a total loss. Typical of American enterprise, a thriving cottage industry soon developed in marketing the ash. One sign that greeted the army of sightseers which flocked into the area advertised 'St. Helens dust 50c gal', with a warning 'Don't be fooled by subsitutes [*sic*].' One of the most original ideas was to fill tiny glass phials with the ash to hang on necklaces and ear-rings.

Although disastrous enough, the 1980 eruption of St Helens ranks low in the volcanic league table. Based on the estimated amount of airborne ash and pumice (light porous rock) ejected, Katmai (1912) rates 12, Krakatoa (1883) 18, and Tambora (1815) 80. St Helens rates 1. (A series of publications on St Helens has been issued by the United States Geological Survey.)

Nearly two years after Mount St Helens erupted, another long-dormant North American volcano awoke. On 28 March 1982 Mexico's El Chichón began erupting, culminating in a massive outpouring of ash and gases on 4 April. Because El Chichón's blasts were directed skyward, it pumped some ten times as much debris into the stratosphere as did St Helens, where the blasts were mainly horizontal. El Chichón expelled an estimated 500 million tons of ash and gases, some of which soared 20 miles above the earth.

The St Helens eruption received far more publicity than El

Heimaey's Landakirkja church silhouetted against fountaining lava. The foreshortening effect of the telephoto lens makes the danger more apparent than real. (Sigurgeir Jónasson)

Chichón's, but it was the latter that had the greatest effect on the world's weather. Robert I. Tilling says: 'Atmospheric scientists report that its volcanic cloud is the largest observed in the Northern Hemisphere in seven decades. To find its equal one has to go back to the 1912 eruption of Katmai in Alaska.' The sunlight-screening debris affects solar radiation, thus reducing temperature; although this reduction is slight, it could noticeably change the weather, possibly for three years after the eruption.

The greatest volume of matter ejected from a volcano within historic times is believed to be about 36 cubic miles: from the eruption of Tambora, Indonesia, on 5–7 April 1815. During the tremendous explosions the volcano lost 3,700 feet in height and a crater 7 miles in diameter was formed. A vast ash cloud turned day into night for hundreds of miles around the volcano, darkness which lasted for three days, as on the island of Madura, 310 miles away.

To witness the birth of a volcano is one of the rarest of all human experiences. A few people have had that privilege, although I doubt if one of them, a Mexican peasant named Dionisio Pulido, would use that word. The volcano was born in his field and eventually destroyed it, together with the surrounding countryside.

At about 4 o'clock on the afternoon of 20 February 1943, Pulido was in his field when he noticed a fissure about 2 feet long. Soon the field trembled, as though a giant hand deep in the earth was shaking it. Then sulphurous smoke arose, accompanied by hissing; sparks came from the fissure and pine trees 100 feet away began to burn. Pulido hurriedly left.

Soon watchers came from several miles away, attracted by the plume of smoke. The fissured hole was now a tiny pear-shaped crater which was erupting ash, sparks and stones, while a choking odour pervaded the area. The ground was 'jumping up and down'. The incipient volcano's activity rapidly increased. By midnight it was hurling huge incandescent rocks into the air with thunderous roars, and a dense pillar of ash was lit with lightning flashes.

When Pulido arrived at 8 o'clock the next morning, the upstart which had taken over his field was a true volcanic cone, 35 feet high. Fumes, incandescent rocks and debris were belching out, causing the cone to grow to over 100 feet by midday. The first lava issued the same day. On the evening of the third day, 22 February, the first volcanologist – Ezequiel Ordonez – arrived, and from then on the new volcano was under constant scientific observation until its activity ceased, nine years later. It was named Parícutin after the village it soon overwhelmed. So great was the rain of ash that a year later it was difficult to realise that a village had ever existed there.

Parícutin grew rapidly. In a week it was 550 feet high and throwing up masses of viscous lava with a thunder heard over 100 miles away. During the first few months it was estimated to be ejecting solid material – lava, cinders and ash – at an average rate of some 2,400 tons a minute, about $3\frac{1}{2}$ million tons every 24 hours. In addition, thousands of tons of steam were discharged every day. In the first seven months, about 2,000 million cubic yards of solid material fell on the surrounding countryside.

The great rain of volcanic material ejected from Parícutin ruined the countryside over an area some 35 miles in diameter, and depopulat-

Opposite above
Many buildings on Heimaey were inundated by the ash which rained down from the volcano. (Sigurgeir Jónasson)

Below *At about 8.40 a.m. on 18 May 1980 the photographer, his wife and pilot were in a light aeroplane near St Helens. As they watched the north face began to 'ripple and churn'. They turned away – just in time. As they looked back they saw the rapidly expanding ash-cloud gaining on them. They took this photograph then dived to gain speed and landed safely in Portland.* (Keith Staffel/Keith Ronnholm)

ed 300 square miles. Everything within a radius of 5 miles of the cone was blanketed with volcanic ash, like black snow, 1–9 feet thick. Lois Mattox Miller, who flew over the area, says:

> 'I first noticed its devastating effects 75 miles away. Black ashes shroud once-green valleys and mountain sides. Gardens and orchards have vanished. Church spires stick up, half buried under a mountain of slag. Springs have gone dry and the river Cupatitzo is now a slow-moving stream of mud.
>
> 'Not a green thing, not a blade of grass, is alive in an area of 100 square miles. Fifty miles away, tender crops wither and only the hardier growth, the trees and shrubs, still lives. The disaster has brought complete desolation to seven villages and damage to many others. Vegetation on the fertile farmlands withers and dies wherever the shifting winds spread a blanket of ashes. Birds drop lifeless from the skies. Water is scarce, for the springs have gone dry.'

Parícutin had a wide repertoire of sounds. In its milder phases it spoke with the roar of a heavy surf breaking on the shore; but when it hurled molten rock 3,000 feet into the air it was as if a score of battleships had fired broadsides simultaneously. A few moments after each violent explosion, there was the noise as of sporadic rifle-fire, the spatter of the ejected rocks falling back on the volcano's slopes.

Vast billowing ash clouds poured from the crater and swirled upward like a giant multicoloured cauliflower stuck in the volcano's mouth. Black, grey, steam-white, sometimes coloured yellowish-red from the glow of molten lava, and lightened by the darts of lightning and 'flashing arcs', this immense plume towered 4 miles above the volcano's summit.

A hail of volcanic bombs frequently shot thousands of feet into the air. At first they were liquid and solidified in the air, but later they were solid red-hot spheres. Parker D. Trask says that they varied in size from that of a walnut to a big house: one was 50 feet in diameter. A bomb 4 feet in diameter landed 25 feet from where he was standing and buried itself in the ground, the top being 1 foot beneath the surface. Another small bomb broke a large oak limb before burying itself 3 feet in the ground.

Although *El Monstruo*, as the Indian peasants called the 'fire monster' in their midst, wrought great destruction, it also brought its compensations. Some of the peasants profited from the thousands of sightseers, and Pulido had at least one offer to buy Parícutin.

To the volcanologist, Parícutin presented the chance of a lifetime to study a volcano almost from the day of its birth. In July 1944, the 'United States Committee for the Study of Parícutin Volcano' was formed to integrate the study of the eruption and its various effects. Parícutin's action was Vulcanian of the most vigorous type. For about a year its activity was almost continuous.

Parícutin finally blew itself out on 4 March 1952 after nine years and 12 days of almost ceaseless activity. It was then 1,500 feet high, having ejected an estimated 3,000 million tons of solid matter.

Although volcanoes on land are obviously the best known, those beneath the sea sometimes make headlines throughout the world.

Early on the morning of 14 November 1963, near the Vestmann Islands, Iceland, men on a fishing vessel saw a red glow just above the sea surface and thought that it was a ship on fire. It was in fact the volcanic birth of the island Surtsey. After two days it was 120 feet high and 1,500 feet long; a week later 300 feet high and half a mile long. It was belching out a 5-mile-high column of steam, ash and fumes, capped with a mushroom-shaped cloud. The Vestmann Islanders stopped work to stand and stare, and school-children were given a holiday to see 'a land of fire' rising newborn from the sea.

The volcano ejected rocks with tremendous force. Robert Anderson says that the crew of an aeroplane which flew over it at about 6,000 feet saw rocks whiz past them, which indicates an initial speed of about 400 mph. At times during the first month, half a million tons were ejected every hour: no wonder that the volcanic island rapidly consolidated itself. When activity finally stopped in 1967, Surtsey – named after the Norse god of fire – covered an area of some 2 miles.

The Icelandic government has declared the island a scientific preserve, administered by the Surtsey Research Society. This rugged and empty land provides an unprecedented natural laboratory on which scientists can observe creation begun anew.

Volcanic islands are a cartographer's nightmare, for some of them appear, disappear, and then rise again. Falcon Island, near Tonga in the Southwest Pacific, was known as a reef in the 18th century. In 1867 the sea in the area became unexpectedly shallow, and seamen passing near saw 'smoke' rising from it. In 1885 an island arose on the site, attaining a height of about 250 feet, but the sea gradually eroded it until, in 1899, Falcon Island was no more. In 1927, however, there was an eruption which built a cone 300 feet high and 3 miles in circumference. Falcon Island was once more on the map. It stayed above the waves until March 1949. Since then it has not been seen again, but by the time this book is published the cartographers may once again be reaching for their pens.

Volcanic eruptions have, at times, affected world weather. Three eruptions took place in 1812, 1814 and 1815 (Tambora). The clouds of ash released by these were so vast that they prevented an appreciable amount of the sun's heat from reaching the earth. The year 1816 was known as 'the year without a summer', and has been called 'Eighteen Hundred and Froze to Death'. In some parts of the United States, 6 inches of snow fell in June; people wore overcoats and gloves in July and a temperature of 37°F was registered in August. The summer of that year was filled with freakish weather, 100°F one day, snow storms the next – almost!

The weather in the immediate area of a volcano is created largely by the effects of the eruption: heat, gases and the great volume of ash. In all violent eruptions there are thunderstorms with brilliant lightning, hail and heavy rain. The great heat in some also causes whirlwinds. During the great eruption of Tambora in April 1815, very powerful whirlwinds formed. They snatched up men, horses, cattle and anything movable. The largest trees were torn out of the ground by the roots and whirled into the air. For several days the surrounding seas were littered with trees and branches.

Volcanic ash in the atmosphere is responsible for brilliant red sunsets and sunrises. As the sun's rays pass obliquely through the dusty upper air, the shorter wavelengths of light are blocked, leaving a preponderance of the longer, reddish waves. Edward Whymper has given a remarkable account of this prism effect of volcanic ash. On 3 July 1880, he and his party were camped on Chimborazo, 16,000 feet above sea level and about 60 miles from the Andean volcano Cotopaxi when it suddenly erupted.

'Several hours elapsed before the ash commenced to intervene between the sun and ourselves, and when it did so we witnessed effects which simply amazed us. We saw a green sun, and such a green as we have never, either before or since, seen in the heavens. We saw smears or patches of something like verdigris-green in the sky, and they changed to equally extreme blood-red, or to coarse brick-dust reds, and they in an instant passed to the colour of tarnished copper or shining brass.' (Quoted by G. J. Symons)

Despite the death and destruction they cause, volcanoes have their blessings for mankind. Peter Francis, in his book *Volcanoes*, has a chapter entitled 'Volcanoes as money-makers'.

Volcanic ash helps to replace eroded topsoil, and the soil resulting from the decomposition of volcanic materials is extremely fertile. Some of the world's most beautiful and fertile areas, such as the Caribbean chain of islands and the Hawaiian area, have been built by volcanic action. Java is a volcanic island and, although only the size of New York State, is so fertile that it supports some 70 million people – about three times the population of New York.

The extreme fineness of volcanic ash makes it an ideal polishing and cleansing agent. Valuable chemical products are obtained from volcanic substances, including gold and silver. The Kimberley 'pipe' in South Africa, which has produced such a wealth of diamonds, is the conduit of an ancient volcano.

Several attempts have been made to harness volcanic energy. With the ever-growing need for power, volcanoes and their by-products are of increasing value, especially in areas where conventional sources of power are lacking. It is likely that in the 1980's several countries will obtain energy from the immense heat of the earth. As drilling and other techniques improve, it will be practicable to bore the several miles necessary to reach hot rocks. Already it has proved possible to pump cold water down one bore hole and receive it back through another at a temperature of 160°C.

Iceland, Italy, New Zealand and California make practical use of volcanic steam. One advantage is that the supply is virtually inexhaustible: magma is heated from below and cools so slowly that it still supplies steam thousands of years after the original eruption. Ninety per cent of the houses in Reykjavik, Iceland's capital, are heated by natural steam. The first power plant in the United States to be operated by this method was opened in 1960 in Sonoma County, California.

To the scientist, volcanoes provide firsthand evidence of the composition of the earth, while geographers and geologists learn much from their distribution and structure. On the credit side also must surely be the terrible beauty of a volcano in action: the most tremendous natural spectacle on earth. An erupting volcano in full

Below and overleaf top *Dream turned nightmare. The St Helens eruption turned one of the most beautiful areas in North America into a lifeless desert. President Carter's verdict was: 'The moon looks like a golf course compared*

to what's up there'. Both photographs were taken about eleven miles from the crater. (Roland V. Emetaz. USDA Forest Service), (Roland V. Emetaz and James W. Hughes. USDA Forest Service)

blast is literally 'the greatest show on earth', and adds immeasurably to our heritage of natural wonders. When watchers saw Parícutin shoot a spectacular display of volcanic fireworks into the sky, they broke into an involuntary cheer.

In view of their devastating results, much thought has been given to forecasting volcanic eruptions. With active volcanoes prediction is relatively easy: small earth tremors, easily detectable by seismographs, almost invariably precede an eruption. Sometimes, however, with no warning, a volcano long thought to be extinct suddenly erupts. The one on Tristan da Cunha had been quiescent since the discovery of the island in 1506, yet on 9 October 1961 it erupted with such violence that the whole population had to be evacuated.

Volcanoes within range of dense populations are monitored. In addition to seismographs, there are tilt-meters which measure deformations of the surface: a frequent prelude to volcanic activity. Magnetometers detect changes in the magnetic field, another precurser of an eruption. Volcano prediction, however, is still far from an exact science. In the summer of 1976, the volcano of La Soufrière on Guadeloupe showed such definite signs of a major eruption that everybody within 6 miles was compulsorily evacuated. After this La Soufrière caused a few flashes and bangs and then subsided. (*The Journal of the Geological Society*, London, published several articles on volcano prediction in May 1979.)

This chapter is concerned primarily with volcanic activity in the past few centuries, but the earth bears witness to ancient eruptions which dwarf anything experienced by modern man. George P. L. Walker, who has made a special study of ancient volcanic eruptions, has recounted what happened when the New Zealand volcano Taupo erupted some 2,000 years ago. The evidence is the volcanic debris still embedded in the earth.

First, a Plinian eruption blasted gas and liquid rock some 30 miles into the stratosphere. An immense mushroom-shaped cloud of volcanic ash blotted out the sun, and there was an ashfall of millions of tons over 1,000 square miles. From the sides of Taupo a vast mass of red-hot ash suspended in hot gases swept across the surrounding countryside. The all-destroying wave is estimated to have been 100 yards high and to have poured out ash and gas at a rate of 1 million cubic yards *a second*. This fiery avalanche filled valleys, overtopped hills, obliterated forests, and was stopped in its northern course only when it reached the Bombay Hills, about 200 miles from Taupo. Its track was marked by a featureless smoking desert which can still be traced today.

Such was the eruption of Taupo two millenia ago, but studies reveal that far greater ones, both in magnitude and violence, have occurred in prehistory. Although this chapter ends with a description of the greatest volcanic eruption of the past 3,000 years, on Krakatoa, Stephen Sparks tells me that this was dwarfed by one on Sumatra which he estimates was some 50 times greater: 'probably the greatest volcanic eruption yet documented from the geologically recent past, about 75,000 years ago'.

Even further back in prehistory, there have been still greater eruptions than either Taupo or Sumatra. About 6 million years ago, the whole of the 88,000-square-mile Columbia River plateau in the Pacific Northwest, North America, was buried 100 feet deep in very fluid magma. There is also evidence of ancient ash flows depositing *250* cubic miles of sandy ash. These super volcanic outbreaks could happen again, a sobering thought (*Volcano*, Time-Life Books, 1982).

Various explanations have been given for the Biblical plagues of Egypt. It has been speculated that they were the result of the great eruption of Santorini, a crescent-shaped island in the Aegean Sea. Radio-carbon dating places the eruption at about 1,500 BC.

From brief descriptions and allusions in ancient writings, from the archaeology of the area, studies of the volcanic remains and know-ledge of volcanic behaviour, it is possible to reconstruct a little of that vast explosion in the dawn of Mediterranean civilisation. Several cubic miles of rock were blasted into the air, and ash and volcanic debris carpeted the earth for tens of thousands of square miles. A vast wall of water, hundreds of feet high at first, surged out from Santorini to swamp islands and all the shorelines of the eastern Mediterranean. The Biblical references to ruined crops, violence in the skies, blood-red waters, pestilence and 'thick darkness, even darkness which may be felt' could result from a vast rain of volcanic ash (J. G. Bennett). It has been suggested that the spectacular parting of the waters, which saved the Israelites but engulfed their pursuers, was the result of a vast tidal wave from Santorini.

Little is known about Santorini, much about Krakatoa. Its eruption in 1883 was the subject of some of the most intensive scientific studies ever accorded a single natural phenomenon. R. D. M. Verbeek wrote a two-volume study in Dutch. The chief British contribution was the Report of the Krakatoa Committee of the Royal Society, published in

Left *Part of the enormous ash-cloud that rose twelve miles above the crater and, in ever attenuated form, circled the earth in 17 days. At Yakima, 100 miles east of St Helens, the ashfall was about half a million tons.* (Keith Ronnholm)

1888. It was edited by G. J. Symons and has chapters by various experts, collating a vast mass of worldwide observations on every aspect of the subject; it runs to over 500 pages and is replete with diagrams, charts, maps and both black-and-white and colour illustrations.

The thoroughness with which this work was done can be gathered from the statement in the Preface: 'We have not only collected the facts, but have done our utmost to enable everyone to verify them.' To this fine monument, not only to the most violent explosion in 3,000 years but also to Victorian science in Britain, all writers on Krakatoa are deeply indebted. Although there is no doubt about the fact of the eruption, there is controversy about some of the details. I shall deal only with the major features, which have been frequently described. More is still being learnt about the eruption, as the findings of the international congress on Krakatoa, held in its centenary year, show.

Krakatoa is a small volcanic island in the Sunda Strait, midway between Java and Sumatra. When it exploded on 27 August 1883, it made its mark in one form or another on every one of earth's 197 million square miles. Krakatoa is in the centre of the area of the earth's greatest volcanic activity. At some unknown period, judging by the effects produced, it had exploded with even greater violence than in 1883; and in May 1680 it erupted and destroyed the rich tropical forests that covered the island. From then until 1883, Krakatoa was inactive.

On the morning of 20 May 1883 booming sounds, like heavy artillery fire, were heard in Batavia (now Djakarta) and Buitzenzorg (now Bogor), 100 miles from Krakatoa. For many hours, doors and windows rattled in these towns and in neighbouring villages. The commander of the German warship *Elisabeth* noticed an ash column rising from Krakatoa, which he estimated to be about 7 miles high. Ash fell 300 miles from the volcano, and for miles around the air was heavy with sulphurous fumes which blackened the brasswork of ships passing through the Strait. After these premonitory rumblings Krakatoa was quiet, but further rumblings and minor eruptions occurred in June and July; several new craters formed, and fresh vents appeared in the main crater.

On 26 August the first of a series of explosions began which, with short intervals, were to culminate in the final paroxysm. Several observations were made about this time by members of ships' crews in or near the Sunda Strait. At 2 p.m., Captain Thomson of the *Medea*, 76 miles from Krakatoa, saw 'a black mass rising up like smoke' to an estimated height of 17 miles. At sunset, Captain Wooldridge of the *Sir Robert Sale* described the sky as presenting 'a most terrible appearance, the dense mass of clouds being covered with a murky tinge, with fierce flashes of lightning'.

All the eye-witnesses refer to the splendour of the electrical phenomena during this 'curtain raiser' to the grand finale. A ship lying 45 miles from Krakatoa was struck by lightning five or six times on the mainmast conductor. A rain of phosphorescent mud covered masts, rigging and deck. Some of the crew tried to extinguish this fire because they thought that it was the work of evil spirits trying to scuttle the ship. 'Our ship looked as if we had been through a shower of mustard' was the comment of another witness.

Robert James Dalby, who was on a ship near Krakatoa, commentated in his journal on a pre-eruption phenomenon that I have

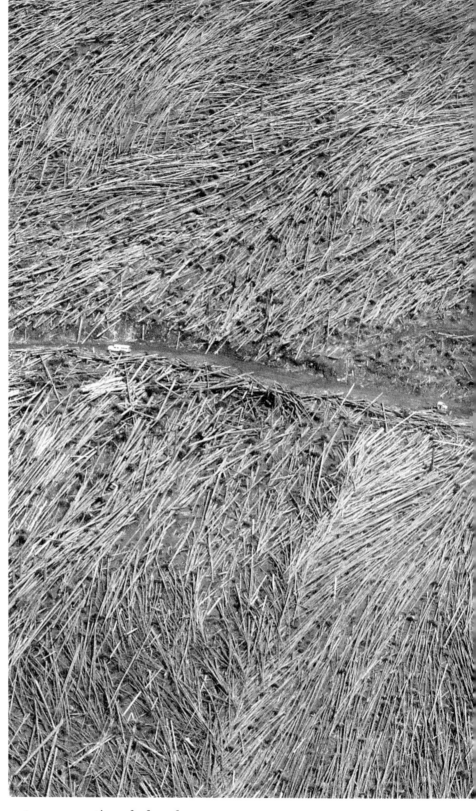

Scattered like straw, mature trees that towered 150-feet were flattened by the millions of tons of ash and burning rock blasted from the volcano. Trees 17 miles away were destroyed. The total: at least six million mature trees felled or seriously damaged, plus countless 'immatures'. (Stephen Sparks)

not seen mentioned elsewhere.

'The gusts of wind increased to such a hurricane as no man had ever experienced before. The wind seemed a solid mass thrusting

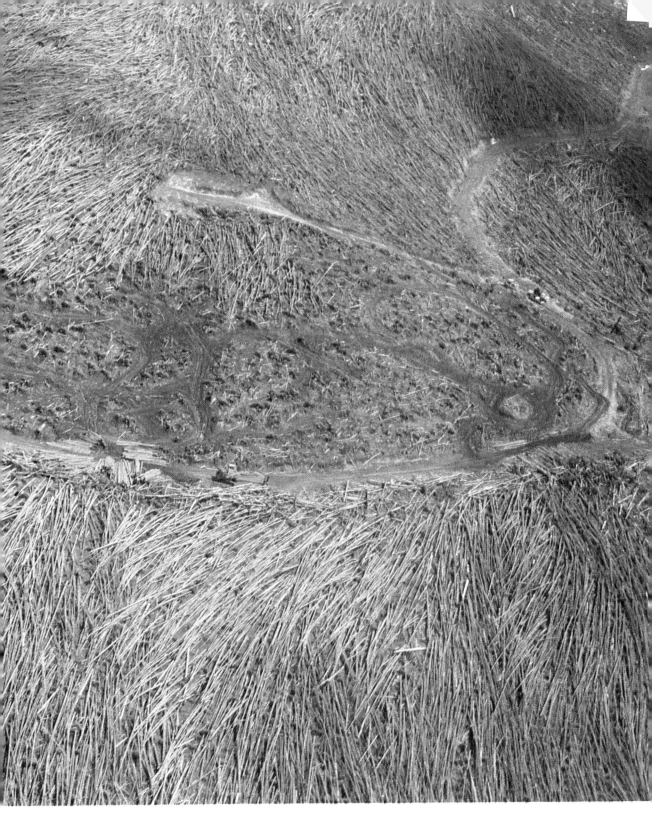

everything before it, and roaring like an enormous engine and
shrieking through the rigging like a demon in torment . . . When we
could get a glimpse of the heavens we could see there a terrible
commotion: the clouds whirled around at terrific speed, and I think

most of us thought that we were in the vortex of a cyclone [tornado?].' (*Sunday Times* Magazine, 21 August 1983)

Presumably the intense heat caused the windstorm.

Shortly before 10 a.m. on the 27th all was comparatively still – but not for long. At two minutes past 10, in a roaring cataclysm of noise, a huge maelstrom of magma, rock and ash blasted into the stratosphere, some of it shooting 50 miles high. Four cubic miles were ejected. In a few seconds the bulk of the 2,600-foot-high volcanic mountain vanished.[4] As a result of his on-the-spot investigations within a few weeks of the eruption, Verbeek considered that when Krakatoa erupted it ejected the magma from a large but shallow chamber beneath the volcano. Much of Krakatoa collapsed into this now empty cavity.

The violence of these literally earth-shaking convulsions triggered a series of tsunami which caused far more devastation than the eruption itself. A vast wall of water, several hundred feet high, shot out in all directions, sweeping across the Sunda Strait at 350 mph. It knocked down lighthouses like matchsticks. Bursting upon the nearby coasts of Sumatra and Java, the monstrous wave, now about 100 feet high, caused immense damage and loss of life along a shoreline of hundreds of miles. Along the shallow shore at Merak, Java, the wave was estimated to be 130 feet high – as tall as a 12-storey building. Altogether, 295 villages and towns were inundated, 3,000 ships destroyed, at least 36,000 people killed (some estimates give much higher figures).

Racing across the Indian and Pacific Oceans with undiminished speed (judging by time and distance, it must have been over 400 mph in some directions), tsunami hit far-distant shores. In the Strait of Surabaya, 500 miles from Krakatoa, tidal gauges were lifted 10 inches. In Port Elizabeth, South Africa, 5,000 miles away, ships were rocked at anchor. According to some reports, the effects of the wave were noted in the English Channel, 11,000 miles away on the other side of the world.

The blast of air from the explosion burst windows and cracked walls in Batavia and Buitenzorg, 100 miles distant. A gasometer, hit by a terrific gust, jumped out of its well. At even greater distances, cracks were made in walls by the impact of this violent air wave.

Krakatoa caused the mightiest noise on record. The thunder was deafening in Java, Sumatra and Borneo, 500 and more miles away. In the Celebes, nearly 1,000 miles away, it was so loud that two ships were sent out to make a reconnaissance. At Daly Waters, Australia, 2,023 miles away, an observer reported: 'On Sunday, the 26th, at midnight, we were awakened by an explosion resembling the blasting of a rock, which lasted for a few minutes.'

On Rodriguez Island, nearly 3,000 miles from Krakatoa, the chief of police recorded 'the distant roar of heavy guns, coming from the eastward'. A Rodriguez coastguard also noted the sound and his detailed note leaves no doubt that it came from Krakatoa. It had taken the sound waves four hours to reach the island. (The theoretical distance for which a one-megaton explosion can be heard is 100 miles.)

Sound travels much better over sea than over land, but it is interesting to envisage such distances in more familiar terms. If Krakatoa had been Pike's Peak, Colorado, the sound would have been heard throughout the Continental United States, from Alaska to Florida. Had it been Vesuvius, the sound would have been heard from the Arctic Circle to the equator, from Siberia to mid-Atlantic. Altogether, Krakatoa was heard across one-thirteenth of the entire surface of the globe – 15 million square miles.

The great mass of volcanic ash injected into the atmosphere at the time of the eruption was carried around the world by jet streams, eventually settling on every sea and country on earth. Some of the dust remained in the atmosphere for years. This dust caused strange optical phenomena and brilliant sunsets. Blue, green, copper- and silver-coloured suns and moons were seen. Owing to the great height to which the dust cloud was carried (some estimates say 50 miles), it reflected sunlight long after darkness would normally have fallen on earth.

The amazing sunsets were Krakatoa's special glory. The dusty haze produced gorgeous hues, and rose-coloured twilights that lasted an hour or more after the sun had set. Men realised that the old European chroniclers may not have been drawing on their imaginations overmuch when they wrote of blood-red skies following the earlier eruption of Krakatoa in 1680.

Descriptions by many observers of these sunsets, together with coloured drawings, are given in the Royal Society Report on the eruption. Here is a description of sunset at New Caledonia, Southwest Pacific, on 6 January 1884, nearly five months after the eruption:

'As soon as the sun's disc has disappeared, a glow comes up from the west like that of white-hot steel, reddening somewhat as it mounts to the zenith, but changing the while to blue. From the zenith it passes into the most exquisite green, deepening as it loses itself in the east. As the sun sinks lower and lower, the red tints overpower the white-hot steel tints, and the blue of the zenith those of the green.

'At 7 p.m., or a little after, nearly the entire western half of the horizon has changed to a fiery crimson: as time goes on, the northern and southern areas lose their glory, and the greys of night contract, from the northern end first, most rapidly; the east is of the normal grey. The south now closes in, and presently, about 8 p.m., there is only a glare in the sky, just over the sun's path, as of a distant conflagration, till the fire in the west dies out . . .'

Thus throughout the world the curtain fell slowly on this mighty spectacle in a literal blaze of glory.

NOTES

1. Stored in the town were numerous casks of rum. These exploded, and ran in blazing torrents through the streets.
2. Holcomb tells me that one blast 'became airborne some distance out from the volcano and travelled far out beyond the limit of tree destruction, to be dissipated in the air and drop its load of ash as air-fall deposits. Tree branches apparently fell on Mt Adams, 30 miles to the east.' The 17-mile figure pertains merely to the limit of tree destruction.
3. The water thus produced has been estimated at 50,000 million gallons.
4. What remained of the island was covered with a blanket of powdered debris several hundred feet thick, yet by the turn of the century trees were growing and rats, snakes and lizards were populating what was left of Krakatoa.

Conversion Tables

1 inch	= 2.5400 centimetres	1 cubic foot	= 0.02832 cubic metre
1 foot	= 0.3048 metre	1 cubic yard	= 0.7646 cubic metre
1 yard	= 0.9144 metre		
1 mile	= 1.6093 kilometres	1 ounce	= 28.3495 grams
		1 pound	= 0.45359 kilogram
1 square inch	= 6.452 square centimetres	1 ton	= 1.01605 tonnes (1,000 kilogrammes)
1 square foot	= 0.0929 square metre		
1 square yard	= 0.8361 square metre	(Celsius × 9/5) + 32	= Fahrenheit
1 square mile	= 2.5900 square kilometres	(Fahrenheit − 32) × 5/9	= Celsius

Bibliography

In general, abbreviations of periodicals follow the *World List of Scientific Periodicals*. References are not repeated where they occur in General Works. The bibliography of *The Elements Rage* (1966) contains some 1,000 entries, most of which are not listed here.

For current references to all meteorological subjects see:
GEO Abstracts: Part B: Climatology. Norwich.
For Meteoroids see:
Mineralogical Abstracts. London.
For Earthquakes and Volcanoes see:
SEAN Bulletin. Smithsonian Institution, Washington DC.

GENERAL WORKS

ANTHES, RICHARD A., *et al.* (1978) *The atmosphere.* 2nd ed. Columbus, Ohio: Charles E. Merrill.

BREUER, GEORG (1980) *Weather modification.* tr. Hans Mörth. Cambridge: Cambridge University Press.

BRITTON, C. E. (1937) *A meteorological chronology to A.D. 1450.* London: HMSO. (Meteorological Office. Geophysical Memoir – No.70)

BROOKS, C. E. P. (1949) *Climate through the ages.* London: Benn.

CORLISS, WILLIAM R. (1977) *Handbook of unusual natural phenomena.* Glen Arm, MD.: Sourcebook.

—— (1983) *Tornadoes, dark days, anomalous precipitation, and related weather phenomena.* Glen Arm, MD.: Sourcebook.

FRAZIER, KENDRICK (1979) *The violent face of nature.* New York: William Morrow.

HOLFORD, INGRID (1976) *British weather disasters.* Newton Abbot: David & Charles.

HUGHES, PATRICK (1974) *American weather stories.* Washington DC: US Department of Commerce.

JENNINGS, GARY (1970) *The killer storms.* Philadelphia: J. B. Lippincott.

LUDLUM, DAVID (1971) *Weather record book.* Princeton NJ: Weatherwise Inc.

McINTOSH, DOUGLAS HAIG, comp. (1963) *Meteorological glossary.* London: HMSO. (M.O. 729 A.P. 827)

MALONE, THOMAS FRANCIS, ed. (1951) *Compendium of meteorology.* Boston: American Meteorological Society.

METEOROLOGICAL OFFICE (1975) *The marine observer's handbook.* London: HMSO.

MILLER, RUSSELL (1983) *Continents in collision.* Amsterdam: Time-Life.

MURCHIE, GUY (1955) *Song of the sky.* London: Secker & Warburg.

NATIONAL GEOGRAPHIC SOCIETY (1978) *Powers of nature.* Washington DC: National Geographic.

WALTHAM, TONY (1978) *Catastrophe: the violent earth.* London: Macmillan.

WHITE, GILBERT F., ed. (1974) *Natural hazards: Local, national, global.* New York: Oxford University Press.

WHIPPLE, A. B. C. (1982) *Storm*. Alexandria, Virginia: Time-Life Books.

WHITTOW, JOHN BYRON (1980) Disasters. Harmondsworth: Penguin.

HURRICANES

AINLEY, GEORGE (1944) 1944 – Year for the great hurricane! *Sci. Dig. 15* May 39–40.

ALBRIGHT, JOHN GROVER (1939) *Physical meteorology*. New York: Prentice-Hall.

ARNOLD, RUDY (1939) After a hurricane. *Pop. Sci. Mon. 134*: 65–70.

BALDWIN, HANSON W. (1951) When the Third Fleet met the great typhoon. *New York Times Magazine* December 16: 18, 48–9, 51–2.

BERGERON, T. (1954) The problem of tropical hurricanes. *Quart. J. R. Met. Soc. 80*: 131–64.

BILHAM, E. G.(1938) *The climate of the British Isles*. London: Macmillan.

BRITTON, C. E. (1937) *A meteorological chronology to A.D. 1450*. London: HMSO. (Meteorological Office. Geophysical memoirs – No. 70)

BROOKS, C. E. P. (1954) *The English climate*. London: English Universities Press

BROOKS, CHARLES F. (1935) *Why the weather?* London: Chapman & Hall.

CARSON, RACHEL L. (1951) *The sea around us*. London: Staples Press.

CLINE, ISAAC MUNROE (1927) *Tropical cyclones*. London: Macmillan.

COLTON, F. BARROWS (1939) The geography of a hurricane [New England hurricane of September 1938] *Nat. geogr. Mag. 75*: 529–52.

DAVIS, ALBERT B., Jr (1961) *Galveston's bulwark against the sea: history of the Galveston sea wall*. Galveston, Texas: US Army Engineer District, Corps of Engineers.

DEFOE, DANIEL (1704) *The storm or, A collection of the most remarkable casualties and disasters which happen'd in the late dreadful tempest, both by sea and land*. London: G. Sawbridge.

DUANE, J. E. Jr (1935) The hurricane of September 2, 1935, at Long Key, Florida. *Bull. Amer. met. Soc. 16*: 238–9.

DUNN, GORDON E., & MILLER, BANNER I. (1960) *Atlantic hurricanes*. Baton rouge: Louisiana State University Press.

DURISCH, PETER, & HOWARTH, ROBERT (1975) *Cyclone! Christmas in Darwin 1974*. Sydney: Sydney Morning Herald.

EMENY, STUART (1942) Tidal wave kills 10,000 people. *News Chronicle* November 14.

FUNK, BEN (1980) Hurricane! *Nat. Geogr. 158*: 346–79.

GAILLARD, D. D. (1904) *Wave action in relation to engineering structures*. Fort Belvoir, Va.: The Engineer School. (US Corps of Engineers Professional Paper – 31)

HUMPHREYS, W. J. (1942) *Ways of the weather . . .* New York: Ronald Press (Humanizing Science series).

LAUGHTON, L. G. CARR, & HEDDON, V. (1930) *Great Storms*. London: P. Allan. (Nautilus Library – No. 13)

LUDLUM, DAVID M. (1963) *Early American hurricanes, 1492–1870*. Boston, Mass.: American Meteorological Society.

MARTYR, WESTON (1937) I am frightened for the men in Enkaba. *News Chronicle* September 21.

MARVIN, CHARLES F., *et al.* (1934) The great wind of April 11–12, 1934, on Mount Washington, N.H., and its measurement. *Mon. Weath. Rev., Wash. 62*: 186–95.

MILHAM, WILLIS I. (1912) *Meteorology*. London: Macmillan.

MINIKIN, R. R. (1963) *Winds, waves and maritime structures*. 2nd rev. ed. London: Griffin.

MOORE, WILLIS LUTHER (1927) I am thinking of Hurricanes. *American Mercury* 12 September: 81–6.

MORISON, SAMUEL ELIOT (1959) *The Liberation of the Philippines: Luzon, Mindanao, the Visayas. 1944–45*. London: Oxford University Press. (History of United States Naval Operations in World War II – Vol. XIII)

MOZAI, TORAO (1982) The lost fleet of Kublai Khan. *Nat. geogr. mag. 162*: 634–48.

NIMITZ, C. W. (1956) [Letter on lessons of damage in typhoon.] *Proc. U.S. nav. Inst. 82*: 83–8.

PAULHUS, J. L. H. (1965) Indian Ocean and Taiwan rainfalls set new records. *Mon. Weath. Rev., Wash. 93*: 331–5.

REID, W. (1846) *An attempt to develop the law of storms by means of facts, arranged according to place and time . . .* 2nd ed. London: John Weale.

REPORT *of the Secretary of the U.S. Navy, 1889* (1890) Disaster at Apia, Samoa. 95–123.

RIEHL, HERBERT (1962) Jet streams of the atmosphere. *Colorado State University. Technical Paper No. 32*: 117, 188.

RODNEY, LORD GEORGE (1932) Letter-books and order-books of George, Lord Rodney, 1780–1782. *Coll. N.Y. Hist. Soc. 65,1*: 91–2.

SIMPSON, R. H. (1954) Hurricanes. *Sci. Amer. 190, 6*: 32–6.

——, & RIEHL, Herbert (1981) *The Hurricane and its impact*. Louisiana State University Press.

SMITH, HENRY (1962) A high wind in Sheffield. *The Guardian* July 4.

STEVENSON, THOMAS (1886) *The design and construction of harbours*. Edinburgh: Black.

TANNEHILL, IVAN RAY (1956) *Hurricanes: their nature and history*. 9th ed. Oxford:

Oxford University Press.

TOWNSEND, C. H. (1936) Two giant tortoises were swept twenty miles by hurricane. *Bull N.Y. Zool. Soc. 39*: 119–20.

TREVELYAN, GEORGE MACAULAY (1930) *England under Queen Anne*. Blenheim, London: Longman.

TORNADOES

ALBRIGHT, JOHN GROVER (1939) *Physical meteorology*. New York: Prentice-Hall.

BATHURST, G. B. (1964) The earliest recorded tornado. *Weather. 19*: 202–4.

BATTAN, LOUIS J. (1959) Duration of tornadoes. *Bull. Amer. met. Soc. 40*: 340–2.

BICKHAM, JACK M. (1976) *Twister*. Garden City, NY: Doubleday & Co.

BIGELOW, FRANK H. (1908) The truncated dumb-bell vortex illustrated by the St. Louis, Mo., tornado of May 27, 1896. *Mon. Weath. Rev., Wash. 36*: 245–50.

BILLET, H. (1914) *The South Wales tornado of October 27, 1913*. London: HMSO. (Meteorological Office. Geophysical Memoir- No. 11)

BONACINA, L. C. W. (1946) The Widecombe calamity of 1638. *Weather 1*: 123–5.

——, **& SIMMONDS, J.** (1950) Tornadoes across England. *Weather 5*: 254–7.

BROWN, R.A., *et al.* (1978) Tornado detection by pulsed Doppler radar. *Mon. Weath. Rev. 106*: 29–38.

BUCK, ROBERT N. (1959) 'What about the weather Captain?' *Air Facts 22, 5*: 11–18.

BUSCH, NOEL FAIRCHILD (1936) *Two minutes to noon*. London: Barker.

FINLEY, JOHN PARK (1887) *Tornadoes*. New York: Insurance Monitor.

FLORA, SNOWDEN D. (1953) *Tornadoes of the United States*. Norman, Okla.: Oklahoma University Press.

FUJITA, THEODORE (1970) The Lubbock tornadoes: a study of suction spots. *Weatherwise 23*: 160–73.

—— (1973) Tornadoes around the world. *Weatherwise 26*: 56–83.

GRAHAM, HOWARD E. (1952) A fire-whirlwind of tornadic violence. *Weatherwise 5*: 59, 62.

GREELY, A. W. (1888) *American weather*. New York: Dodd, Mead & Co.

HANNA, V. C. (1904) *The Eads bridge story*. Terminal Railroad Association.

HARRIS, SIR ARTHUR (1947) *Bomber offensive*. London: Collins.

HARRISON, H. T. (1952) *Certain tornado and squall line features*. Denver, Col.: United Airlines. (Meteorology circular- No. 36)

HAWKE, E. L. (1938) The tornado of July 7, 1938, in the Chiltern Hills. *Quart. J.R. met. Soc. 64*: 616–18.

HAZEN, HENRY ALLEN (1890) *The tornado*. New York: N. D. C. Hodges

HERSEY, JOHN (1946) *Hiroshima*. Harmondsworth: Penguin Books.

HESS, W. N., ed. (1974) *Weather and climate modification*. New York: Wiley.

HUMPHREYS, W. J. (1937) *Weather rambles*. London: Bailliere & Co.

IRVING, DAVID (1963) *The destruction of Dresden*. London: Kimber.

JUSTICE, ALONZO A. (1930) Seeing the inside of a tornado. *Mon. Weath. Rev., Wash. 58*: 205–6.

KELLY, D. L.; *et al.* (1978) An augmented tornado climatology. *Mon. Weath. Rev. 106*, 1172–83.

KESSLER, E., ed. (1981) *Thunderstorms: a social, scientific and technological documentary*, vol 2. Washington DC: US Government Printing Office.

KIESLING, ERNST W., *et al.* (1977) *Protection of property and occupants in windstorms*. Paper presented at the American Society of Civil Engineers National Convention, Dallas, Texas. April 29.

LAMB, H. H. (1957) *Tornadoes in England May 21, 1950*. London: HMSO. (Meteorological Office. Geophysical memoir- No. 99)

LEE, J. T., ed. (1980) *Summary of AEC-ERDA-NRC supported research at NSSL 1973–1979*. Norman, Oklahoma: National Severe Storms Laboratory.

LINEHAN, URBAN J. (1957) *Tornado deaths in the United States*. Washington DC: US Weather Bureau. (Technical paper- No. 30)

LOWE, A. B., & McKAY, G. A. (1962) *The tornadoes of Western Canada*. Ottawa: Meteorological Branch, Dept. of Transport.

LUDLUM, DAVID M. (1970) *Early American tornadoes 1586–1870*. Boston: American Meteorological Society.

LYELL, SIR CHARLES (1875) *Principles of geology*. Edited by L. Lyell. London: John Murray.

MEADEN, G. T. (1976) Tornadoes in Britain: their intensities and distribution in space and time. *J. Meteorol. 1*: 242–51.

MILLIGEN-JOHNSTON, GEORGE (1770) *A short description of the province of South Carolina*. London: John Hinton. Reprinted in *Colonial South Carolina . . .* Columbia S.C.: University of South Carolina Press, 1951.

MINOR, JOSEPH E., & PETERSON, RICHARD E. (1979) *Characteristics of Australian tornadoes*. (Preprint vol.: 11th. Conference on severe local storms, Kansas City, Missouri, Oct. 2–5) 208–15. Boston: American Meteorological Society.

MOORE, ELY (1908) A buffalo hunt with the Miamis in 1854. *Kansas Hist. Coll. 10*: 402.

MOORE, WILLIS L. (1922) *The new air world*. Boston, Mass.: Little, Brown.

MURPHY, J. J. (1935) Meteorological features

and history of tornado at Norfolk, Virginia. *Bull. Amer. met. Soc. 16*: 252–5.

PARKER, SYBIL P., ed. (1980) *Encyclopaedia of ocean and atmospheric sciences*. New York: McGraw-Hill.

PETERSON, RICHARD E., ed. (1976) *Proceedings of the Symposium on tornadoes assessment of knowledge and implications for man. June 22–24*. Lubbock, Texas: Texas Technical University.

POUGH, FREDERICK H. (1943) Parícutin is born. *Nat. Hist., N.Y. 52*: 134–42.

ROGER DE HOVEDEN (1853) *The annals of Roger de Hoveden*. Translated from the Latin by H. T. Riley. London: Bohn. 2 vols.

[RÓWE, J. B.] (1905) *The two Widecombe tracts, 1638 giving a contemporary account of the great storm*. Reprinted with an introduction. Exeter: Commin.

ROWE, M. W. (1975) A history of tornado study in Britain. *J. Meteorol. 1*: 20–24.

—— (1976) Tornadoes in mediaeval Britain. *J. Meteorol. 1*: 219–22.

SHAW, SIR WILLIAM NAPIER (1923) *The air and its ways*. Cambridge: Cambridge University Press.

SMITH, ROGER (1980) Untwisting the mysteries of tornadoes. *New Scientist 85*: 650–52.

STONE & WEBSTER ENGINEERING CORPORATION (1976) Engineering Mechanics Division Technical Report Appendix A. *Data on tornadoes producing severe damage (1871–1974)*. EMTR-800-0.

SUTTON, SIR GRAHAM (1959) Tornadoes. *New Scientist 5*: 400–1.

TALMAN, CHARLES F. (1931) *The realm of the air*. Indianapolis, Ind.: Bobbs–Merrill.

TEPPER, MORRIS (1958) Tornadoes. *Sci. Amer. 198, 5*: 31–7.

TOLL, JOHN (1980) *Tornado*. St Catherines, Ontario: Stonehouse Publications.

VAN EVERDINGEN, E. (1925) The cyclone-like whirlwinds of August 10, 1925. *Proc. Sect. Sci. K. ned. Akad. Wet. 28*: 871–99.

VONNEGUT, B., & WEYER, JAMES R. (1966) Luminous phenomena in nocturnal tornadoes. *Science 153*: 1213–20.

WOLFORD, LAURA V. (1960) *Tornado occurrences in the United States*. Rev. ed. Washington DC: US Weather Bureau. (Technical Paper- No. 20)

WOOD, ELIOTT COLPOYS (1962) *A guide to the parish church at Widecombe-in-the-Moor*. Exeter: James Townsend.

WATERSPOUTS

BAJKOV, A. D. (1949) Do fish fall from the sky? *Science 109*: 402.

BIGELOW, FRANK H. (1906) Studies on the thermodynamics of the atmosphere. VI: The waterspout seen off Cottage City, Mass., in Vineyard Sound, on August 19, 1896. *Mon. Weath. Rev., Wash. 34*: 307–15. [Bigelow wrote several other papers on this waterspout in later issues of the *Monthly Weather Review*]

EVANS, BERGEN (1946) Concerning rains of fishes. *Science 103*: 713.

GOLDEN, JOSEPH H. (1971) Waterspouts and tornadoes over South Florida. *Mon. Weath. Rev. 99*: 146–54.

—— (1973) Some statistical aspects of waterspout formation. *Weatherwise 26*: 108–17.

—— (1974) The life cycle of Florida Keys' waterspouts. 1. *J. Appl. Meteorol. 13*: 676–92.

GORDON, A. H. (1948) Waterspouts and their danger to aircraft. *Met. Mag., Lond. 77*: 253–4.

—— (1951) Waterspouts. *Mar. Obs. 21*: 47–60, 87–93.

GUDGER, E. W. (1921) Rains of fishes. *Nat. Hist., N.Y. 21*: 607–19.

—— (1922) Rains of fishes and of frogs. *Nat. Hist. N.Y. 22*: 84.

—— (1929) Do fishes fall from the sky with rain? *Sci. -Mon., N.Y. 29*: 523–7.

—— (1929) More rains of fishes. *Ann. Mag. nat. Hist. ser. 10, 3*: 1–26.

—— (1946) Rains of fishes – myth or fact? *Science 103*: 693–4.

HARDY, R. N. (1971) The Cyprus waterspouts and tornadoes of 22 December 1969. *Met. Mag. Lond. 100*: 74–82.

HERSEY, JOHN (1962) *Here to stay*. London: Hamish Hamilton.

HOLDER, CHARLES F. (1887) *Living lights*. London: Sampson Low.

HURD, WILLIS EDWIN (1948) Waterspouts. *H.O. Pilot Chart Central American Waters*. No. 3500.

LEVERSON, VERNE H., et al. (1977) Waterspout wind, temperature and pressure structure deduced from aircraft measurements. *Mon. Weath. Rev. 105*: 725–33.

LUCRETIUS (1937) *De rerum natura*. With an English translation by W. H. D. Rouse, 3rd ed. rev. London: Heinemann. (Loeb Classical Library).

McATEE, WALDO L. (1917) Showers of organic matter. *Mon. Weath. Rev. 45*: 217–24.

MAJOR, T. W. (1929) Waterspouts between clouds. *Mar. Obs. 6*: 127.

MEADEN, G. T. (1976) A meteorological explanation for some of the mysterious sightings on Loch Ness and other lakes and rivers. *J. Meteorol. 1*: 118–24.

—— (1976) Devils and the Loch Ness Monster: I: some Questions by Sir Peter Scott. II: The reply. *J. Meteorol. 2*: 19–21.

MURPHY, J. J. (1935) Meteorological features and history of tornado at Norfolk, Virginia. *Bull. Amer. met. Soc. 16*: 252–5.

ROWE, MICHAEL W. (1982) Remarkable showers associated with whirlwinds.

J. Meteorol. 7: 177–8.

RUSSELL, HENRY CHAMBERLAINE (1898) Waterspouts on the coast of New South Wales. *J. Roy. Soc. N.S.W. 32*: 132–49.

STONE & WEBSTER ENGINEERING CORPORATION (1976) Engineering Mechanics Division Technical Report Appendix A. *Data on tornadoes producing severe damage (1871–1974)*. EMTR-800-0.

TALMAN, CHARLES F. (1931) *The realm of the air*. Indianapolis, Ind.: Bobbs–Merrill.

THE TIMES (1939) A shower of frogs. *The Times* June 17 [and subsequent correspondence to July 11].

WEGENER, ALFRED (1917) *Wind- und Wasserhosen in Europa*. Braunschweig: Vieweg.

WHITE, GILBERT (1789) *The natural history of Selborne*. London: B. White (and many subsequent editions).

HAIL

ALUSA, ALEXANDER L. (1976) The occurence and nature of hailstorms in Kericho, Kenya. *Proceedings* of 2nd Scientific Conference on weather modification, Boulder, Colorado, USA. 2–6 August.

ANON (1935) The great Northamptonshire hailstorm of 22nd September, 1935. *British Rainf.* 1935: 281–5.

BEEBE, WILLIAM (1918) A Kashmir barrage of hail. *Bull. N.Y. Zool. Soc. 21*: 1616–19.

BILHAM, E. G., & RELF, E. F. (1937) The dynamics of large hailstones. *Quart. J.R. met. Soc. 63*: 149–62.

BLAIR, THOMAS A. (1928) Hailstones of great size at Potter, Nebraska. *Mon. Weath. Rev., Wash. 56*: 313.

BOTLEY, C. M. (1938) *The air and its mysteries*. London: Bell.

BROOKS, CHARLES F. (1935) *Why the weather?* London: Chapman & Hall.

BROWN, W. G. (1912) Explosive hail. *Nature, London 88*: 350.

BROWNING, K. A. (1966) The lobe structure of giant hailstones. *Quart. J.R. met. Soc. 92*: 1–14.

—— (1978) *The structure and mechanisms of hailstorms*. American Meteorological Society Monograph 38.

—— *et al.* (1963) The density and structure of hailstones. *Quart. J.R. met. Soc. 89*: 75–84.

BUCK, ROBERT N. (1959) 'What about the weather Captain?' *Air Facts 22, 5*: 11–18.

BUIST, GEORGE (1856) Remarkable hailstorms in India, from March 1851 to May 1855. *Rep. Brit. Ass.*, 1855.

CELLINI, B. (1949) *The life of Benvenuto Cellini*. New York: Phaidon.

CHANGNON, STANLEY A., & IVENS, J. LOREENA (1981) History repeated: the forgotten hail cannons of Europe. *Bull*

Amer. met. Soc. 62: 368–75.

CHANGNON, STANLEY A., *et al.* (1977) *Hail suppression: Impacts and issues*. Final report, Technology assessment of the Suppression of Hail. Urbana: Illinois State Water Survey.

CLARKE, ARTHUR C. (1980) *Mysterious world*. London: Collins.

CROSSLEY, A. F. (1961) Hail in relation to the risk of encounters in flight. *Met. Mag., London. 90*: 101–10.

DUFF, D.V. (1936) *Palestine picture*. London: Hodder & Stoughton.

ELIOT, J. (1899) Hailstorms in India during the period 1883–97. *Indian met. Mem. 6*: 237–315.

FLORA, SNOWDEN D. (1956) *Hailstorms of the United States*. Norman, Oklahoma: University of Oklahoma Press.

FORT, CHARLES (1941) *Book of the damned*. (In *Books of Charles Fort*. New York: Holt)

FROISSART, SIR JOHN (1847) *The Chronicles of England, France, Spain, etc.* Translated by H. P. Dunster. London: James Burns.

GREELY, A. W. (1888) *American weather*. New York: Dodd, Mead & Co.

GRIFFITHS, R. F. (1975) Observation and analysis of an ice hydrometer of extraordinary size. *Met. Mag. 104*: 253–60.

GRIMMINGER, G. (1933) The upward speed of an air current necessary to sustain a hailstone. *Mon. Weath. Rev., Wash. 61*: 198–200.

KENDREW, W. G. (1957) *Climatology*. Oxford: Clarendon Press.

KNIGHT, NANCY C., & CHARLES, A. (1978) Some observations on foreign material in hailstones. *Bull. Amer. met. Soc. 59*: 282–6.

LAPIE, P. O. (1943) *My travels through Chad*. London: John Murray.

LONG, IAN F. (1963) Fossil hail prints. *Weather 18*: 115.

LOVELAND, GEORGE A. (1917) Nebraska hailstorm of August 8, 1917. *Mon. Weath. Rev., Wash. 45*: 540–2.

LUDLAM, F. H. (1980) *Clouds and storms: the behavior and effect of water in the atmosphere*. University Park, PA: Pennsylvania State University Press.

LUDLAM, F. H. & MACKLIN, W. C. (1960) The Horsham hailstorm of 5 September 1958. *Met. Mag., Lond. 89*: 245–51.

LUDLUM, DAVID M. (1971) *Weather record book*. Princeton, NJ: Weatherwise.

MULL, S., & KULSHRESTHA, S. M. (1962) The severe hailstorm of 27 May 1959 near Sikar (Rajasthan): a synoptic and radar study. *Indian J. Met. Geophys. 13* Special No. March: 81–94.

MURCHIE, GUY (1955) *Song of the sky*. London: Secker & Warburg.

NORMAN, JOHN ROXBOROUGH (1963) *A history of fishes*. 2nd ed. by P. H.

Greenwood. London: Benn.

ODDIE, B. C. V. (1965) The hail cannon. *Weather 20*: 154–6.

PRUPPACHER, H. R., & KLETT, J. D. (1978) *Microphysics of clouds and precipitation*. Dordrecht: Reidel.

ROGERS, R. R. (1970) *A short course in cloud physics*. Oxford: Pergamon.

SCHONLAND, SIR BASIL (1964) *The flight of thunderbolts*. London: Oxford University Press.

SMITH, ALLEN G. (1960) Hail, great destroyer of wildlife. *Audubon Mag. 62*: 170–1, 189.

SMITH, ALLEN G., & WEBSTER, H. R. (1955) Effects of hailstorms on waterfowl population in Alberta, Canada. *J. Wildlife Mgmt 19*: 368–74.

STEYN, KEEVE (1950) The Pretoria hailstorm. *Public Works of South Africa 10*: 75: February [A subsequent reprint corrected inaccuracies].

SUPF, PETER (1933) *Airman's world*. London: Routledge.

TALMAN, CHARLES F. (1931) *The realm of the air*. Indianapolis, Ind: Bobbs-Merrill.

THOMPSON, PHILIP D., & O'BRIEN, ROBERT (1965) *Weather*. New York: Time.

VITTORI, OTTAVIO (1960) Preliminary note on the effects of pressure waves upon hailstones. *Nubila 3, 1*: 34–52.

VOSBURGH, FREDERICK G. (1938) Menbirds soar on boiling air. *Nat. geogr. Mag. 74*: 123–40.

WORLD METEOROLOGICAL ORGANIZATION; WEATHER MODIFICATION PROGRAMME (1981) *Report . . . on the dynamic of hailstones and related uncertainties of hail suppression*. Geneva: Hail Report No. 3.

LIGHTNING

ARAGO, FRANÇOIS (1855) *Meteorological essays*. Trans. Col. Sabine. London: Longman.

BARRY, J. D. (1980) *Ball lightning and bead lightning: extreme forms of atmospheric electricity*. New York: Plenum.

BERGER, K. (1973) Kugelblitz und Blitzforschung. *Naturwissenschaften 60*: 485–92.

BROOKS, CHARLES F. (1938) *Why the weather?* London: Chapman & Hall.

BUCK, ROBERT N. (1959) 'What about the weather Captain?' *Air Facts 25, 5*: 11–18.

CLIFFORD, DON W. (1981) *Aircraft mishap experience from atmospheric electricity hazards*. Agard Lecture Series No. 110-NATO.

CORLISS, WILLIAM R. (1982) *Lightning, auroras, nocturnal lights, and related luminous phenomena*. Glen Arm, Md: Sourcebook.

COUNCIL FOR CODES OF PRACTICE. Committee for Electrical Engineering (1965) *The protection of structures against lightning*. 2nd revision. London: British Standards Institution (CP 326: 1965).

CREW, E. W. (1982) Localised violent air disturbances apparently caused by lightning. *Speculations in Sci. & Tech. 5*: 67–75.

DAVIES, D. W., & STANDLER, R. B. (1972) Ball lightning. *Nature 240*; 144.

FLAMMARION, CAMILLE (1905) *Thunder and lightning*. Translated by W. Mostyn. London: Chatto & Windus.

FLETCHER, COLIN (1963) Ordeal by lightning on Glacier Mountain. *Reader's Digest*: July.

GOLD, E. (1952) Thunderbolts. The electric phenomena of thunderstorms. *Nature, 169*: 561–3.

GOLDE, R. H. (1977) *Lightning*. New York: Academic Press.

HAGENGUTH, J. H. (1961) *Memorandum on ball lightning*. Pittsfield, Mass.: General Electric Company [typescript].

HARRIS, SIR WILLIAM SNOW (1847) *Remarkable instances of the protection of certain ships . . . from the destructive effects of lightning . . .* London.

—— (1854) *Shipwrecks by lightning: copies of papers relative to shipwrecks by lightning, as prepared by Sir Snow Harris, and presented by him to the Admiralty*. Parliamentary Papers, 1854 (453) Vol XLII.

HUMPHREYS, W. J. (1936) Ball lightning. *Proc. Amer. phil. Soc. 76*: 613–26.

JENSEN, J. C. (1933) Ball lightning. *Physics 4*: 372–4.

—— (1933) Ball lightning. *Sci. Mon., N.Y. 37*: 190–2.

KAPITZA, P. L. (1961) *The nature of ball lightning*. In Ritchie, Donald J., editor (1961) *Ball Lightning: a collection of Soviet research in English translation*. New York: Consultants Bureau.

KLASS, PHILIP J. (1968) *UFOs identified*. New York: Random House.

LOEB, LEONARD B. (1961) *Thunderstorms and Lightning: a summary*. Berkeley, Calif.: University of California, Department of Physics [typescript].

LUDLAM, F. H. (1980) *Clouds and storms; The behavior and effect of water in the atmosphere*. University Park, PA: Pennsylvania State University Press.

LUERS, JAMES K., & HAINES, PATRICK (1982) *Heavy rain/wind shear accidents*. University of Dayton Research Institute.

McEACHRON, KARL B. (1938) Lightning to the Empire State Building. *Elect. Engng. N.Y. 57*: 493–505, 507.

MALLINSON, A. B. (1937) [A floating fireball.] *J. Instn. elect. Engrs. 81*: 487, July: 46.

MATTHIAS, B. T., & BUCHSBAUM, S. J. (1962) Pinched lightning. *Nature 194*: 327.

REMILLARD, WILFRED J. (1960) *The acoustics of thunder*. Cambridge, Mass.: Acoustics Research Laboratory, Division of Engineering and Applied Science, Harvard University. (Technical memorandum- No. 44)

RITCHIE, DONALD J. (1963) Ball lightning in nature and in the laboratory. *J. Inst. elect. Engrs. 9*: 202–6.

RYDER, P. (1981) *Met. O. 15 Internal Report No. 31 Lightning*. Bracknell: Meteorological Office.

SAINT-PRIVAT-D'ALLIER RESEARCH GROUP (1978) *Development of research on lightning in France*. 14th International Conference on Lightning Protection, Gdansk.

SHIPLEY, JOHN F. (1946) Lightning and trees. *Weather 1*: 206–10.

TALJAARD, J. J. (1952) How far can thunder be heard? *Weather 7*: 245–6.

TALMAGE, STERLING B. (1929) The spoor of a thunderbolt. *Scientific Monthly* April.

TALMAN, C. F. (1931) The strangest lightning. *Amer. met. Soc. Bull. 12*: 130.

TREVINO, LEE (1983) *They call me Super Mex*. London: Hutchinson.

UMAN, MARTIN A. (1969) *Lightning*. New York: McGraw-Hill.

—— (1971) *Understanding lightning*. Carnegie, PA: Bek Technical.

WALLINGTON, C. E. (1964) Lightning strikes on aircraft – 1. *Weather 19*: 206–08.

WASSON, R. GORDON (1956) Lightning-bolt and mushrooms: an essay in early cultural exploration. (In *For Roman Jakobson*. The Hague: Monton)

WORTH, L. H. (1973) Atmospheric mystery. *Weather 28*: 86.

YOUNG, GEORGE A. (1962) *A lightning strike of an underwater explosion plume*. White Oak Md: US Naval Ordnance Laboratory, Explosions Research Department (NOLTR 61–43).

AVALANCHES

ALTER, J. CECIL (1926) Avalanche at Bingham, Utah. *Mon. Weath. Rev., Wash. 54*: 60.

BAILEY, RONALD H. (1982) *Glacier*. Amsterdam: Time-Life.

BENTLEY, WILSON A. (1904) Work on snow crystals. *Nat. geogr. Mag. 15*: 30–7.

—— (1923) The magic beauty of snow and dew. *Nat. geogr. Mag. 43*: 103–12.

——, & HUMPHREYS, W. J. (1931) *Snow crystals*. New York & London: McGraw-Hill.

BROOKS, CHARLES F. (1935) *Why the weather?* London: Chapman & Hall.

BROWN, T. GRAHAM, & DE BEER, SIR GAVIN (1957) *The first ascent of Mont Blanc*. London: Oxford University Press.

BUSS, ERNST, & HEIM, ALBERT (1881) *Der Bergsturz von Elm den 11 September 1881*. Denkschrift, Zurich: J. Wurster.

CONWAY, SIR MARTIN (1895) *The alps from end to end*. Westminster: Archibald Constable.

DOLLFUS, OLIVIER, & DEL AGUILA, CARLOS PEÑAHERRERA (1962) Informe de la Comisión Peruana de Geomorfolgiá sobre la Catástrofe ocurrida en el Callejón de Huaylas, el 10 de Enero de 1962. *Boln. Soc. Geogr. Lima 79*: 3–18.

FLAIG, WALTHER (1955) *Lawinen*. Wiesbaden: F. A. Brockhaus.

FRASER, COLIN (1978) *Avalanches and snow safety*. London: Murray.

HARDING, JOHN, et al., ed. (1980) *Avalanche*. Proceedings of a symposium. London: Alpine Club.

HEIM, ALBERT (1932) Bergsturz und Menschenleben. Supplement to *Vgschr. Naturf. Ges. Zurich 77, 20*. Geologische Nachlese. No. 30.

HIRZEL, HEINRICH (1809) *Eugenias Briefe an ihre Mutter. Geschrieben auf einer Reise nach den Bädern von Lenk im Sommer 1806*. Zürich: Orell Füssli.

LA CHAPELLE, EDWARD R. (1966) The control of snow avalanches. *Sci. Amer. 214, 2*: 92–101.

McDOWELL, BART (1962) Avalanche! *Nat. geogr. Mag. 121*: 855–80.

MORRISON, C. F., et al. (1960) *The Collapse of the Listowel arena*. Ottawa: National Research Council, Division of Building Research. (Technical paper- No. 97)

NATIONAL INFORMATION BUREAU (1970) *Cataclysm in Peru!* Lima: O.N.I.

PLAFKER, GEORGE, et al. (1971) Geological aspects of the May 31, 1970, Peru earthquake. *Bull. seismol. Soc. Amer. 61*: 543–78.

QUERVAIN, M. R. DE (1957) Avalanche classification. *International Association of Scientific Hydrology. General Assembly of Toronto 4*: 387–92.

——, & ZINGG, T. H. (1951) Die aussergewöhnlichen Schneefälle vom Januar und Februar 1951 in den Schweizer Alpen und ihr Folgen. *Wass u. Energ. Wirt. 43*: 205–19.

ROCH, ANDRÉ (1960/1) *Mesure de la force des avalanches*. Davos: Swiss Institute for Snow and Avalanche Research. (Report No. 25)

—— (1964) Possibilités de protection en déviant ou en freinant l'avalanche. *Strasse und Verkehr 50*: 19–22.

—— (1980) *Neve e Valanghe*. Milan: Club Alpino Italiano.

SCHAEFER, VINCENT J. (1943) How to fingerprint a snowstorm. *Nat. Hist., N.Y. 51*: 20–7.

SELIGMAN, GERALD (1936) *Snow structure*

and ski fields. London: Macmillan.

—— (1937) The nature of snow. *Nature 139*: 1090–94.

—— (1937) Physical investigations on falling snow. *Nature 140*: 345–8.

—— (1947) Snow avalanches. *Geogr. Mag., Lond. 19*: 467—8.

TUCKETT, F. F. (1920) *A pioneer in the high Alps*. London: Arnold.

VOELLMY, A. (1955) Über die Zerstörungskraft von Lawinen. *Schweiz. Bauztg 73*: 159–65, 212–17, 246–9, 280–5. [An English translation by the US Dept of Agriculture, Forest Service. Alta Avalanche Study Centre, Wasatch National Forest was published in 1964.]

VOIGHT, B. (1978) *Rockslides and avalanches vol. 1. Natural Phenomena*. Amsterdam: Elsevier.

VOKES, H. E. (1942) Landslide. *Nat. Hist., N.Y. 49*: 32–7.

WECHSBERG, JOSEPH (1958) *Avalanche*. London: Weidenfeld & Nicolson.

WORKING GROUP ON AVALANCHE CLASSIFICATION, INTERNATIONAL COMMISSION ON SNOW & ICE (1973) Avalanche classification. *Hydrological Sciences Bulletin 18*: 391–402.

FLOODS

ALLEY, REWI (1956) *Man against flood: a story of the 1954 flood on the Yangste and the reconstruction that followed it*. Peking: New World Press.

ANON (1953) *The battle of the floods: Holland in February 1953*. Amsterdam: Netherlands Booksellers and Publishers Association. London: Newman Neame.

—— (1962) *1962 floods in East Pakistan: the story of an unprecedented calamity*. Dacca: East Pakistan Government Press.

—— (1964) *Flood control in the Lower Mississippi River Valley*. Vicksburg, Miss.: Mississippi River Commission and US Army Engineer Division.

BARKER, DUDLEY (1948) *Harvest home*. London: HMSO.

BARROWS, H. K. (1948) *Floods: their hydrology and control*. New York & London: McGraw-Hill.

BLEASDALE, A. (1959) The measurement of rainfall. *Weather 14*: 12–18.

——, & DOUGLAS, C. K. M. (1952) Storm over Exmoor on August 15, 1952. *Met. Mag., London 81*: 353–67.

BROOKS, C. E. P., & GLASSPOOLE, J. (1928) *British floods and droughts*. London: Benn.

BURTON, S. H. (1952) The 'Chains' of Exmoor. *Weather 7*: 334–6.

CHANTER, JOHN FREDERICK (1907) *The history of the parishes of Lynton and Countisbury* . . . Exeter: Commin.

CLARK, CHAMP (1983) *Flood*. Amsterdam: Time-Life Books.

COLTON, F. BARROWS (1939) The geography of a hurricane. [New England hurricane of September 1938] *Nat. geogr. Mag. 75*: 529–52.

CONFERENCE ON THE NORTH SEA FLOODS OF 31 JANUARY/1 FEBRUARY, 1953 (1954) *A collection of papers presented to the Institute in December 1953*. London: Institution of Civil Engineers.

DELDERFIELD, ERIC R. (1958) *The Lynmouth flood disaster*. Exmouth: Raleigh Press.

DOBBIE, CHARLES HERBERT, & WOLF, PETER OTTO (1953) The Lynmouth flood of August 1952. *Min. Proc. Instn. Civ. Engrs. 2, 3*: 522–88.

DOYLE, RICHARD (1976) *Deluge*. London: Arlington Books.

EVANS, B. C. J. (1979) Thames barrier navigation. *Port of London 54*: 610: 81–4.

FARB, PETER (1956) A flood prevention plan that works. *National Municipal Review* May.

FARQUHARSON, WILLIAM IAN (1953) *Storm surges on the East coast of England*. Institution of Civil Engineers. Conference on the North Sea Floods.

FRYE, RALPH (1955) The great molasses flood. *Reader's Digest* September.

GREATER LONDON COUNCIL: Research Library (1979) *The Thames Barrier*. London Topics No. 32. (Contains bibliography)

GRIEVE, HILDA (1959) *The great tide: the story of the 1953 flood disaster in Essex*. Chelmsford: County Council of Essex.

[HARRISON, ROBERT] (1682) *A strange relation of the suddain and violent tempest, which happened at Oxford May 31. Anno Domini 1682* . . . Oxford: Richard Sherlock.

HARRISON, SAMUEL (1864) *A complete history of the great flood of Sheffield on March 11 and 12, 1864*. Sheffield: Harrison.

HAWKE, E. L. (1952) Rainfall in a cloudburst. *Nature 165*: 204.

HERSEY, JOHN (1962) *Here to stay*. London: Hamish Hamilton.

HOOD, J. DENNIS (1892) *Waterspout on the Yorkshire Wolds: cataclysm at Langtoft, and Driffield*. Driffield: Frank Fawcett.

HORNER, R. W. (1977) *Thames tidal flood works in the London excluded area*. Paper presented at Metropolitan District Centre.

HOYT, WILLIAM G., & LANGBEIN, WALTER B. (1955) *Floods*. Princeton NJ: Princeton University Press.

HUANG WEI (1978) *Conquering the Yellow River*. Peking: Foreign Languages Press.

KELLER, WERNER (1980) *The Bible as history*. London: Hodder & Stoughton.

KENYON, FREDERIC (1940) *The Bible and archaeology*. London: Harrap.

LOVELL, JOHN (1893) Thunderstorm,

cloudburst and flood at Langtoft, East Yorkshire July 3rd 1892. *Quart. J.R. met. Soc. 19*: 1–15.

McCULLOUGH, DAVID G. (1968) *The Johnstown Flood*. London: Hutchinson.

McGONAGALL, WILLIAM (1934) *Poetic gems, selected from the works of William McGonagall*. Dundee: David Winter.

McMASTER, JOHN BACH (1933) The Johnstown flood. *Pennsylvania Magazine of History and Biography. 57*: 209–43, 316–54.

MARK, ROBERT (1979) *The Thames barrier*. London: Greater London Council.

MINISTRY OF TRANSPORT AND PUBLIC WORKS, THE HAGUE (1980) *The storm surge barrier in the eastern Scheldt*. Verkeer en waterstaat informatieblad No. 22E.

NEWSON, MALCOLM D. (1975) *Flooding and flood hazard*. Oxford: Oxford University Press.

O'CONNOR, RICHARD (1959) *Johnstown: the day the dam broke*. London: Redman.

PAULHUS, J. L. H. (1965) Indian Ocean and Taiwan rainfalls set new records. *Mon. Weath. Rev., Wash. 93*: 331–5.

RAMSAY, CYNTHIA RUSS (1978) Water: Time's relentless sculptor (*In Powers of Nature*. Washington D.C. National Geographic).

REPORT OF THE COMMITTEE ON THE CAUSE OF THE FAILURE OF THE SOUTH FORK DAM [Johnstown Flood] (1891) *Trans. Amer. Soc. civil Engrs*. 24 June: 431–69.

SIMPICH, FREDERICK (1927) The great Mississippi flood of 1927. *Nat. geogr. Mag. 52*: 243–89.

STEERS, J. A. (1953) The East coast floods. *Geogr. J. 119*: 280–98.

TODD, OLIVER J. (1942) Taming 'Flood Dragons' along China's Hwang Ho. *Nat. Geogr. Mag. 81*: 205–34.

UFFORD, H. A. QUARLES V. (1953) The disastrous storm surge of 1 February. *Weather 8*: 116–20.

WOOLEY, SIR LEONARD (1954) *Excavations at Ur*. London: Benn.

METEOROIDS

BALL, SIR ROBERT (1904) *The story of the heavens*. London: Cassell.

BARRINGER, DANIEL MOREAU (1905) Coon Mountain and its crater. *Proc. Acad. nat. sci. Philad. 57*: 861–6.

BAXTER, JOHN (1976) *The fire came by*. London: Macdonald & Janes.

BERNHARD, HUBERT J. (1936) Stardust. *Nat. Hist., N.Y. 38*: 300–303.

BIOT, J. B. (1803) *Relation d'un voyage fait dans le département de l'Orne, pour constater la réalité d'un météore observé à l'Aigle le 26 floréal an 11*. Paris

BREZINA, A. (1940) The arrangement of collections of meteorites. *Proc. Amer. phil. Soc. 43*: 211–47.

CEPLECHA, ZDENĚK (1979) Earth-grazing fireballs. *Bulletin of the Astronomical Institutes of Czechoslovakia 30*: 349–56.

CEPLECHA, Z. (1960) Experimental data on the final mass of the body landed on the earth after penetrating the atmosphere at cosmical velocity. *Bulletin of the Astronomical Institutes of Czechoslovakia 11*: 9–13.

CHALDNI, ERNEST FLORENS FRIEDRICH (1794) *Ueber den Ursprung der von Pallas gefundenen und an der ihr ähnlicher Eisenmassen, und über einige damit in Verbindung stehende Naturerschlingungen*. Riga: Hartknoch.

DUNLAP, J. L., & GEHRELS, TOM (1979) The shape of Geographos and other asteroids. *Nat. Geog. Soc. Research Reports* 125–34.

FERNIE, J. D. (1967) Journey via Otjiwarongo, *Il. R. Astr. Soc. Can. 61*: 127–40.

GRIBBIN, JOHN (1980) Cosmic disaster shock, *New Scientist 1980*: 750–2.

HOWARD, EDWARD (1802) *Experiments and observations on certain stony and metalline substances, which at different times are said to have fallen on the earth; also on various kinds of native iron*. (From the *Philosophical Transactions*) London: W. Bulmer.

KING, EDWARD (1796) *Remarks concerning stones said to have fallen from the clouds, both in these days, and in ancient times*. London: G. Nicol.

KRINOV, E. L. (1966) *Giant meteorites*. New York: Pergamon.

KUIPER, G. P., et al. (1958) Survey of asteroids. *Astrophys. J.* Supplement Series No. 32, 3: 289–428.

LAPAZ, LINCOLN (1951) Injuries from falling meteorites. *Pop. Astr. 59*: 433–9.

—— (1958) The effects of meteorites upon the earth (including its inhabitants, atmosphere and satellites) *Adv. Geophys. 4*: 217–350.

LE MAIRE, T. R. (1980) *Stones from the stars*. Englewood Cliffs, New Jersey: Prentice-Hall.

LEY, WILLY (1964) *Watchers of the sky*. London: Sidgwick & Jackson.

LIVY [Livius Titus] (1935) *History of Rome*. Translated by James Brodie. Book 1, Section 3. London: James Brodie.

McCALL, G.J.H. (1973) *Meteorites and their origins*. Newton Abbot: David & Charles.

MILLMAN, PETER M. (1962) Sous-commission pour normaliser la terminologie et les notations concernant les météors. *Trans. int. aster. Un. XIA*- Reports: 228–30.

—— (1971) The meteoric hazard of interplanetary travel. *Am. Scient. 59*: 700–5.

MUCK, OTTO HEINRICH (1978) *The secret of*

Atlantis. Translated by Fred Brodley. London: William Collins.

NININGER, H. H. (1933) *Our stone-pelted planet*. Boston, Mass.: Houghton.

—— (1959) *Out of the sky*. London: Constable.

O'KEEFE, J. A., ed. (1964) *Tektites*. Chicago, Ill., & London: University of Chicago Press.

OLIVIER, CHARLES P. (1925) *Meteors*. Baltimore, Md: Williams & Wilkins.

ROMIG, MARY F. (1965) *Space ice*. Santa Monica, Calif.: The Rand Corporation [typescript].

SCHLESINGER, FRANK (1910) Pwdre Ser. *Nature: 84*: 105–6.

SPENCER, L. J. (1932) Hoba (South-West Africa), the largest known meteorite. *Mineralogical Mag. 23*: 1–18.

VOAS, ROBERT B. (1962) John Glenn's three orbits in Friendship 7. *Nat. geogr. Mag. 121*: 792–827.

WARLOW, PETER (1982) *The reversing earth*. London: Dent.

WATSON, FLETCHER G. (1956) *Between the planets*. London: Oxford University Press.

WHIPPLE, FRED L. (1952) *Meteoritic phenomena and meteorites*. (In White, Clayton S., & Benson, Otis O. Jr., editors (1952) *Physics and medicine of the upper atmosphere*.) Albuquerque, NM: University of New Mexico Press.

EARTHQUAKES

ADAMS, WILLIAM MANSFIELD (1964) *Earthquakes: an introduction to observational seismology*. Boston, Mass.: Heath.

ALDEN, WILLIAM C. (1928) Landslide and flood at Gros Ventre, Wyoming. *Trans. Amer. Inst. min. (metall.) Engrs. 76*: 347–61.

ANON (1962) *The Agadir, Morocco earthquake February 29, 1960*. New York: Committee of Structural Steel Producers of American Iron and Steel Institute.

BERG, GLEN V., & STRATTA, JAMES L. (1964) *Anchorage and the Alaska earthquake of March 27, 1964*. New York: American Iron and Steel Institute.

BERKMAN, S. C., & SYMONS, J. M. (1964) *The tsunami of May 22, 1960 as recorded at tide stations*. Washington DC: US Department of Commerce (Coast and geodetic survey).

BILLINGS, L. G. (1915) Some personal experiences with earthquakes. *Nat. geogr. Mag. 27*: 57–71.

BJERRUM, LAURITS (1966) *Mechanism of progressive failure in slopes of overconsolidated plastic clays and clay shales*. Oslo: Norwegian Geotechnical Institute. (Third Terzaghi Lecture).

BOESEN, VICTOR HUGO (1941) America's greatest earthquake. *Coronet 9*: 75–80.

BOLT, BRUCE A. (1978) *Earthquakes – a primer*. San Francisco: W. H. Freeman.

BOOTH, BASIL, & FITCH, FRANK (1979) *Earthshock*. London: Dent.

BROADHURST, GARLAND C. (1902) The new Madrid earthquakes. *Am. Geologist 30*: 78–9.

BULLEN, K. E. (1963) *An introduction to the theory of seismology*. Cambridge: Cambridge University Press.

BUSCH, NOEL FAIRCHILD (1963) *Two minutes to noon*. London: Barker.

CALIFORNIA STATE EARTHQUAKE INVESTIGATION COMMITTEE (1908–1910) *The Californian earthquake of April 18, 1906*. Report . . . Washington DC: Carnegie Institution of Washington.

CANBY, THOMAS Y. (1973) California's San Andreas fault. *Nat. Geogr. Mag. 143*: 38–53.

—— (1976) Can we predict quakes? *Nat. Geogr. Mag. 149*: 830–5.

COMMITTEE ON THE ALASKA EARTHQUAKE OF THE DIVISION OF EARTH SCIENCES, NATIONAL RESEARCH COUNCIL (1973) *The Great Alaska Earthquake of 1964*. [US] National Academy of Sciences.

CONFERENCE OF EXPERTS TO STUDY THE METHODS OF DETECTING VIOLATIONS OF A POSSIBLE AGREEMENT ON THE SUSPENSION OF NUCLEAR TESTS, GENEVA, JULY 1 TO AUGUST 21, 1958 (1958) *Report*. London: HMSO (Cmnd 551)

DAVISON, CHARLES (1924) *A history of British earthquakes*. Cambridge: Cambridge University Press.

—— (1931) *The Japanese earthquake of 1923*. London: Thomas Murby.

—— (1936) *Great earthquakes*. London: Thomas Murby.

—— (1937) Luminous phenomena of earthquakes. *Discovery 18*: 278–9.

—— (1938) The effects of earthquakes on animals. *Chambers' Journal 7*: 263–5.

DERR, JOHN S. (1973) Earthquake lights: a review of observations and present theories. *Bull. seismol. Soc. Amer. 63*: 2177–87.

EARTHQUAKE HAZARDS REDUCTION PROGRAM CONFERENCE, I. (1976) *Abnormal animal behavior prior to earthquakes, I*. Menlo Park, California: Office of Earthquake studies, US Geological Survey.

ECKEL, EDWIN B., ed. (1958) *Landslides and engineering practice*, [by] the Committee on Landslide Investigations. Washington DC: Highway Research Board. (Special report 29)

EIBY, G. (1980) *Earthquakes*. London: Heinemann.

GALANOPOULOS, A. G. (1960) Tsunamis observed on the coasts of Greece from antiquity to present time. *Annali di Geofisica 13*: 369–86.

GEIKIE, ARCHIBALD (1897) *Ancient*

volcanoes of Great Britain. London: Macmillan.

GRIBBIN, JOHN, & PLAGEMANN, STEPHEN (1977) *The Jupiter effect*. London: Fontana.

HECK, NICHOLAS HUNTER (1958) Earthquake history of the United States Part 1: *Continental United States and Alaska* (exclusive of California and Western Nevada), revised ed. (through 1956) by R. A. Eppley. Washington DC: US Government Printing Office (No. 41–1).

HODGSON, JOHN (1964) *Earthquakes and earth structure*. Englewood Cliffs, NJ, & London: Prentice-Hall.

HOLMES, ARTHUR (1982) *Principles of physical geology*. London: Van Nostrand Reinholdt.

HOLMSEN, GUNNAR (1936) De siste bergskred i Tafjord og Loen, Norge. *Svensk geogr. Årsb. 12*: 171–90.

HOLMSEN, PER (1953) Landslips in Norwegian quick-clays. *Géotechnique 3*: 187–200.

IACOPI, ROBERT (1964) *Earthquake country*. Menlo Park, Calif.: Lane Book Co. (A Sunset Book)

IMAMURA, A. (1937) *Theoretical and applied seismology*. Tokyo: Maruzen.

JACKSON, ROBERT (1960) *Thirty seconds at Quetta: the story of an earthquake*. London: Evans Brothers.

JAMES, WILLIAM (1906) On some mental effects of the earthquake. *Youth's Companion: 80*: 283–4.

KANAMORI, HIROO (1978) Quantification of earthquakes. *Nature 271*: 411–14.

KENDRICK, SIR THOMAS D. (1956) *The Lisbon earthquake*. London: Methuen.

KINGDON-WARD, F. (1951) Notes on the Assam earthquake. *Nature: 167*: 130–1.

—— (1952) Caught in the Assam-Tibet earthquake. *Nat. geogr. Mag. 101*: 402–16.

KINGDON-WARD, JEAN (1952) *My hill so strong*. London: Cape.

LEET, L. DON (1948) *Causes of catastrophe: earthquakes, volcanoes, tidal waves and hurricanes*. New York, London: McGraw-Hill.

LYELL, SIR CHARLES (1875) *Principles of geology*. Edited by L. Lyell. London: John Murray.

MELDOLA, RAPHAEL, & WHITE, WILLIAM (1885) Report on the East Anglian earthquake of 1884. *Essex Field Club Special memoirs 1*.

MERCALLI, GIUSEPPE (1902) Sulle modificazioni proposte alla scala sismica De Rossi-Forel. *Società Sismologica Italiana 8*: 184–91.

MILLER, DON J. (1960) *Giant waves in Lituya Bay, Alaska*. Washington DC: US Government Printing Office. (Geological Survey professional paper- 354-C)

MOHOROVIČIĆ, A. (1909) Das Beben vom 8. × 1909. *Godiš, Izv. Kv. zem. Zav. Met. Geodin. 9*: 1–63.

NIDDRIE, DAVID (1961) *When the earth shook*. London: Hollis & Carter.

OLDHAM, R. D., *et al.* (1899) Report on the great earthquake of 12th. June 1897. *Memoirs of the Geological Survey of India 29*.

PANEL ON PUBLIC POLICY IMPLICATIONS OF EARTHQUAKE PREDICTION (1975) *Earthquake prediction and public policy*. Washington DC: Advisory Committee on Emergency Planning, National Academy of Sciences.

PENICK, JAMES, Jr (1976) *The new Madrid earthquakes of 1811–12*. Columbia, MO: University of Missouri Press.

RICHTER, CHARLES F. (1935) An instrumental earthquake magnitude scale. *Bull. seismol. Soc. Amer. 25*: 1–32.

—— (1958) *Elementary seismology*. San Francisco, Calif., & London: W. H. Freeman.

SHARPE, C. F. STEWART (1938) *Landslides and related phenomena*. New York: Columbia University Press.

SHAW, EVELYN (1977) Can animals anticipate earthquakes? *Nat. Hist. N.Y. 86*, No. 9: 14–20.

SHEPARD, EDWARD M. (1905) New Madrid earthquake. *J. of Geology 13*: 47.

SMITH, DAVID G., ed. (1981) *The Cambridge Encyclopedia of earth sciences*. Cambridge: Cambridge University Press.

TAZIEFF, HAROUN (1964) *When the earth trembles*. Translated from the French by Patrick O'Brian. London: Hart-Davis.

TSUYA, H., ed. (1950) *The Fukui earthquake of June 28, 1948* Report of the Special Committee for the study of the Fukui earthquake. Tokyo: The Committee.

WALKER, BRYCE (1982) *Earthquake*. Amsterdam: Time-Life Books.

WALL, A. E. P. (1960) *The big wave, May 23, 1960*. Hilo, Hawaii: Hilo Tribune-Herald.

WALLACE, ROBERT E., & TA-LIANG TENG (1980) Prediction of the Sungpan-Pingwu earthquakes, August 1976. *Bull. seismol. Soc. Amer. 70*: 1199–223.

WRIGHT, FRANK LLOYD (1945) *An autobiography*. London: Faber.

VOLCANOES

ANDERSON, ROBERT, *et al.* (1965) Electricity in volcanic clouds. *Science*, Washington DC *148*: 1179–89.

BENNETT, J. G. (1963) Geophysics and human history. *Systematics 1*: 127–56.

BULLARD, FRED MASON (1962) *Volcanoes, in history, in theory, in eruption*. London: Nelson.

—— (1976) *Volcanoes of the earth*. London: University of Texas Press.

COBHAM, SIR ALAN (1940) *Tight Corners, tales of adventure on land, sea & in the air.* London: Allen & Unwin.

COLTON, F. BURROWS (1952) Our home-town planet, earth. *Nat. geogr. Mag. 101*: 116–39.

COLUMBIAN INC. (1980) *Mount St. Helens Holocaust.* Lubbock, Texas: C. F. Boone Publishers Inc.

DANA, J. D. (1890) *Characteristics of volcanoes, with contributions of facts and principles from the Hawaiian Islands.* New York: Dodd, Mead & Co.

DECKER, ROBERT & BARBARA (1981) *Volcanoes.* San Francisco: W. H. Freeman.

FINDLEY, ROWE (1981) Mount St Helens. *Nat. Geogr. Mag. 159*: 3–65.

—— (1981) Mount St. Helens aftermath. The mountain that was- and will be. *Nat. geogr. mag. 160*: 713–33.

FOSHAG, WILLIAM F. (1954) The life and death of a volcano [Parícutin]. *Geogr. Mag., Lond. 27*: 159–68.

FRANCIS, PETER (1978) *Volcanoes.* Harmondsworth, Middx: Penguin Books.

FURNEAUX, RUPERT (1965) *Krakatoa.* London: Secker & Warburg.

GALANOPOULOS, ANGELOS G. (1963) Die Denkalionische Flut ans geologischer Sicht. *Das Altertum 9,1*: 3–7.

—— (1964) Die ägyptischen Plagen und der Auszug Israels ans geologischer Sicht. *Das Altertum 10, 3*: 131–8.

GREEN, JAMES A. (1944) Parícutin: the cornfield that grew a volcano. *Nat. geogr. Mag. 84*: 129–64.

GRIGGS, ROBERT FISKE (1922) *The valley of ten thousand smokes.* Washington DC: National Geographic Society.

KELLER, WERNER (1980) *The Bible as history.* London: Hodder & Stoughton.

KENNAN, GEORGE (1902) *The tragedy of Pelée.* New York: Outlook Company.

KOSTER, A. L. (1956) City of the dead. *Nat. Hist., N.Y. 65*: 412–15.

LEET, L. DON (1948) *Causes of catastrophe: earthquakes, volcanoes, tidal waves and hurricanes.* New York & London: McGraw-Hill.

LIPMAN, PETER W., & MULLINEAUX, DONAL R. (1981) *The 1980 eruptions of Mount St. Helens, Washington.* Washington DC: US Geological Survey.

MACDONALD, GORDON A. (1972) *Volcanoes.* Englewood Cliffs, NJ: Prentice-Hall Inc.

MILLER, LOIS MATTOX (1943) *Pan-American Magazine.* October.

PERRET, FRANK A. (1924) *The Vesuvius eruption of 1906: study of a volcanic cycle.* Washington DC: Carnegie Institution of Washington. (Publication No. 339)

—— (1935) *The eruption of Mount Pelée 1929–32.* Washington DC: Carnegie Institution of Washington. (Publication No. 458)

PLINY THE YOUNGER (1915) *Letters.* With an English translation by William Melmoth, revised by W. M. L. Hutchinson. London: Heinemann. (The Loeb classical library)

POUGH, FREDERICK H. (1943) Parícutin is born. *Nat. Hist., N.Y. 52*: 134–42.

—— (1944) Parícutin comes of age. *Nat. Hist., N.Y. 53*: 342–9.

—— (1948) Parícutin has a birthday. *Nat. Hist., N.Y. 57*: 206-8.

ROSS, J. T. (1816) Narrative of the effects of the eruption from the Tambora Mountain, in the island of Sumbawa, on the 11th. and 12th. of April 1815. *Verhandelingen van het Bataviaasch Genootschap van Kunsten en Wetenschappen 8.*

SHEETS, PAYSAN D., & GRAYSON, DONALD K. eds. (1979) *Volcanic activity and human ecology.* New York: Academic Press.

SIMKIN, T., et al. (1981) *Volcanoes of the world.* Stroudsberg, Pa: Hutchinson Press.

SMITH, DAVID G., ed. (1981) *The Cambridge Encyclopedia of earth sciences.* Cambridge: Cambridge University Press.

SPARKS, R. S. J. (1979) The Santorini eruption and its consequences. *Endeavour 3*: 27–31.

SYMONS, G. J., ed. (1888) *The eruption of Krakatoa, and subsequent phenomena.* Report of the Krakatoa Committee of the Royal Society, London: Trübner.

THORARINSSON, SIGURDUR (1965) Surtsey: Island born of fire. *Nat. geogr. Mag: 127*: 713–26.

—— (1964) *Surtsey: the new island in the North Atlantic.* Reykjavík: Almenna Bókafélagid.

TILLING, ROBERT I. (1982) Volcanic cloud may alter earth's climate. *Nat. geogr. Mag. 162*: 672–5.

TOON, OWEN B., & POLLACK, JAMES B. (1977) Volcanoes and the climate. *Nat. Hist. N.Y. 86*: 8–26.

TRASK, PARKER D. (1943) The Mexican volcano Parícutin. *Science 98*: 501–5.

VERBEEK, R. W. M. (1885–1886) *Krakatau.* Batavia: Imprimerie de l'état.

WALKER, G. P. L. (1980) The Taupo pumice: product of the most powerful known (Ultraplinian) eruption? *Journal of Volcanology and Geothermal Research 8*: 69–94.

WEINTRAUB, BORIS (1982) Fire and ash, darkness at noon. *Nat. geogr. Mag. 162*: 660–71, 676–84.

Index